# JAPAN REARMED

# JAPAN REARMED

*The Politics of Military Power*

Sheila A. Smith

*A Council on Foreign Relations Book*

Harvard University Press

*Cambridge, Massachusetts*
*London, England*
2019

The Council on Foreign Relations (CFR) is an independent, nonpartisan membership organization, think tank, and publisher dedicated to being a resource for its members, government officials, business executives, journalists, educators and students, civic and religious leaders, and other interested citizens in order to help them better understand the world and the foreign policy choices facing the United States and other countries. Founded in 1921, CFR carries out its mission by maintaining a diverse membership, with special programs to promote interest and develop expertise in the next generation of foreign policy leaders; convening meetings at its headquarters in New York and in Washington, DC, and other cities where senior government officials, members of Congress, global leaders, and prominent thinkers come together with CFR members to discuss and debate major international issues; supporting a Studies Program that fosters independent research, enabling CFR scholars to produce articles, reports, and books and hold roundtables that analyze foreign policy issues and make concrete policy recommendations; publishing *Foreign Affairs*, the preeminent journal on international affairs and U.S. foreign policy; sponsoring Independent Task Forces that produce reports with both findings and policy prescriptions on the most important foreign policy topics; and providing up-to-date information and analysis about world events and American foreign policy on its website, www.cfr.org.

The Council on Foreign Relations takes no institutional positions on policy issues and has no affiliation with the U.S. government. All views expressed in its publications and on its website are the sole responsibility of the author or authors.

*Library of Congress Cataloging-in-Publication Data*
Names: Smith, Sheila A., 1959- author.
Title: Japan rearmed : the politics of military power / Sheila A. Smith.
Description: Cambridge, Massachusetts : Harvard University Press, 2019. |
Includes bibliographical references and index.
Identifiers: LCCN 2018042063 | ISBN 9780674987647
Subjects: LCSH: Japan—Armed Forces—History—20th century. |
Japan—Armed Forces—History—21st century. | Japan—Military policy. |
Japan. Kenpō (1946) | Japan—Foreign relations—United States. |
United States—Foreign relations—Japan.
Classification: LCC UA845 .S625 2019 | DDC 355.00952—dc23
LC record available at https://lccn.loc.gov/2018042063

For Ralph Edward Smith

# · CONTENTS ·

# · ABBREVIATIONS ·

| | |
|---|---|
| ADIZ | Air Defense Identification Zone |
| Antiterror Law | Antiterrorism Special Measures Law |
| APEC | Asia Pacific Economic Community |
| ARF | ASEAN Regional Forum |
| ASDF | Air Self-Defense Force |
| BADGE | Base Air Defense Ground Environment |
| BMD | Ballistic Missile Defense |
| $C_3I$ | Command, Control, Communications, and Intelligence |
| CLB | Cabinet Legislation Bureau |
| DPJ | Democratic Party of Japan |
| DPRK | Democratic People's Republic of Korea |
| EEZ | Exclusive Economic Zone |
| G-7 | Group of Seven (United States, United Kingdom, Japan, Italy, Germany, France, Canada) |
| GCC | Gulf Cooperation Council or Cooperation Council for the Arab States of the Gulf |
| GDP | Gross Domestic Product |
| GHQ | General Headquarters |
| GSDF | Ground Self-Defense Force |
| HNS | Host Nation Support |

| | |
|---|---|
| IMO | International Maritime Organization |
| INF | Intermediate-Range Nuclear Forces |
| IRAF | Iraq Reconstruction Assistance Force |
| Iraq Special Measures Law | Special Measures on Humanitarian and Reconstruction Assistance in Iraq |
| ISR | Intelligence, Surveillance, and Reconnaissance |
| JCG | Japan Coast Guard |
| JCP | Japan Communist Party |
| JCS | Joint Chiefs of Staff |
| JICA | Japan International Cooperation Agency |
| JSP | Japan Socialist Party |
| LDP | Liberal Democratic Party |
| METI | Ministry of Economy, Trade, and Industry |
| MINUSTAH | United Nations Stabilization Mission in Haiti |
| MITI | Ministry of International Trade and Industry |
| MLIT | Ministry of Land, Infrastructure, Transport, and Tourism |
| MOD | Ministry of Defense |
| MOF | Ministry of Finance |
| MOFA | Ministry of Foreign Affairs |
| MSA | Maritime Safety Agency |
| MSDF | Maritime Self-Defense Force |
| MSO | Maritime Security Operations |
| NATO | North Atlantic Treaty Organization |
| NDPO | National Defense Program Outline |
| NGO | Non-Governmental Organization |
| NPT | Treaty on the Nonproliferation of Nuclear Weapons |
| NSC | National Security Council |
| ODA | Official Development Assistance |
| PAC-3 | Patriot Advanced Capability-3 |
| PKO | Peacekeeping Operations |
| PLAN | Chinese People's Liberation Army Navy |
| PRC | People's Republic of China |
| ReCAAP | Regional Cooperation Agreement on Combating Piracy and Armed Robbery against Ships in Asia |

| | |
|---|---|
| RIMPAC | Rim of the Pacific Exercise |
| ROC | Republic of China |
| ROE | Rules of Engagement |
| ROK | Republic of Korea |
| SACO | Special Action Committee on Okinawa |
| SCAP | Supreme Commander for the Allied Powers |
| SDF | Self-Defense Force |
| SDP | Social Democratic Party |
| SLBM | Submarine-Launched Ballistic Missile |
| SOFA | Status of Forces Agreement |
| SOSUS | Sound Surveillance System |
| TPP | Trans-Pacific Partnership |
| UK | United Kingdom |
| UN | United Nations |
| UNCLOS | United Nations Convention on the Law of the Sea |
| UNHCR | United Nations High Commissioner for Refugees |
| UNMISS | United Nations Mission in South Sudan |
| UNOMOZ | United Nations Operation in Mozambique |
| UNTAC | United Nations Transitional Authority in Cambodia |
| UNTAET | United Nations Transitional Administration in East Timor |
| USAID | United States Agency for International Development |
| USSR | Union of Soviet Socialist Republics |
| WMD | Weapons of Mass Destruction |

JAPAN REARMED

# Introduction

MORE THAN SEVENTY YEARS after the atomic bombings of
Hiroshima and Nagasaki, the Japanese people remain deeply
skeptical of the benefits of military power. When Barack Obama
became the first sitting U.S. president to visit Hiroshima in
May 2016, he spoke of the horror of the use of force in the nuclear
age: "Seventy-one years ago, on a bright cloudless morning, death
fell from the sky and the world was changed. A flash of light and a
wall of fire destroyed a city and demonstrated that mankind possessed the means to destroy itself. Why do we come to this place,
to Hiroshima? We come to ponder a terrible force unleashed in a
not so distant past." The Japanese people welcomed his visit and
overwhelmingly approved of his message. As more nations gave
into the temptation of acquiring nuclear weapons, Japan steadfastly
resisted and became a staunch advocate of the Nuclear Nonproliferation Treaty.[1]

Generations of postwar Japanese leaders have grappled with
how to ensure their nation's defenses in the nuclear age while limiting the power of its military. The Japanese constitution remains

as it was written in 1947, with Article Nine committing the Japanese people to eschew the "use of force to settle international disputes." Prime Minister Abe Shinzō reciprocated Obama's visit to Hiroshima in December 2016 by visiting the site of the Japanese attack on the United States. At Pearl Harbor, Abe repeated a commitment that Japanese leaders have made for three-quarters of a century: "We must never repeat the horrors of war again. This is the solemn vow we, the people of Japan, have taken. Since the war, we have created a free and democratic country that values the rule of law, and have resolutely upheld our vow never again to wage war. We, the people of Japan, will continue to uphold this unwavering principle while harboring quiet pride in the path we have walked as a peace-loving nation over these seventy years since the war ended."[2]

As both Abe and Obama noted in their long-awaited visits to these war memorials, the relationship between the United States and Japan has been transformed, from adversaries in war to strategic allies in the postwar period. The security treaty that codifies this alliance provides for U.S. defense assistance to Japan and for Japanese provision of bases and facilities for the United States. Allying with the world's strongest military power has provided strategic protection for Japan, deterring its nuclear neighbors with America's nuclear umbrella. In return, Japanese citizens host over 50,000 U.S. military personnel in their country, as well as the only U.S. aircraft carrier home ported abroad. The U.S. and Japanese militaries operate together not only in and around the Japanese islands but have also worked in coalition with other armed forces across maritime Asia to the Indian Ocean and Persian Gulf.

Japan's strategy of possessing limited military power and relying on its alliance with the United States has served it well, and yet in today's Asia, Tokyo's approach to military power is being tested.

Northeast Asia has become a far more contested region as Chinese military power increases and as North Korea seeks to become a nuclear state. Japan's Self-Defense Force (SDF) now regularly runs up against the expanding armed forces of its neighbors. China's growing military has led to serious clashes with Japan. Chinese maritime and air patrols operate with increasing frequency and regularity in proximity to Japan, and Beijing has challenged Japanese sovereignty over the Senkaku Islands (Diaoyu in China), sending its coast guard and naval vessels to the East China Sea to assert its claims. The failure of diplomacy to resolve these tensions has at times all but broken communication between Tokyo and Beijing, and rising contact between Japanese and Chinese militaries has intensified concern that a miscalculation or unintended incident could easily bring the two Asian nations into conflict. The lack of agreement between Japan and China on their maritime boundary also exacerbates this risk. Tokyo has consulted with Washington on how to de-escalate tensions during these moments of crisis with Beijing. Japanese officials worry about "gray zone" contingencies— clashes below the actual use of armed forces but which could easily escalate to a military conflict.

Japan's military is being tested not only by China, however. Other neighbors challenge Japan's defenses. In the north, Russia continues to assert its military presence in and around Japanese air and waters.[3] North Korea's growing missile arsenal has raised serious questions about Japan's ability to cope with a ballistic missile attack. In the face of these threats, the U.S. president has restated the U.S. commitment to Japan's defenses several times. President Obama announced on a visit to Tokyo in 2014 that Article Five protections in the U.S.-Japan security treaty would extend to the Senkakus if force were used against Japan. When President Donald Trump met with Prime Minister Abe in Washington in February 2017, he restated this policy. Days later, when North Korea tested its missiles in the direction of Japanese territory, President Trump stood beside Prime Minister Abe at Mar-a-Lago to provide assurances that the United States would be "behind Japan, 100%" in dealing with Pyongyang's threat. Part reassurance to the Japanese people, and part deterrence against China and North Korea, these declarations of American intentions reflect a growing worry about military activity around Japan.

And yet for all of these assurances, the political mood in the United States has unsettled the Japanese. Just months earlier during the 2016 presidential campaign, candidate Trump had suggested that Japan should defend itself against North Korea. A survey from Pew Research Center in spring 2017 showed only 24 percent of the Japanese have confidence in Trump's foreign policy.[4] Serious trade tensions also simmer just below the surface of the U.S.-Japan relationship. As Japan faces increasing pressure on its defenses, the reliability of the United States seems less certain.

Japanese thinking about their military is changing as the possibility of a military conflict in Northeast Asia becomes more easily imagined. However, Japan's leaders are unlikely to use armed force before relying on diplomacy to resolve their grievances. Since the end of the Cold War, Japanese security choices have continued to be defined by the political tug of war over how to interpret Article Nine and how to meet alliance demands from Washington. Japan has relaxed its restraints on its military, and the SDF today plays a far more visible role in national policy. The SDF has been deployed abroad repeatedly and has extensive experience in U.S.- and UN-led military coalitions. Like Japan's civilian leaders, SDF commanders now work alongside a variety of partners in the Asia-Pacific region, especially in maritime security cooperation.

Article Nine still organizes debate in Japan over its military, but it does not limit the size or the lethality of Japan's armed forces.

Threat perception, long dormant as a factor in Japanese military planning, now assumes a larger role in shaping decisions about Japan's defense needs. The experiences of Japan's SDF in recent years suggest it must prepare to be tested. Should armed conflict erupt in Northeast Asia, Japan's choices with regard to the use of force will have tremendous consequences for the region. While Japan's military has never engaged in combat, changes have been made to clarify when and how Tokyo's leaders will order their armed forces to defend Japan. Japan's leaders have become far more comfortable using the military as an instrument of statecraft.[5]

## Article Nine and Japan's Defenses

The uniqueness of Japan's constitution has drawn the world's attention and is the focus of considerable scholarly inquiry.[6] However, it remains a politically charged issue within Japan. Drafted under occupation, Article Nine was designed to demilitarize Japan. Imperial Japan's devastating defeat in World War II led to an occupation headed by the Supreme Commander of the Allied Powers, General Douglas MacArthur. MacArthur ordered the drafting of a new constitution. In a note to aides, he offered three principles to guide their efforts. The institutions that had led Japan's modernization—the emperor, the military, and the aristocracy—would be reformed. The emperor would no longer exercise supreme authority in governing his nation, and Japan's aristocrats would no longer inherit power. Japan's citizens would choose their leaders and, through them, their national priorities.

The "no war" clause offered a legacy of contention, one that remains today within Japan as well as beyond. MacArthur's initial vision was the complete pacification of Japan, a revolutionary aim for a culture that had prided itself on its martial spirit. MacArthur's vision for reforming Japan went hand in hand with similar U.S. ambitions to transform the world order. Tying Japan to the emerging architecture of collective security seemed just as important as democratizing political power. In his note, MacArthur wrote, "War as a sovereign right to the nation is abolished, Japan renounces it as an instrumentality for settling its disputes and even for preserving its own security. *It relies upon the higher ideals which are now stirring the world for its defense and its protection.* No Japanese Army, Navy or Air Force will ever be authorized and no rights of belligerency will ever be conferred upon any Japanese force [emphasis added]."[7]

Thus, in the immediate aftermath of World War II's devastation, the American idealism that informed the occupation's reformers saw this new constitution as complementing the construction of a new global order, organized around the United Nations, which promised collective security and the peaceful settlement of disputes. The world changed quickly as the postwar peace brought conflict and a Cold War between the United States and the Soviet Union. U.S. policy toward Japan shifted abruptly too, in what the Japanese refer to as the "reverse course." Before the occupation was over, Americans were urging Japan to rearm, as war broke out on the Korean Peninsula.

The Japanese government insisted on interpreting Japan's new constitution to allow for self-defense. Even as the document was being drafted in 1946, Japanese leaders sought to temper General MacArthur's zeal for pacifying their nation.[8] The Committee to Consider the Problem of the Constitution, tasked with working with the occupation authorities on the draft, sought to tone down MacArthur's language. Once the draft of the new constitution went to the Japanese House of Representatives, the chair of its Committee on the Bill for Revising the Imperial Constitution, Ashida Hitoshi, reportedly tweaked it even further to open the way to allowing Japan to acquire military force for self-defense. The final version of Article Nine, Japan's renunciation of war, reads as follows:

> Aspiring sincerely to an international peace based on justice and order, the Japanese people forever renounce war as a sovereign right of the nation and the threat or use of force as means of settling international disputes.
>
> In order to accomplish the aim of the preceding paragraph, land, sea, and air forces, as well as other war potential, will never be maintained. The right of belligerency of the state will not be recognized.

Like MacArthur, Japan's drafters referenced the larger global effort to avoid indiscriminate use of force, yet they argued that the use of force for self-defense was legitimate under the charter of the newly created United Nations, which endowed all nations with the right to defend themselves. Japanese leaders ever since have interpreted Article Nine as allowing for military power sufficient to defend their nation. But they have done so cautiously and often in the face of deep domestic criticism.

Japan's early debates in the Diet focused largely on this interpretation over the purpose of military power. In 1954, the SDF was established alongside the Defense Agency—a civilian bureaucracy that would manage military planning. Rather than debating Japan's external security challenges, Diet debates focused on how to limit the growth of the SDF and curtail the political influence of the military over policy. Periodically, Japanese cabinets would be weakened by controversies over the behavior of the SDF, with opposition critics charging the ruling party with failing to exercise sufficient control over the military institution.[9] From 1955, the LDP dominated Japanese politics and governed Japan as the majority party or in coalition, however, giving the conservatives the ability to define their country's postwar defense choices. Nonetheless, tension between progressives and conservatives over the legitimacy of the SDF continued for decades.

The language of Article Nine mattered in these legislative tangles. While few argued that Japan should be able to use force to settle its international disputes, the ambiguous second paragraph invited contention. For opposition critics, Article Nine banned armed force of any kind. They blamed Washington for urging Japan to rearm and accused government officials of concluding "secret agreements" with the United States that violated the spirit of the constitution and, even worse, would draw Japan into war. Japan's conservatives continued to interpret it as Ashida had intended. Yet more recently, even conservatives take issue with the ambiguity, suggesting it is disingenuous and misleading. In 2017, a new approach was put forward by Prime Minister Abe: to add a third paragraph to Article Nine stating that Japan's SDF is constitutional.[10] Rather than addressing the core proscription on the use of force, Abe argues for ending domestic squabbling over the legitimacy of Japan's military.

In practice, Japanese government interpretation of Article Nine has always been elastic. The most consequential debates about the constitution's influence over how to arm Japan and how to use force to defend it took place decades ago. At that time, questions such as whether it would be legitimate for Japan to maintain nuclear weapons or launch a preemptive strike if its security were threatened were directly addressed. Indeed, early postwar political leaders were unabashed in their concern with how to defend their country in the nuclear era. Hence the Japanese government has never argued that Article Nine would prevent the nuclear option or the acquisition of the ability to strike offensively with armed force should Japan's security be threatened.

Japan has been surrounded by countries with considerable military forces. The former Soviet Union, while not identified as a direct threat to Japan, had considerable military might positioned close by and maintained a substantial nuclear arsenal. The successful acquisition of nuclear weapons by China in the mid-1960s also raised a new source of concern for Japan. But it has really been in the wake of the Cold War that Tokyo has felt that it is increasingly facing adversaries who might use force against Japan. Thus, it remains difficult to know if the normative constraints of Article Nine defeated the impulse to respond to threat of the use of force by others. In theory, at least, Japan's leaders have not excluded any type of military capability. Instead, they have wielded Article Nine as a statement of Japanese intentions.

## Threat Perception and Japanese Military Power

This choice of military self-restraint, however, has changed the logic of military planning. Rather than being driven by threat perception, postwar military planning instead focused on a basic force posture deemed sufficient for territorial defense. The first formal defense plan, drafted in 1976, in fact, was preceded by sustained debate within the Defense Agency over what the proper basis for defense planning should be. The civilians within the agency argued that more practical concerns, such as fiscal and resource constraints, effectively limited Japan's military capability. And, of course, threat-based analysis was associated with uniformed planners as it was their job to consider the worst case scenarios. Senior civilians in the agency wanted to move away from the idea that Japan had to keep pace with the military power of its neighbors. The National Defense Program Outline thus reflected less of Japanese assessments of what was happening outside of

Japan and instead set the stage for steady funding and a low profile for Japan's military.

U.S. assessments of threat also shaped Japanese thinking and framed the alliance conversation on Japan's military capability. Early on, as the Cold War intensified, Washington hoped for a much bigger Japanese military buildup than Tokyo imagined. Japan had little interest in rebuilding its own intelligence-gathering apparatus, given how its prewar intelligence organizations had spied abroad and at home, terrorizing Japanese citizens as the country turned toward militarism. Without a developed institutional capacity for intelligence gathering or assessment, Tokyo planners largely relied on Washington's reading of the capabilities and operations of foreign militaries across the globe. The Cold War competition with the Soviet Union became the basis for U.S. intelligence gathering that was unprecedented in scope and in scale. But Washington did not always share what it knew, and by the 1970s, when the Richard Nixon administration radically altered Asia's geopolitics by opening secret negotiations with China, Japanese leaders understood they could not trust the United States to protect Japan's interests. The National Police Agency was Japan's repository of domestic intelligence but also began to develop the capacity to share information with U.S. and other national policing agencies on third countries and on global terror networks. Yet it took decades more for Japan to begin to develop its own military intelligence architecture. The Defense Intelligence Headquarters, a signals intelligence agency, was established in 1997, and after the North Korean *Taepodong* launch, Japan began to invest in its own military satellite capabilities.[11]

Needless to say, Tokyo's hesitancy in identifying threat has not impeded its appreciation for military power. Japan invested in acquiring advanced weaponry produced by the leading industries in the United States and domestically, and it emerged from the Cold War with one of Asia's most advanced militaries.[12] Japan has consistently ranked in the top ten globally in its military spending, despite its commitment to spend only 1 percent of its GDP on defense. In 1990, Japan ranked sixth in military spending, with an annual budget of $37.7 billion. The SDF was armed with some of the most technologically advanced aircraft, produced under license from the United States, and Japan could claim to have Asia's most powerful navy. But during the 1990s, Japan's economy lost steam and so too did its military spending. Within a decade, China had overtaken Japan, ranking fourth in the world with an annual military budget of $43 billion to Japan's $41 billion. Even more striking was the difference between Asia's major powers in 2010: China spent $144 billion on its military while Japanese spending had remained constant at $41 billion. China now had the world's second-largest defense budget, while Japan had remained in sixth place.[13]

As Japan's economic downturn in the 1990s stalled its military investment, successive cabinets wrestled with U.S. expectations that Japan would join in global coalition efforts to contend with post–Cold War security challenges. New demands on Japan's military emerged in the 1990s and 2000s, especially from the United States. Initially wary of sending its forces abroad, Tokyo decided the SDF could join in UN peacekeeping operations. In 2001, however, the Japanese government was faced with an even greater challenge—the 9/11 attacks on the United States. The Koizumi Junichirō cabinet crafted a plan that provided rear area support and, with Diet approval, the SDF joined the military coalition that assisted U.S. combat in Iraq. Later, the SDF would be sent around the globe in humanitarian and disaster relief activities. But Japanese leaders stopped short of committing their military to combat.

Japan's leaders remain cautious about using their military as a tool of foreign policy, but they have accepted that the SDF can make a contribution to global security. Yet in the decades since the end of the Cold War, Tokyo policy makers have been pressed to consider new ways to contribute militarily to collective efforts to provide for global and regional security. The United States asked Japan to participate in coalition activities in and around the Persian Gulf and in the U.S. antiterrorism coalition after September 11. As the world's second-largest economy, Japan was expected to demonstrate its responsibility in global security management, and the SDF became an instrument of Japan's global contribution rather than an instrument of national ambition. In this new era of forming ad hoc military coalitions to cope with global security problems, Japan's leaders came to rely more heavily on their military as an instrument of global strategy, a demonstration of Tokyo's willingness to contribute to peace. The Abe cabinet continues to assert that the overarching goal is to make a "proactive contribution to peace."[14]

Today, Japanese officials are far more ready to discuss threats closer to home. The most conspicuous source of threat to Japan is North Korea. From the late 1990s, Japan confronted North Korea's "suspicious ships" in its waters, prompting defensive operations by both the Japan Coast Guard and the Maritime Self-Defense Force (MSDF). Pyongyang's growing ballistic missile capabilities have also been a concern, and Japan has invested heavily in ballistic missile defense systems developed with the United States. More recently, Prime Minister Abe has been unrestrained in his view of the North Korean threat and has actively pursued global cooperation to sanction the Kim Jong-un regime for its increasing missile launches over Japanese territory.[15]

Japanese government documents do not name other countries as threats, however. While China clearly worries Japanese planners, official statements do not identify China as a threat to Japan. Instead the Ministry of Defense and the Ministry of Foreign Affairs prefer statements that identify worrisome behaviors as threatening or potentially threatening. Threats or potential threats to Japan include nuclear proliferation, cyberattacks, terrorism, and environmental damage. Moreover, Japanese military leaders do not assert their interests, nor do they project their military capabilities in ways that other nations' militaries might. For example, in 2010, even as tensions between Japan and China were growing in the East China Sea and in other international waters, Admiral Sugimoto Masahiko, the MSDF chief of staff, argued the need for greater confidence building in the region to "create an atmosphere that is free from potential threat."[16]

Nonetheless, Japanese strategic planners understand that it is not in their interests to limit their military as others invest in their own. In Asia's changing military balance, Japanese officials clearly feel they are being left behind.

## Japan and the Use of Force

With major-power rivalry coming to define the post–Cold War order, Japanese leaders increasingly see the value of their military as an instrument of national power. Security planners have become more sensitive to the growing military prowess of Japan's neighbors, worried that they might seek advantage in using their military power to coercive ends. Japan's conservatives, back in power after a stint in the opposition, have become impatient with their domestic struggles over the legalities of interpreting the constitution and yet feel unable to express their policy aims in any other language. In Tokyo, the law matters when it comes to the exercise of military power, as does Japanese public opinion.

Even Prime Minister Abe, with his reputation as being one of Japan's more hawkish postwar leaders, does not advocate for a muscular use of military power by his country. Abe has, however, reenergized Japan's debate over its postwar constitution, arguing in the Diet that it is time for the Japanese to place their imprimatur on the document that guides the governance of their society. Abe too has introduced a flurry of security policy reforms and raised defense spending for the first time in over a decade; he actively sought to enlist U.S. support for Japan and its defense needs. But even when conservatives such as Abe argue for a stronger Japanese military, they do so using the language of deterrence, fully persuaded by the strategic logic of the nuclear era. Deterring war rather than waging it has become the purpose of Japan's military power.[17]

One of the biggest unknowns is how Japanese leaders will actually apply armed force should they perceive a threat. The military continues to be educated to use force as a last resort and only with explicit authority. In recent years, the SDF has been ordered to defend the nation's territory against specific incursions, or expected incursions, by foreign forces. The SDF has yet to shoot down an aircraft or to sink a ship, however, and has largely used its considerable military might to persuade intruders that it is not in their interests to test its commitment to defend Japan. Only the Japan Coast Guard has used lethal force against an intruder, sinking a North Korean ship after pursuing it out of Japan's territorial waters in 2001. Japan does not signal its intent to use force, however. There are no red lines being offered, no defining of thresholds across which potential adversaries should not test Japan's mettle.

One thing is clear, however, and that is that Japanese leaders are more willing to demonstrate their capability. Japan now has laws that specifically outline what to do in case of aggression against it. Moreover, new laws now allow the SDF to use force in crises short of conventional war and in coalition with other partners should Japan's security be threatened. Abroad, the SDF is slowly being given greater latitude as its experience in security cooperation with the United States and other partners grows. The MSDF has perhaps the most experience in coalition activities and has led in the thinking about how Japan's laws affect its ship commanders. Japan's role in maritime patrols in the South China Sea, however, remains cautious, while its antipiracy mission in the Gulf of Aden seems far less problematic.

Unlike other U.S. alliances, such as the North Atlantic Treaty Organization or the U.S.-South Korea alliance, formal contingency planning that commits military force to combined operations has not been part of the U.S.-Japan alliance. As Japan considers the possibility that it might have to fight a war, its leaders will have to decide whether it will integrate its forces into a combined command with the forces of the United States or whether it will seek to build its capacity to deter or repel an aggressor without U.S. help. To date, Tokyo's answer has been clear: Japanese threat perception has driven it closer to the United States as Asia has become more uncertain; and yet, Washington seems somewhat at odds about the future of its alliances. An unpredictable president, who seems disinterested in using American power for the defense of others, could easily upend Japanese expectations. The reliability of the United States, more than the military capabilities of its neighbors, will in the end decide the future of Japan's approach to military power.

While Tokyo has increasingly embraced the SDF as an instrument of statecraft, Japanese leaders must now question their longstanding assumption that the United States will defend Japan. Throughout the Cold War and in the decades since, the United States and Japan have adjusted their military responsibilities in the alliance, but the core strategic bargain that the United States would provide the military capability to strike offensively from Japanese bases while Japan's military would maintain the capability to defend its home islands is shifting. As American political leaders openly debate their commitment to allied defenses, Japanese politicians are beginning to argue for greater military capability, including limited strike capability, to ensure potential adversaries do not miscalculate SDF readiness.

Japan has choices to make. The military pressure on Japan, largely from China and North Korea, will only increase. Japan will want to increase its ability to respond, and will seek greater demonstrations from the United States that it too is willing to respond on Japan's behalf. With calls for burden sharing growing in the United States again, the Japanese government will need to prove it is doing all it can to defend itself. Far more difficult decisions could be ahead, however. Several scenarios could deal a blow to Japan's confidence in U.S. protection. First, a missile launch by North Korea could strike Japanese territory, revealing the inability of ballistic missile defense to ensure Japanese security. This scenario created worry in 2017 as Pyongyang intensified its missile testing, and while negotiations between the United States and North Korea may produce a moratorium on missile and nuclear testing, there is little optimism in Japan that North Korea's nuclear and missile threat will dissipate any time soon. A more robust deterrent capability under Japanese control would be the logical remedy, and indeed has already been recommended by some in the ruling party.

Second, the U.S. abandonment of its longstanding maritime dominance in Asia would leave Japan open to greater Chinese pressure. Coalition building with other Asian maritime powers could offset this somewhat, and Japan is already exercising with Australian and Indian navies as well as helping other maritime nations build their capacity to defend their own waters. A U.S. retreat from or loss of dominance, however, would require Japan to build greater maritime capabilities to protect its sea lanes. This adjustment would occur incrementally, but a more robust Japanese maritime role would require considerable investment.

Finally, the worst-case scenario for Tokyo policymakers is a failure of the alliance in a crisis. As Asia's militaries come into greater proximity, and as tensions increase, the risk of a military incident or use of force increases. Already Japanese policymakers confronted the possibility of a military clash with China over the Senkaku Islands. Alliance managers in Tokyo and Washington sought to upgrade their preparations for crisis management as a result, and Japan has sought also to reduce risk in the East China Sea with China. But the possibility that Washington might sit on the sidelines, or worse yet, advocate against Japanese interests, in a crisis haunts military planners in Tokyo. This type of demonstrated alliance failure would undermine decades of Japanese strategic planning, and likely prompt Tokyo to consider alternative options for guaranteeing its security. As unpalatable as it may seem, this would entail thinking about an alliance with another great power or a review of Japan's nuclear options. Without a doubt, it would accelerate the acquisition of greater Japanese military power. Already, all of these scenarios have been considered by Japan's political leaders and by Japan's military. While they have been successfully managed to date, a less predictable U.S.-Japan alliance would make any one of them a game changer for Japanese decision makers, and especially for the SDF.

• • •

*Japan Rearmed* traces this trajectory of Japan's increasing embrace of the military as an instrument of statecraft. Chapter 1 begins with the Cold War context of Japan's rearmament.

The fits and starts of designing an "exclusively defensive military" in the era of superpower nuclear competition reveal how difficult it was for Tokyo to determine the contours of its military rearmament. Asia was far from quiet during the Cold War; it was rocked by the Korea and Vietnam wars, and the Japanese looked beyond their borders with trepidation. For many, U.S. bases on their soil seemed more likely to drag them into a war than to protect them from one. Meanwhile, Japan's military might grew slowly but significantly, organized as it was in support of a U.S. strategy of containment but fueled by Japan's growing wealth. By the end of the 1980s, rearmament was long completed, and the SDF had become a modern, technologically advanced force. In Chapter 1, four dimensions of this policy debate are examined, all part of the political deliberations involved in navigating Japan's post–Cold War experience.

The remaining chapters chronicle the change in Japanese thinking about the utility of the military instrument as the currents of global power shifted in the Cold War's wake. Demand from the United States for a greater Japanese contribution to Western security grew, and the 1990 Gulf War revealed the limits of relying on wealth when the rest of the U.S.-led coalition of industrial democracies was sending troops. Chapter 2 tracks the events and the decision-making that allowed Japan's military to become an active participant in global coalitions, organized by the United Nations for peacekeeping and by the United States in response to terrorism and piracy.

Chapter 3 tackles the more complex changes that have been under way to ready the SDF to defend Japan. Prodded initially by crises at home, the Japanese government recognized it was unprepared to deploy its military—even within Japanese territory—and thus significant policy changes were needed. Japan was forced to make decisions on defense operations more frequently as foreign forces encroached on Japanese waters and airspace. Rules of engagement and a civilian-military chain of command had to be clarified as new technologies required timely decision-making, particularly in response to ballistic missiles. In the increasingly fraught military interactions between Japan and China, ensuring that Japan could fully respond to prevent escalation to military conflict also required some rethinking of where Tokyo deployed its forces and what missions ought to take priority.

Chapter 4 takes a closer look at the rising interest in Japan in constitutional revision and analyzes how the military has been affected by Article Nine and the government's shifting interpretation of its meaning. The Abe cabinet's decision to reinterpret Article Nine to allow for the "right of collective self-defense" reignited popular protest and legislative drama. In 2015, Japanese young and old took to the streets to protest their prime minister's "war bills." Prime Minister Abe's personal goal of amending the language of this "no war" clause has similarly drawn criticism, and yet for those who seek to clarify the legitimacy of and greater latitude for Japan's armed forces, even Abe has not gone far enough.

Finally, Chapter 5 points out what we often fail to consider when thinking of Japanese views on the use of force: the expectations of Tokyo when it comes to deploying and, if necessary, using U.S. military power on Japan's behalf. Managing a second national military has been a core task of U.S. allies since the end of World War II, and sustaining the support of the Japanese who host U.S. bases in their communities has taken considerable resources and policy attention. The costs Tokyo is willing to bear as it considers the value of its strategic bargain with the United States remain high. The premise, of course, is that U.S. forces will be there to deter aggression should Japan need them. As Asia becomes more fraught, and the United States debates the benefits of its long-standing alliance network, Japan's reliance on borrowed military power may prove unwise.[18] But it may take a failure of the alliance to reorient Japan's thinking about its strategic alternatives.

# ONE

# Japan in the Cold War

CREATED IN 1954, Japan's postwar military, the Self-Defense Force (SDF), was given an exclusively defensive mission, and the Defense Agency was provided with a modest budget to rearm. From their inception, the Japanese ground, maritime, and air forces were built in the shadow of the world's preeminent military. U.S. forces stationed in Japan were no longer occupation forces but rather formed the front line of Washington's new Cold War competition with the Soviet Union. The Korean War spurred this global forward deployment of U.S. forces, and although the United States rapidly reduced its forces in Asia afterward, the precedent was set for a garrison of American military forces on Japanese soil. In fact, the United States continued to occupy the southern Ryūkyū Islands through the end of the Vietnam War, making it possible to deploy U.S. air forces, navy, and marines across Asia. The dynamics of U.S. Cold War strategy, as much as the constitution, shaped Japan's thinking about its military capabilities and operations.[1]

Japan's immediate postwar priority was to rebuild its economy and restore diplomatic ties with its neighbors in Asia, many of whom it had invaded and occupied during World War II. Three decades later, Japan's staggering economic accomplishments brought greater support across Asia as Japan began to lead others in the region on a trajectory of economic growth and development. The opening to China in the 1970s, of course, presented an opportunity for Tokyo, as it had for Washington, to change the regional balance of power. Negotiations with Beijing were protracted, largely over China's interest in opposing Soviet hegemony in the region. While Tokyo was not opposed to countering Moscow's influence in Asia, Japanese negotiators preferred to emphasize the opportunity of close economic ties with China. Although talks had lain dormant since the mid-1950s, Japan still hoped to conclude a peace treaty with the Soviet Union. Economic cooperation remained Tokyo's preferred instrument of national power as it sought better relations with its adversaries.

For much of the Cold War, Japan's leaders relied almost exclusively on the United States to shape the regional military balance while they pursued economic recovery. In time, Japan would accrue considerable economic influence across Asia. As Japan's gross domestic product (GDP) grew, so too could its largesse. Peace treaties negotiated bilaterally with those who had not signed the San Francisco Peace Treaty included hefty side agreements for trade and investment. Official development assistance to China, for example, far outstripped that given to other nations in Asia and underwrote Deng Xiaoping's vision of transforming China's economy. Decades later, however, it seems that Japan got little strategic benefit for its early investment in China's transformation.

By the 1980s, Japan was a global economic power and firmly ensconced in managing the global economy as a member of the influential Group of Seven advanced industrial economies. Reconciliation with its neighbors largely accomplished, Japan's trading interests across the globe were made possible by a global order sustained by the United States and European nations, and successive Japanese prime ministers reassured its Asian neighbors that Japan had no desire to turn its wealth into military power. Japan had become adept at navigating the ups and downs of the global Cold War rivalry and had emerged as one of the most consequential supporters of the liberal economic order.

Japan did nevertheless develop its military power. Yet the extent of that power was often overshadowed by the strained politics within Japan between right and left over the interpretation of Article Nine and over the continued presence on Japanese soil of American military forces. Political battles raged in the Diet between conservatives and progressives. Early on, Japan's position as a U.S. ally irked many within Japan but was welcomed by defense planners seeking to rebuild a military. The alliance provided the new SDF with military aid. Over time, the Cold War alliance with the United States sheltered Japanese leaders from many of the more difficult questions regarding their use of force. Japan's SDF would face no combat, nor would Japan's civilian leaders have to worry about a series of direct threats to their nation's security. Instead, civilian and uniformed leaders quietly sought to rebuild their relationship and design a military planning process that constrained the military's power.

## A Peace Treaty, an Alliance, and Article Nine

Peace came to Japan formally in the negotiations of September 1951 in San Francisco. Forty-nine countries—members of the expanded Allied coalition that had defeated Imperial Japan—signed the treaty. Absent, however, were the countries Japan's leaders would face to their north and east, countries that were now in an opposing camp in the newly unfolding Cold War. Seven years after General Douglas MacArthur had arrived to "democratize and demilitarize" Japan, Prime Minister Yoshida Shigeru, a former diplomat and now the leader of the Liberal Party, would represent his country's interests and regain its sovereignty.[2]

The terms of the peace were deliberately designed to avoid the punitive effects of the Versailles Treaty that followed World War I. Japan would pay no reparations to those nations it had invaded, nor would it be bound by any financial obligations that would constrain its own economic recovery. Included in the treaty, however, was a provision for the return of all territory won by Japan in previous wars. Japan's colonial acquisitions Taiwan (Formosa) and Korea would become independent nations. Islands across the Pacific acquired through war and expansion would become independent or fall under UN mandate. The Soviet Union had already claimed the Northern Territories, or Kuriles, although its diplomats were absent from San Francisco, and to this day this territorial dispute between Moscow and Tokyo precludes a formal end to their conflict. And to the south, the Ryūkyū and Bonin Islands would remain occupied by the United States until the early 1970s. Some of the loose ends of the San Francisco negotiations would create serious territorial disputes over offshore islands with Japan's neighbors in the twenty-first century.

Also included in the treaty was a provision for managing those who had been tried and convicted at the Tokyo War Crimes Tribunal as well as the regional tribunals across Asia. The San Francisco Peace Treaty brought an end to Japan's extended occupation by the Allied Powers and restored Japanese sovereign control over its much-diminished territory and almost its entire people. But

Article Three of the peace treaty provided for the continued stationing of U.S. forces on Japanese soil.

Prime Minister Yoshida had to provide for his nation's defenses. As a vital first step, he needed to persuade his party and his fellow legislators that Japan's best path to security lay in aligning with the United States against the Communist states. A bilateral security treaty would accomplish that. The security pact concluded alongside the peace treaty in 1951 thus began a new relationship between Japan and the United States. From victor and vanquished, the United States and Japan became allies in emerging global competition between liberal and Communist blocs. The security agreement was straightforward—U.S. forces would remain on Japanese soil after independence until Japan's own forces could be organized to defend the country. The context of that pact was war on the Korean Peninsula. By October 1950, Chinese forces had entered the war and pushed U.S. forces back, raising the possibility of a Communist takeover of the entire peninsula. The Korean War would ultimately end in a negotiated draw, and in July 1953, generals from China, North Korea, and the United States signed the armistice agreement that quieted military action but became the basis of a continued state of war on the peninsula. This divided Korea defined tensions in Northeast Asia for generations. When Yoshida traveled to San Francisco, the Korean War had shaken the world and prompted the formation of alliances that would separate the "free world" from the "communist world." Undoubtedly few there could imagine that sixty-five years later the peninsula would remain divided across the thirty-eighth parallel. What was obvious, however, was that Japan's postwar security environment would be shaped by events on the Korean Peninsula.

For decades, the scenario of a conflict on the Korean Peninsula defined how Japanese military planners imagined the SDF might become involved in war. Rather than a direct attack against Japan, it was the spillover from a repeated war on the Korean Peninsula that seemed the most likely genesis of regional war. Japan's rearmament began as U.S. forces left their occupation duties for war on the peninsula. At the request of U.S. occupation authorities, Prime Minister Yoshida hastily ordered up the National Police Reserve to ensure peace within Japan. A nascent maritime force was also mobilized to help U.S. forces rid Korean waters of mines in 1950. The presence of U.S. forces in Japan—forces organized to support the UN Command after the armistice was concluded—meant that while Japanese forces would not be directly involved, the United States would need those bases and Japanese support for them should war erupt.[3]

In 1960, Tokyo and Washington renegotiated their security treaty. This was not due to external threat. Rather it was a result of growing political pressure within Japan on the Japanese government over the alliance with the United States. Incidents involving U.S. forces and Japanese citizens soured public opinion on the alliance. A highly publicized case of violence against a Japanese woman by a U.S. army guard drew particular anger. In 1957, Kishi Nobusuke would become prime minister, arguing the time had come to make a basing agreement into a more substantive alliance. Japan would agree to provide U.S. regional forces with bases on its territory in exchange for an explicit commitment of defense assistance from the United States. Alongside this new treaty was a memorandum of understanding that bound Washington to consult with Tokyo if it wanted to use these forces to initiate combat, to reduce or introduce major weapons systems, or to change the composition of its forces significantly.[4]

Meanwhile, Japan's own military was quietly reformed, and rearmament began. Once back from San Francisco in 1951, Prime

Minister Yoshida began to rebuild a military capable of defending the country. With all of the other governing tasks that awaited when the occupation ended, it took time to focus on how to design Japan's new military. The Yoshida cabinet understood the fine line between ensuring Japan's defense and upholding the spirit of restraint embedded in Article Nine's first paragraph. American occupation authorities had not drafted the Japanese constitution alone. Consultations with Japanese authorities, notably the Liberal Party's Ashida Hitoshi, had produced language that gave Yoshida and his successors a legal basis for providing for self-defense. But two issues had to be addressed. First, the new postwar military had to be subordinated to civilian power; and second, a new institutional setting for overseeing military affairs was needed. Japan's postwar military had to be firmly under the control of the democratically elected prime minister and his cabinet, and a new cadre of appointed officials would be assigned to define and implement defense policy. In 1954, two years after the San Francisco Peace Treaty went into effect, the Japanese Diet passed the law that would establish a new postwar military—one that would provide for the nation's self-defense while conforming to Article Nine's proscription on the use of force as "a means of settling international disputes."

At the time, 210,235 U.S. military personnel remained on Japanese soil; 185,705 were on the main Japanese islands and an additional were 24,530 in Okinawa, which remained under U.S. administration. U.S.-Japan consultations on a new naval force for Japan began early and continued after Japan regained sovereignty. In October 1951, a small group of Japanese naval officers created a study group, referred to as the "Y Iinkai," or Y Committee, to design a postwar navy. These officers did not work alone, however. They were advised by the United States, and the lead on the American side was Admiral Arleigh Burke, deputy chief of staff to the commander of U.S. Naval Forces, Far East, then working as a member of the allied cease-fire commission in Korea. According to James Auer, a historian of U.S.-Japan naval cooperation, Burke understood that the Japanese needed to rebuild their navy if they were to secure their interests. He also appreciated Japan's naval prowess and fostered the promise of U.S.-Japan maritime cooperation after the occupation ended. These fledgling forces organized during the occupation years—the National Police Reserve and the National Safety Force—became the beginnings of Japan's postwar military, the SDF.[5]

Prime Minister Yoshida needed to create the legal basis for Japan's new military, and the Diet would have to approve it. Yoshida formed a partnership with the Progressive Party, led by Shigemitsu Mamoru. Shigemitsu's party had actively discussed the need for Japan's defenses. On September 27, 1953, Yoshida and Shigemitsu announced their agreement on two points. First, they recognized that with the changes afoot in the region and "the growing spirit of independence" in Japan, it was time to create a long-term plan for national defense; and second, they would begin by turning the National Safety Force into the Self-Defense Force.[6]

A committee of members from both parties was formed to outline what was needed, and this became the outline for the new legislation drafted by the government. This outline contained the defining components of Japan's postwar defense policy, the Defense Agency and the SDF. Second, the prime minister would be given the right of command, and a civilian national defense council would be established. A new air force would be also created, separating air power from the army and the navy, and the rules of engagement for responding to violations of Japan's airspace would be set. Japan's new military services—ground, maritime, and air—would have a joint staff council. A reserve force would also be required. The committee also addressed perhaps the most difficult aspect of the new law: how to mobilize this new military and use force during a national emergency.[7]

The set of bills was presented to the Diet in March 1954: one bill to create the SDF and a second to establish the Defense Agency (see figure 1.1). In two months, these passed into law. Compared to the protracted debate over many of the policies on the SDF that followed in later years, the Diet debate over Japan's new military was matter-of-fact. Nonetheless, it revealed the new realities of defining a defensive military. Article Nine provided a new frame for thinking about military power, and the debate centered on how to apply this thinking to the design of a new type of military. Interpreting what this meant for the SDF drove policy decisions for decades to come.

Once the SDF was formed, however, the language of Article Nine continued to define Japan's debate over military policy. Eradicated from the vernacular of military policy was the term *war* and *military*—no *senryoku* (war potential), no *senkan* (battleships), and no *guntai* (military forces). From the beginning, Japanese leaders incorporated the term *self-defense* into all that was military, semantically embedding the intent of self-defense in all policy deliberations. Thus, from its conception, Japan's postwar military was the SDF, and its mission emphatic: *senshu bōei,* or "exclusive self-defense." Later, this language would be applied to the weaponry it acquired. A destroyer would be called a *goeikan*—a "defensive escort ship"—and much later in the 1980s, the reflexivity of this semantic cover was confirmed when, in Diet deliberations, the Japanese government described a Harrier carrier with a flight deck for helicopters as a "defensive" aircraft carrier.

In 1954, the concerns debated seemed less about disguising Japan's new military and more about handling the practical challenges

FIG. 1.1  Defense Agency Director General Kimura Tokutarō with the flags of the newly created Ground and Maritime Self-Defense Forces with hand-painted signs for Japan's new Defense Agency and National Defense Academy, June 26, 1954. © *Asahi Shimbun*

that confronted a newly independent Japan. One focal point was the set of requirements embodied in terms of the Mutual Defense Assistance Agreement with the United States. In the Lower House Foreign Affairs Committee deliberations, the Ministry of Foreign Affairs presented in detail the new treaty arrangements that would guide U.S. arms sales to its allies. After a devastating military defeat and seven years of occupation, Japan needed access to critical new weapons and technology. Japan had not successfully developed nuclear weapons during the war, nor was it technologically prepared for the age of the jet engine. While there was little interest in pursuing nuclear weaponry, new modern jet fighters would be needed. U.S. policy makers advised Tokyo it needed to catch up technologically if it wanted to provide adequately for its defenses.

Resources remained scarce for this early phase of Japan's recovery. Diet deliberations in the Budget Committee focused on the fact that Japan could not afford a massive investment in military weapons. In the early years after regaining sovereignty, the Japanese government was hard pressed to meet the demands of its citizens for poverty relief. Veterans' families protested in front of the prime minister's residence demanding state support. Rebuilding industrial strength required large infusions of government funding. Education and other basic services also badly needed support. Spending money on a new military had few advocates.

Even Japan's conservatives were divided on how to approach building a new military. The Yoshida cabinet and its partners in the Progressive Party saw the legislation through the Diet, but by the end of the year, Yoshida's political rival, the Liberal Democratic Party's Hatoyama Ichirō, was in the prime minister's office and Diet debate over Japan's military took on a new cast. Hatoyama was far more suspect of Washington's motives for rearming Japan. In his first month in office, he called on the Cabinet Legislative Bureau, the legal advisory body that ensured government bills were consistent with the constitution, to clarify some of the most important premises regarding Japan's newly reformed military. The Hatoyama cabinet stepped back from the idea that Japan needed to build a military capable of engaging in modern warfare, an argument repeatedly used by his predecessor, and instead sought to articulate a set of principles derived from Japan's constitution.[8]

Several aspects of that Diet debate of December 1954 continue to shape Japanese understanding of their military today. First, the discussion sought to clarify the difference between forces built for self-defense and those forces that could be described as having war potential, or *senryoku,* proscribed by Article Nine. This attempt at a distinction between offensive and defensive weapons would blossom into a serious handicap for Japanese military planners as Japanese capabilities grew, but in the early years, opposition Diet members sought to ensure that all weapons purchased by the SDF were unable to be used for striking other nations. Little discussion was had on whether Japan could defend itself without being able to strike other forces beyond Japanese territory. Second, the Japanese government sought clarity in international law regarding the right of all sovereign nations for self-defense. This basic premise of the right of self-defense was the justification for maintaining a military, and yet Japan would use this right of self-defense to limit the use of force to the minimal amount necessary and only in response to an attack on Japan. Finally, Hatoyama believed that Japan should develop a force consistent with the constraints on its use implied by Article Nine. Nonetheless, even the Hatoyama cabinet did not prohibit specific types of weapons or capabilities, relying instead on the ability of future governments to properly decide what was necessary for self-defense.[9]

## Civilians in Control

Asserting civilian authority over the use of Japan's new military was just as important as defining the limits on its capabilities. In the early decades of the postwar period, deep divisions between the conservative Liberal Democratic Party (LDP) and the progressive opposition parties, mainly the Japan Socialist Party (JSP) and the Japan Communist Party, were often focused more on this principle of democratic governance than on a debate over the country's strategic needs. The agency responsible for military policy, the Defense Agency, had been placed directly under the guidance of the prime minister. Although the agency's director general was given cabinet status, the agency itself was not accorded full ministerial powers. Defense policymaking ranked below Japan's other priorities. Officials from the Ministry of Foreign Affairs, the Ministry of Finance, and the Ministry of International Trade and Industry were seconded to populate its ranks, ensuring oversight by Japan's more powerful civilian bureaucracies. Diplomacy, finance, and trade were far more valued instruments of national policy.

Much wrangling over who was best suited to assert civilian control took place within and across the bureaucracies. Within the Defense Agency during these early years, civilian control was translated as *sebiro contorōru,* or "the control of the suits"—a reference to the primacy of the Internal Bureau run by civilian policy makers. It took time, however, to develop a new cadre of civilian defense experts. For decades, the Defense Agency was populated by bureaucrats seconded from other ministries—and thus defense policy was crafted by those with loyalties that lay in other ministries and without expertise in military planning. Not until well into the 1980s did those who began their careers in the Defense Agency rise to senior positions.[10] With the SDF barred from serious input into what was required to defend Japan and civilian bureaucrats who had little operational expertise, Japan's defense planning became dominated by fiscal and political goals rather than by debates over what constituted an effective means to defend the country.

Keeping the SDF out of the policymaking process had its costs. Fears about what the military was actually up to peppered Diet debates, and opposition party critics frequently charged the government with allowing Japan's military to plan with U.S. forces for Cold War conflicts beyond Japan. In 1965, as Japan and South Korea negotiated their postwar peace treaty, the Diet erupted in a furor over a leaked contingency study conducted by the SDF that considered what to do if war erupted on the Korean Peninsula. The Three Arrows Study (*Mitsuya Kenkyū*) was a joint staff study conducted in 1963 that included eighty-four military officers from all three services of the SDF. The study included research on various aspects of Japan's defense planning as well as situational exercises for a Korean contingency. A JSP member, Okada Haruo, nicknamed "Okapparu" and known for his hard-hitting and relentless style in Diet debates, charged the military with secret collusion with the United States, and the ensuing political uproar was a significant setback to military planning. Yet the details of the Mitsuya Kenkyū revealed just how little strategic coordination there was between the SDF and the U.S. military. Its conclusions suggested the need for a formal dialogue between the two militaries that would help clarify U.S. planning for Korea as well as how Japan's military could best defend Japan.[11]

Preventing the military from exerting control over the government was important in 1947 as many saw Japanese military expansion as being driven by uniformed ambitions. Article Sixty-Six of the constitution explicitly banned those in uniform from serving in government, and the Japanese Diet refused to allow anyone wearing the uniform to testify in hearings. In fact, the JSP recognized the constitutionality of the SDF in 1984, eight years after a decade of coalition governments in Japan had produced the first long-term planning document, the National Defense Program Outline. Even then, the JSP only accepted that the SDF had been formed in a constitutional manner, and when a JSP Diet member became prime minister in 1994, many wondered whether he truly accepted the SDF as a legitimate instrument of the state.[12] An unintended consequence of this awkward debate over civilian control was that the SDF was barred from planning, and civilian leaders became wary of advocating publicly on defense policy.

In most democracies, civilian control is exercised by the legislative branch as well as by the executive branch. These divisions in the Diet also prevented the establishment of committees responsible for overseeing Japan's defense policy. In preparation of the National Defense Program Outline in the mid-1970s, the head of the Defense Agency at the time, Sakata Michita, argued the need for the parliament to play its role in the making of national security policy. Until then, debates over defense policy were handled within the policy committees of the LDP only. Sakata was persuasive, and the first Diet committees to consider *anzen hoshō,* or "national security," were created. These were not standing committees, however, until 1991.[13]

As the political battle over civilian control raged in the Diet, Japan's bureaucrats struggled to build a new policy-making process that ensured civilians dominated defense policy. The Defense Agency was tasked with managing the rearmament process, and the Mutual Defense Assistance Agreement provided Japanese access to American military aid. Defense procurement enmeshed the SDF in a broader strategic embrace with Washington and guided the rearmament priorities of the new Defense Agency through the 1960s.

U.S. policy makers encouraged Japan to undertake a significant rearmament effort and to have the Japanese military take over primary responsibility for their country's defenses. On August 31, 1955, U.S. Secretary of State John Foster Dulles met with visiting Japanese foreign minister Shigemitsu to discuss the future of the alliance. An array of U.S. officials attended, including deputy secretaries of the Departments of State and Defense, the chairman of the Joint Chiefs of Staff, and the director of the Agency for International Development. The chairman of the Joint Chiefs of Staff at the time was Admiral Arthur Radford, who as commander of the Pacific Fleet had welcomed Prime Minister Yoshida to Hawaii on his way to and from the San Francisco Peace Treaty negotiations. With Japan's foreign minister was Minister of Agriculture Kōno Ichirō, as well as then Secretary General of the Japan Democratic Party Kishi. Just four years after diplomats met in San Francisco to declare peace, the United States wanted Japan to invest in greater defense capability and to cooperate strategically with Washington in Asia. Japanese negotiators, however, wanted a more equitable security treaty, one in which they had greater voice in the management of the alliance.

In a few years, Kishi would be Japan's prime minister, and Washington and Tokyo would begin the process of renegotiating their bilateral treaty.[14] But first a new Japanese statement of its military aims was drafted. In 1957, three years after the SDF's creation, the Japanese cabinet announced its first statement on its defense ambitions, the Basic Policy on National Defense. Four aims defined Japan's approach to national security:

- Support the UN and promote international cooperation for world peace

- Stabilize the Japanese people's livelihoods and establish the foundation for national security
- Establish effective defense capabilities
- Defend the nation on the basis of the U.S.-Japan security treaty

Spare and symbolic, the Basic Policy spoke to the limits on Japan's military ambition rather than to the international context within which Japan would pursue its strategic needs.[15]

The SDF was armed gradually, with successive procurement plans targeting capabilities that would allow it to take over defense missions performed by U.S. forces. Budgets were slim in the difficult 1950s but grew as Japan's economy took off in the 1960s. The Ground Self-Defense Force (GSDF) consumed the largest share of the budget, largely in personnel costs. But Japan's new Maritime Self-Defense Force (MSDF) needed ships, and the Air Self-Defense Force (ASDF) needed costly modern aircraft bought from the United States. By the end of the Third Defense Build-up Plan in 1972, rearmament was deemed complete. To be sure, Japan's three services were equipped with modern weaponry, but Japan had yet to articulate a national strategy for its military that would ensure the SDF's ability to defend the country.

A definitive shift in U.S. Cold War priorities forced Tokyo planners to review their approach to their military and introduced a new era of alliance attention to the military division of labor in the U.S.-Japan alliance. The Vietnam War had altered American perceptions of the U.S. military role in Asia. Richard M. Nixon wrote a well-known article in *Foreign Affairs* magazine in 1967 on the need for the United States to pull back from its commitments to its allies. The United States had spent too much money in Vietnam, and its economy was struggling. A new approach to the use of American military power was called for. It was not until 1969, however, that Nixon's ideas were translated into U.S. policy.[16]

In Tokyo, the Nixon Doctrine signaled the time had come for more careful thought about Japanese ambitions for its military. For some in the LDP, including the newly appointed Defense Agency director general, Nakasone Yasuhiro, this signaled the need for Japan to define a more "autonomous" defense posture (see figure 1.2). Nakasone's time as the director was short—only eighteen months— but it was enough to shake things up. He wanted to make the Defense Agency a stronger and more assertive player in Japan's bureaucratic politics. Because the agency had been populated by bureaucrats from other, more powerful ministries, it had developed the habit of sharing budgetary plans with these ministries in an attempt to get buy-in before taking it to the Ministry of Finance, the final arbiter of all government agencies' budgets. Nakasone ordered his bureaucrats to stop this and instead draft an integrated budget that would be presented to—and advocated for—with the Ministry of Finance directly. He also initiated the publication of an annual white paper on Japan's defense, outlining the agency's work and SDF policy goals, to explain its work to the public, just as other ministries did. Years later, when Nakasone became prime minister, he believed the time had come to make the Defense Agency a full-fledged ministry, but this would not happen until 2007.[17]

What drew most political attention, however, was Nakasone's attempt to define an autonomous defense posture (*jishu bōei*) for Japan. Arguing that the Nixon Doctrine created the need for greater self-reliance by Japan, Nakasone took aim at the fourth principle of the Basic Plan of 1957, Japan's reliance on the United States for its defenses. Under Nakasone, the Defense Agency drew up an expansive plan, departing from the gradualist five-year procurement

FIG. I.2  Defense Agency Director General Nakasone Yasuhiro inspects personnel from the Maritime Self-Defense Force, June 30, 1970. © *Asahi Shimbun*

plans that it had relied on in the past. Conspicuous was the growth in naval forces Nakasone envisioned. The procurement plan attached to this new vision came with a hefty price tag—almost double that of the previous five-year plan.[18]

Nakasone's use of the term *autonomous defense* was not new. His predecessors had begun to use this language in an effort to respond to the Nixon Doctrine. Yet Nakasone seemed far more ambitious in his vision for Japan's military. When asked in an interview in August 1970 whether he had an intent similar to his predecessors' or instead wanted Japan to go it alone militarily, Nakasone responded, "I mean both. The [Japanese] people vaguely feel that it is all right to depend on the United States. I think that this [vague feeling of reliance] is apparent also in Japan's defense strategy and defense policy-making." The political controversy caused by Nakasone's flirtation with the idea of breaking away from strategic dependence on the United States in the end was a setback for SDF planning. With the Defense Agency's small budget and its excessive ambitions, the Nakasone plan was set aside by his successor, and the Defense Agency was sent back to the drawing board.[19]

The Tanaka Kakuei cabinet, which came into office in 1972, took a far different tack. Global and regional Cold War tensions were receding. Détente between Moscow and Washington, and the Nixon White House's opening to China in 1971, suggested a different logic for thinking about Japan's defense planning. Consistent with the SDF mission of exclusive self-defense, this plan laid out what the Defense Agency called "a peacetime force posture," marking an end to the buildup plans for the SDF. Politics and finances both came into play as the defense budget was deliberated. Rising inflation and the first oil shock rattled the pace of Japanese economic growth and severely constrained the Japanese government budget. Moreover, this was a time of uncertainty for the ruling LDP. The LDP's grip on power was weakening. New reformist parties, such as the Buddhist Kōmei party and the Liberal Club were coming to the fore, and the progressive parties seemed to be gaining. Governing in the majority seemed less and less likely, and by the mid-1970s, senior leaders in the party were aware that their defense policy needed a stronger base of support among the Japanese public. The time had come to articulate a national policy that could withstand a change in government. Sakata, Defense Agency director general from 1974 to 1976, became focused on building what he called a "small but significant" military—one that was understood and supported by the public.[20]

Civilian planners within the Defense Agency also began to make their voices heard, emboldened in part by the politics surrounding Nakasone's attempt to put Japan on an ambitious path of military expansion. Rather than building bigger military forces, planners in the Internal Affairs Bureau argued that the time had come to call an end to Japanese rearmament now that the SDF had been rebuilt. Unlike the Nakasone proposal to ramp up Japan's navy and air force to match the capabilities of others, senior Defense Agency officials such as Kubo Takuya sought to bring civilian and military planners into a more constructive dialogue on the premises of Japan's defense needs. Kubo had been involved in the first three defense buildup plans, having been seconded repeatedly to the Defense Agency from the police agency, and he had also served on the National Defense Council.

Within the agency, Kubo circulated an anonymous paper entitled "Thinking about Defense Planning" to elicit debate, and over several years, he successfully drew the military into a conversation about how best to provide for Japanese security. He argued that there was little probability that Japan would be faced with a traditional attack. Therefore, Kubo believed instead that Japanese security had to include not only the military instrument but other instruments as well, including diplomacy and closer alliance cooperation with the United States. Kubo acknowledged that a limited war was the most likely scenario the SDF would have to face, and thus defense capabilities should be developed accordingly. Finally, he argued that it was vital for the Defense Agency to have the support of the Japanese people.[21]

What ultimately emerged from this internal conversation between civilian and military planners in the Defense Agency was the National Defense Program Outline of 1976, the first major statement of the SDF's force posture goals. Based on the standard defense posture (*kibanteki bōeiryoku*) concept developed by Kubo, this force posture outline presented the foundation upon which the

SDF could build rapidly if the security environment worsened. Investments in research and development would continue so that Japan's SDF would not fall behind the technological curve, but there would be no further expansion in the size and scale of Japan's three military services. U.S.-Soviet détente eased tensions in Asia as well as in Europe, and this greatly facilitated Kubo's effort to set military planning on a more predictable peacetime footing.[22]

## The U.S. Military in Japan

As their government quietly sought to rebuild a Japanese military, Japanese citizens experienced the vagaries of the Cold War largely through the prism of U.S. bases in Japan. Japan's participation in the Cold War was highly contested by the progressives in parliament, but popular opinion on the alliance with Washington was deeply affected by the conflicts first in Korea and then in Vietnam. U.S. bases in Japan prompted civil suits against the government for violating the spirit of the constitution. Crimes and misbehaviors of U.S. military personnel soured host communities and again led the Japanese government to court.

Residents of Okinawa were separated from the rest of Japan as the islands remained under U.S. administration until 1972. Protest against the extended U.S. occupation of Okinawa came to a boil when U.S. B-52 bombers took off from bases there headed for Vietnam, and a powerful local reversion movement fused with a growing national antiwar movement to call for an end to U.S. military use of Japan's southernmost islands.

In 1968, Prime Minister Satō Eisaku led negotiations with the Nixon administration for returning Okinawa, based on Japan's "residual sovereignty."[23] Satō argued that the islands must be returned to Japan under the same conditions as the main islands, that there should be no nuclear weapons, and that the U.S. military should be subjected to the same terms of consultation as discussed in the 1960 treaty. The legacy of extended U.S. occupation of Okinawa shaped politics in the prefecture as well as politics between the prefecture and the national government after reversion. Once these islands reverted to Japan, the Japanese government sought to craft leases with those landowners whose land had been forcibly expropriated by the U.S. military during the occupation. A committed group of landowners refused the leases, claiming that land expropriation violated Japan's postwar constitution. This group, the antiwar landowners (*hansen jinushi*), became the core of a broader social movement organized around the U.S. bases in Okinawa. In addition, successive governors called for a renegotiation of the Status of Forces Agreement to address with greater transparency the issues associated with the large U.S. military presence there.

Both the renegotiation of the security treaty and the negotiations over the reversion of Okinawa to Japanese sovereignty were moments of broad popular unrest and protest of the ruling party's support of alliance with the United States. Yet by the end of the Cold War, these protests had faded, as U.S. forces were reduced and consolidated and as Japan's own economy soared to the second largest in the world. In the final decade of the Cold War, Japan's technological might was harnessed to the western alliance, and then Japanese Prime Minister Nakasone, British Prime Minister Margaret Thatcher, and U.S. President Ronald Reagan worked hand-in-hand to cultivate a conservative renaissance at home and to forge a united partnership against the failing Soviet Communist vision abroad.

In the final decade of the Cold War, Japanese military power became more useful to U.S. military planners. The SDF's naval and air power offshore the Soviet Far East was an important capability for U.S. forces operating in the Western Pacific. Exercises between the Japanese and U.S. militaries had increased, and a greater level of understanding between the allied militaries led to more confident sharing of ideas about how the SDF's defensive missions could support U.S. efforts to contain Soviet forces in the Pacific. Calls for greater burden sharing led to greater financial support for U.S. forces in Japan, freeing up the U.S. budget for activities in other parts of the globe. And in the emerging technological competition between the United States and the USSR over missile defenses, Japanese technology became an important asset.[24]

The SDF began formal military consultations with the U.S. military when the two allies agreed in 1978 on Guidelines for U.S.-Japan Defense Cooperation, a division of labor between their militaries. This expanded from bilateral exercises between counterpart services to combined exercises among multiple services, then finally to combined command exercises that began to address how the two nations' militaries might think about synchronizing their operations in wartime.[25] The premise of these exercises conformed to the limited mission of the SDF, however, and thus stopped well short of an integrated contingency plan. Scenarios initially remained limited to Japan, and the two militaries practiced how they would defend Japan together. Yet, by the end of the Cold War, new proposals emerged from the SDF on how Japanese forces could support U.S. operations in the Pacific.[26]

By the mid-1980s, however, U.S. policy makers surprised Japan by asking Tokyo to send its military to an allied naval coalition in the Persian Gulf. The Iran-Iraq War had endangered shipping from the Gulf and risked halting oil shipments to the advanced industrial economies. A maritime coalition was formed that included the United States, the United Kingdom, France, Belgium, the Netherlands, and Italy. Japan's prime minister at the time was Nakasone, long an advocate of a more active role for Japan's military. Nakasone wanted Japan to join the European allies and contribute to the U.S.-led coalition. One idea was to send minesweepers, just as Japan had done during the Korean War. He asked for a concrete proposal from the MSDF and raised this option with his cabinet. He met with strenuous objections, however, particularly from his chief cabinet secretary, Gotōda Masaharu. Gotōda had experienced World War II and was strongly opposed to allowing Japan's military abroad. Japan did not in the end send its minesweepers to the Persian Gulf and instead sought to mitigate U.S. disappointment by addressing complaints from the U.S. Congress on burden sharing.[27]

Tokyo's inability to send its military abroad raised new questions about reciprocity in the U.S.-Japan alliance. Japan's economic stature had grown considerably, and Congress was particularly sensitive to the rising trade frictions with Japan. Moreover, Japan's GDP rose by 178 percent over the 1980s, stimulating a huge wave of Japanese foreign direct investment to the United States. This too drew criticism. Representative Patricia Schroeder, a Democrat from Colorado, assumed leadership of a subcommittee in the House Armed Services Committee assigned to monitor allied burden sharing. This was also a time of considerable U.S. military outlays led by the Reagan administration, and Schroeder's anger was equally directed at the Department of Defense. Schroeder did not hesitate to point out Japan's lack of contributions to the alliance and its role as America's most challenging trade competitor. Tokyo policy makers were asked to quantify all of the expenses they contributed to the alliance, always coming up short for those in Congress who saw U.S. allies as taking unfair advantage of U.S. military spending. By 1987, when the Toshiba Corporation was found to have sold sensitive technology to the Soviets, congressional tempers flared against Japan, and members of Congress smashed Toshiba televisions on the steps of the U.S. Capitol. Japan was failing the U.S. ally test and free riding on the American taxpayer.[28]

This required a political response by the LDP, and Kanemaru Shin, then director general of the Defense Agency, took on the task of persuading his fellow legislators that Japan needed to find a way to pay more for the U.S. forces in Japan. Kanemaru pitched this in terms of the need to be more compassionate toward the United States as it declined in power. Kanemaru persuaded his party and those in the opposition that they should spend Japanese tax dollars to help the U.S. forces in Japan. The *omoiyari yosan*, or "sympathy budget," began as a way of compensating for the disappointment from not sending the SDF abroad, but it became institutionalized as acceptance grew within Japan of the need for funding the U.S. military presence.

Japan increased its spending on the U.S. military and took over more and more responsibility for costs of supporting the U.S. presence in Japan. Japanese spending on the U.S. military expanded from covering the costs of Japanese workers on U.S. bases, to providing basic utilities and other regular costs associated with their presence, to building new and improved facilities for U.S. military personnel. This budget grew quickly over the 1980s and was assigned its own budget line outside of the Defense Agency's budget. Nonetheless, this spending on the U.S. military was perceived as money that could have been spent on the SDF or on other domestic causes. What started as a package of 6.2 billion yen in 1978 reached its peak in 1999 at an annual contribution of 275.6 billion yen. Even after the Cold War ended, Japan's spending on U.S. forces in Japan continued to grow.[29]

# The SDF at the Cold War's End

Japan's SDF was a formidable force, despite the country's nonnuclear status. Its navy was second to none in the Asia Pacific, with considerable antisubmarine warfare and minesweeping prowess, and fully integrated with the U.S. Navy's Western Pacific operations. The MSDF had claimed responsibility for sea lanes south of Japan up to one thousand nautical miles and conducted indispensable intelligence gathering across the East China Sea and in the Western Pacific. In the north, Japan's ASDF, equipped with the latest in fighter aircraft and with the Base Air Defense Ground Environment (BADGE) system, fended off Soviet fighters and Backfire bombers in the heightened tensions of the Cold War's final decade and conducted air defense operations from the southern islands of Okinawa, home to the Eighteenth Wing of the U.S. Air Force. The GSDF was based throughout the archipelago, from Okinawa to Hokkaido. Largely mobilized for disaster relief missions, Japan's ground forces remained focused on territorial defenses and thus had the least contact with the U.S. military. The GSDF was the largest of Japan's three services—in terms of both personnel and budget—and by the end of the Cold War, as interoperability between U.S. and Japanese forces became the goal, even the GSDF sought to contribute to the U.S. Western Pacific strategy by upgrading its coastal missile defenses in the north to contain Soviet strategic forces based at Vladivostok and Petropavlovsk.

The SDF operated alongside the U.S. military in Japan, building networks of personal relationships with generations of U.S. military personnel. U.S. legislators clamored for greater financial burden sharing during the 1980s, but Japan's military contribution to U.S. strategy in Asia in the waning years of the Cold War was

also significant. Bases in Japan, of course, had always been important to the U.S. military. U.S. destroyers and submarines patrolled
the southwestern waters near Taiwan and the Philippines from
their bases in Kyūshū and Okinawa, and the United States maintained some of its most sophisticated intelligence listening stations
on Japanese soil. With a significant portion of the U.S. Navy's
Seventh Fleet, including its only aircraft carrier based abroad, in
Yokosuka and Sasebo, these bases were indispensable to the navy in
the Pacific. Sound surveillance system networks to detect the
USSR's nuclear subs were also laid along the steep sea slopes of
Japan's extensive archipelago. The U.S. Air Force operated from
bases in the north and south, maintaining a strike force capable of
reaching the Korean Peninsula and the Asian mainland. Reconnaissance and surveillance operations conducted from Japanese
bases were critical to U.S. strategy.

During the Cold War, Soviet military operations off of its
far eastern coast provided ample opportunity for U.S.-Japan cooperation. Two conspicuous episodes of Cold War contest revealed the depth of that military cooperation. The first was when
a Soviet pilot named Viktor Belenko defected with a highly secret MiG-25, landing in a small local airport in Hakodate on
Japan's northern island of Hokkaido. Despite angry demands by
Moscow to return the fighter jet immediately, the Japanese government dismantled the aircraft piece by piece, sharing data
with the United States. Belenko defected to the United States,
where he became an adviser to the U.S. government. A second
episode was more tragic. The value of Japanese cooperation in
northern Japan with U.S. intelligence gathering was inestimable,
but it was a quiet story known largely to those who served in
Japan's northern islands and to intelligence analysts in Washington. In September 1983, however, the Soviet Union mistak-

enly shot down a Korean Airlines civilian jet, killing all 269 persons aboard. The Korean Airlines jet may have veered off course.[30] The tragedy revealed just how tense Cold War military tensions were to Japan's north.

The SDF also provided critical assets that, while not officially organized in support of the U.S. military, were welcome additions by U.S. forces beyond Japan. Japan's own maritime interests called for an extended maritime presence out to one thousand nautical miles, as Prime Minister Suzuki Zenko and President Reagan made clear in 1981. The MSDF's sea lane protection mission increasingly supplemented the U.S. Navy's regional operations. As the SDF became ever more capable of shielding Japan, the U.S. military had greater latitude and concentrated its offensive capabilities across the region from bases in Japan and elsewhere.[31]

As important as Japan—and its military—were to the United States during the Cold War, few imagined Japan as a direct target of aggression or invasion. It seemed unlikely that the SDF would be involved in combat. Deterrence through the U.S.-Japan alliance seemed to work nicely, and the standard defense posture for Japan's military outlined in its first National Defense Program of 1976 was largely a peacetime posture, designed to maintain a military capable of ramping up its capabilities should a regionwide war break out. Thus, while the SDF trained and studied with U.S. forces in Japan, little attention was paid to getting ready to fight. When the head of the SDF, Chairman of the Joint Staff Council General Kurisu Hiroomi, argued in July 1978 that Japan's civilians might want to think of how they might call up their military in case of need, he was summarily fired, ostensibly for challenging civilian control. Yet the general was warmly received within the agency tasked with preparing Japan's defenses, and given full honors upon his departure (see figure 1.3). Political attention to the critical task of drafting the

FIG. 1.3  General Kurisu Hiroomi is given a formal send-off with full honors by the SDF on July 28, 1978, after he was forced to resign for calling on Japan's civilian leaders to plan for how the military should respond to an armed attack. © *Asahi Shimbun*

legal procedures for mobilizing the military to defend Japan was sorely lacking. General Kurisu was ahead of his time; it would take repeated crises before Japan's political leaders understood that their country's ability to manage large-scale threats to public safety required a much more detailed legal mandate for a military response. Japan's civilians would need to know how to deploy their military and allow it significant latitude to do its job.[32]

The U.S. and Japanese militaries too would need to consider how they would cooperate in case of a conflict. From north to south, Japanese bases continued to offer the United States a prime location for its military operations in the Asia Pacific and beyond. Japan's military became increasingly strong, but in the decades that followed the Cold War, the United States began to demand even greater clarity about how the SDF could be deployed in a crisis. Multiple crises arose in the 1990s for Japanese policy makers, laying bare their lack of attention to military mobilization and the unfortunate way in which political efforts to restrain the SDF had in fact made it difficult for the force to conduct defense operations, especially operational cooperation with the U.S. forces needed to provide for Japan's security.

• • •

While Washington seemed persistent in its demand for a stronger military for Japan during the Cold War, most of Asia's leaders did not. Other instruments of Japan's national power were vital to restoring Japan's relations with the newly independent states of Asia. Trade and investment became the primary instruments of diplomacy for a recovering Tokyo. As Japan's economy recovered and its influence in Southeast Asia grew, it became necessary once again to reassure those neighbors that Japan had abandoned the pursuit of military power and would not return to its prewar imperial ambitions. This meant keeping the SDF at home. As the barriers to normalizing relations with the Republic of Korea (1965) and finally with China (1972) diminished, again Tokyo relied on nonmilitary instruments to persuade the countries subjected to Imperial Japan's wartime aggression of the newly reformed postwar Japan's peaceful intent.[33]

Yet Japan rearmed, and the SDF's growing capability suggested the Japanese had not abandoned completely their pursuit of military power. Repeatedly, Japanese leaders reiterated their intention to use this capability solely for the purpose of self-defense. Still, the United States urged a collective effort of European, Japanese, and U.S. military power to contend with the armies of the Soviet Union and its allies. Washington considered its alliance with Tokyo as part of a global balancing of the "free world" against the

"Communist bloc." Material power mattered in this Cold War equation, and for many in Washington, more rather than less military might was ideal. Thus, the pace and the scale of Japanese rearmament became a persistent point of contention between Tokyo and Washington. Washington wanted Japan to invest more in military might for the collective good; Tokyo wanted to limit its military to its own shores. For Japan's neighbors, the U.S.-Japan alliance began to be seen as the real barrier to Japan's return to aggression, with Washington acting as the "cap in the bottle" that kept that genie at bay. When a U.S. Marine Corps general on Okinawa said this out loud, however, it drew harsh criticism in Japan.[34]

By the end of the Cold War, Japan's SDF emerged as one of Asia's most technologically advanced—and lethal—militaries. Moreover, Japan's military was increasingly designed to complement the capabilities of U.S. forces in the Pacific. As the SDF became more capable of defending Japan, the Defense Agency began to consider ways in which the SDF might supplement and support U.S. regional offensive capabilities. A formal discussion of the roles and missions each military played for the defense of Japan opened the way to exercises between the U.S. and Japanese militaries. By the end of the Cold War, Japan's global interests began to shape alliance thinking about how the SDF might be able to play a bigger role beyond Japanese territory.

Changes in Japanese thinking about its military, however, did not correspond exactly to U.S. policy transitions in the Cold War. At times, it seemed Japanese military planning was impervious to the changes outside of the country and instead was driven largely by politics in Tokyo. LDP dominance, which lasted from 1955 until 1993, pitted conservative politicians against progressives from the Japan Communist and Socialist Parties. While much of the debate was couched in the ideological cleavages of Washington versus Moscow, the conservatives differed greatly in their views over purpose and size of their postwar military. The complex and at times inconsistent views within the LDP on the utility of the military puzzled U.S. policy makers. Alliance policy change thus took time and repeated discussion. Washington was not always successful in persuading Tokyo to take its advice when it came to thinking about Japan's military needs.

Yet the desire to build greater military self-reliance remained an undercurrent of conservative thinking on Japanese security. Self-reliance meant a larger military force and primary dependence on that military capability for Japan's defenses. This appeal to reduce Japan's dependency on the United States through greater military power never dominated the debate, but it appeared largely in response to shifts in U.S. military deployments in Japan. The first drawdown of U.S. forces came in the 1950s, and the SDF gradually took over their missions for defending Japan. The timing of the U.S. drawdown differed by mission and thus had a different impact on each of Japan's services. The last to transfer command to Japan's SDF was the U.S. Air Force, and it was not until the 1960s that the ASDF assumed full responsibility for Japan's air defenses. The U.S. Navy never really left and instead decided to homeport the only U.S. aircraft carrier abroad in Yokosuka. The U.S. Army would come and go, depending on wars in the theater. After Vietnam, however, the U.S. Marines stayed in Japan as expeditionary ground forces. Until 1972, Okinawa remained under U.S. control—largely run by the military until the Kennedy administration insisted on a civilian administration there. The Japanese government thus had two national militaries on its soil, the emerging SDF and the borrowed military power of the United States, crucial to deter aggression in the Cold War.[35]

The arguments that shaped Japanese military policy in the Cold War have continued in the decades since it ended. But as new missions for the SDF abroad have emerged, new and more lethal challenges to Japan's own defenses have appeared, new ideas about Article Nine have taken hold, and U.S. military protection now comes at a greater price. Indeed, the difficult predicament of sustaining U.S. protection has become more acute as Japan's security environment has worsened.

# TWO

# The Self-Defense Force Abroad

WITH THE COLD WAR OVER, the United States and its allies began to consider new ways to cooperate militarily, and Japan was invited to participate in ad hoc coalitions formed to cope with global sources of instability. Initially, Japan's leaders were ill prepared to respond to these emerging expectations for security cooperation outside their country. The Gulf War of 1991 dealt a difficult blow to Japan's international prestige, as the world's second-largest economy stood by while other nations gathered to help defend Kuwait against Iraq's invasion. But over time, and at times in the face of sharp criticism, the Japanese government began to send its military abroad.

From Prime Minister Kaifu Toshiki in 1990, a weak and indecisive leader overshadowed by his party's powerful secretary general, Ozawa Ichirō, to the far bolder and steadfast Koizumi Junichirō, who did not hesitate to respond to the U.S. call for assistance after 9/11, the leader at the top of Japan's government mattered greatly to decision-making on the dispatch of the Self-Defense Force (SDF) abroad. Opposition parties cried foul at the notion that

Japan's military should go beyond Japanese territory, a concern not only about Article Nine but also about the precedent of the prewar era when many blamed the imperial army for dragging Japan into war. Even within the ruling Liberal Democratic Party (LDP), there were similar voices, although the idea of military cooperation with the United States eased some of their fears. But it was the Ministry of Foreign Affairs (MOFA) that saw the benefits of SDF participation in international military coalitions and argued that this was a necessary demonstration of Japan's contribution to global security. MOFA became a strong proponent of dispatching the SDF for UN Peacekeeping Operations (PKOs). By the time the Democratic Party of Japan (DPJ) came to power in 2009, the SDF had become a regular participant in UN peacekeeping and had played an important role in the international response to global terrorism.

As its experience grew, Japan's SDF took on a more significant role in shaping policy affecting its capabilities and its missions abroad. The SDF has been going abroad now for twenty or more years, and the officers have learned from their experiences. Demand for a military voice in decision-making has grown among civilian policy makers, and the SDF's preferences have far greater weight in considering not only the operational requirements of a given mission, but also the impact of legal constraints on its ability to perform that mission adequately. While Japan's politicians still struggle with the legal intricacies of interpreting Article Nine, its military leaders struggle to clarify the latitude they have to respond to the risks they encounter on the ground, in the air, and in the seas far from Japan. From UN peacekeeping, to support for the U.S. war on terror, to antipiracy in the Gulf of Aden, Japan's SDF has experience in operating around the globe with an array of partners. Yet the restrictions placed on its operations by Tokyo continue to limit the value of SDF participation in military coalitions.

# The First Gulf War and Japan's UN Peacekeeping

The Gulf War created a political crisis in Tokyo, as Japanese leaders were asked to send their military abroad. In December 1990, U.S. Ambassador to Japan Michael Armacost called upon Prime Minister Kaifu to request Japanese participation in a coalition response to Iraq's invasion of Kuwait. By then, the ambassador had already advocated publicly for a Japanese military contribution to the Gulf War, meeting with his counterparts in MOFA as well as LDP Secretary General Ozawa and other senior leaders of the ruling party. The government was divided, the prime minister himself reluctant, and opposition parties in the Diet apoplectic.

Nonetheless, Armacost continued to argue for Japanese participation, pointing out that this was a challenge to international order, and Japan's own interests were at stake. This was not only a UN request for collective action but also a clear signal from Washington that Tokyo should assume more responsibility (and risk) in maintaining global security and reconsider its position on the aptness of using Japan's postwar military capabilities.[1] Japan's restraints on the use of its military capability would become an integral question of alliance cooperation in the decades to follow.

In the end, the Kaifu cabinet did not send the SDF to the Gulf, opting instead to provide financial support to the Cooperation Council for the Arab States of the Gulf. Yet this time the economic power of Japan did not suffice, and global media branded the country as a "checkbook power." Japan's absence from this coalition became a diplomatic liability in the new post–Cold War era. Even the government of Kuwait failed to recognize Japan's contribution when it thanked coalition members for coming to its aid, Wealth alone could not ensure Japanese interests abroad. Moreover, Japan's protracted debate over how to respond left the Japanese government vulnerable to charges that it had done too little, too late.[2]

The decision not to send Japan's military to the Gulf War haunted Japanese decision makers for a decade. As a major importer of energy from the Middle East, Japan had strong interests in the region, and its absence from the coalition drew criticism especially within the United States. Like Japan, Germany too had refused to send its military to the Gulf War coalition force, but on March 6, 1991, Chancellor Helmut Kohl announced he would send German vessels out of Europe for the first time since the end of World War II. Two months earlier, Kohl had argued in the Bundestag that "there can be no safe little corner in world politics for us Germans. . . . we have to face up to our responsibility, whether we like it or not. Until now, we have worked actively and successfully for the world's economic stability. This will no longer be enough." German minesweepers would help clean up the Persian Gulf for humanitarian purposes.[3]

Tokyo considered making a similar contribution. James Auer, the former Japan desk officer at the Pentagon, urged Japan's Defense Agency to send minesweepers to help clear the waters of Iraqi mines. Japan's navy had long maintained excellent minesweeping capabilities—a must-have for an island nation. During the Korean War, while Japan was still under occupation, the U.S. military had asked Japan's new Maritime Safety Force to assist it in the dangerous waters off of Korea. That deployment was Japan's first overseas deployment of maritime forces, albeit under the guise of Japan's newly reorganized postwar coast guard. Forty years later, however, it was Japan's navy, the Maritime Self-Defense Force (MSDF), that maintained minesweepers, and most Japanese fiercely opposed sending their military abroad. While many in the LDP, including the prime minister, hesitated, the secretary general of the party,

Ozawa Ichirō, sent an emissary to Washington to discuss what Japan might be able to contribute. Lower House member and head of the LDP's Foreign Affairs Committee Funada Hajime returned to advocate strongly for sending minesweepers, and, backed by bureaucrats in both MOFA and the Defense Agency, he took the case to the prime minister. In mid-April, Kaifu ordered the MSDF to prepare quietly for dispatch to the Persian Gulf.[4]

Thus, after Desert Storm ended and a cease-fire was concluded, a small fleet of six MSDF ships departed for the Persian Gulf (see figure 2.1). The United States, the United Kingdom, Belgium, and Saudi Arabia were already beginning to sweep mines, and four other countries, including Germany, were on their way. Japan's minesweepers would travel the farthest, south past the Philippines, through the Straits of Malacca, and across the Indian Ocean to reach the Persian Gulf. Since 1952, Japan's minesweepers had stayed in Japanese waters, and unlike the MSDF's modern destroyers, the minesweeping ships of 1991 were now vintage. They were small— around five hundred tons each—and still made of wood. Led by the MSDF minesweeper flagship, the *Hayase*, four minesweepers (the *Hikoshima*, *Yurishima*, *Awashima*, and *Sakushima*) and a supply ship, the *Tokiwa*, set out from their naval bases at Yokosuka, Sasebo, and Kure, with a total of 511 sailors on board under the command of Captain Ochiai Taosa.[5]

The Persian Gulf minesweeping mission presented senior SDF leaders in Tokyo with issues they had yet to consider. During planning, for example, the MSDF had little information about how to conduct minesweeping operations in the Gulf, and planners had to rely on reports written by those Maritime Safety Force officers who had participated in the Korean War. Japan had lost men during that conflict, a reality that the MSDF had had no reason to consider to date. For the first time, the Defense Agency had to provide

FIG. 2.1   MSDF minesweeping ships depart from Yokosuka on
April 26, 1991, for minesweeping operations in the Persian Gulf in the
aftermath of Desert Storm. © *Asahi Shimbun*

special insurance for MSDF personnel dispatched abroad so that their families would be provided for in case of death or injury, and later, once MSDF minesweepers were operating in the Gulf, MSDF staff in Tokyo struggled to find ways of supporting their sailors who were deployed far from their families for the first time.[6]

The mission itself was a success. Although they were the last to arrive, the Japanese force soon got to work. But with no modern equipment, such as underwater cameras or other high-tech gear, many of the mines had to be identified by divers. According to their commander, MSDF personnel faced their first mission abroad without hesitation in the exceedingly high temperatures of the Gulf, under assault by flies and diving in shark-filled waters. Interacting with so many other navies was also a first, but so too was the support and pride shared by Japanese citizens in Dubai and other ports. For those Japanese living and working in the Gulf, the decision to send a Japanese military contingent to join the multilateral force was welcomed, and Japanese working in the oil industry in particular were grateful that their nation's navy was there in the Gulf helping restore peaceful shipping.

Meanwhile, back in Tokyo, MOFA prepared to present the Diet with a more ambitious new law that would allow the SDF to join in UN peacekeeping operations. Japan's diplomats had long wanted to expand their collaboration with the UN, and peacekeeping offered a unique opportunity. The first Japanese to participate in a UN PKO were twenty-seven electoral observers sent to Namibia in 1989. MOFA saw a potential opportunity then for a larger Japanese role in peacekeeping, and they would go on to play a significant role in the peace process in Cambodia. The new UN authority in Cambodia was to be headed by a Japanese official, Akashi Yasushi, then the UN undersecretary general. Thus, it was a perfect first assignment for the SDF in UN peacekeeping.[7]

The debate over peacekeeping legislation consumed the parliament and delayed Japan's participation in UNTAC. Three political missteps explain the delay. First, the ruling party, the LDP, was not fully behind the idea of sending Japan's military abroad and wanted to design safeguards on how it would operate. Second, the LDP sought to push legislation through a special committee, overriding any opposition from its coalition partner, the Kōmeitō. The Kōmeitō was strongly against the idea of sending Japan's military overseas. Finally, the LDP simply ran out of time on the legislative clock, which meant the PKO legislation had to be carried over to the spring 1992 Diet session. The Kōmeitō's secretary general, Ichikawa Yūichi, put forward an amendment that limited the SDF's role to noncombat activities. Faced with this hurdle, the LDP was torn but eventually conceded to what became known as the "peacekeeping force freeze."[8]

Again in the Upper House, political opposition to the deployment overseas slowed Japanese decision-making. By mid-1992, the legislation reached the Upper House, where opposition parties had greater influence. Members of the small Japan Socialist Party staged a last-ditch effort to derail the government's bill, walking out of the proceedings. But on June 9, the Upper House passed the legislation, returning it to the Lower House. In a final demonstration of opposition, the Socialist Party members in the Lower House resigned en masse, but on June 15, the bill passed into law with a vote of 329 to 17. Japan's military would join the UN peacekeeping mission in Cambodia after all.[9]

Under the new law, however, SDF participation in UN PKOs was severely restricted. Five principles were to guide SDF dispatch to peacekeeping operations: (1) agreement on a cease-fire must be reached among the parties to armed conflicts; (2) consent for a UN PKO must be obtained from the host countries and all parties to

the armed conflicts, and consent specifically for Japanese participation in that UN PKO must also be obtained; (3) peacekeeping
operations must maintain strict impartiality, not favoring any of the
parties to the armed conflict; (4) should any of the above requirements cease to be satisfied, the government of Japan may withdraw
its military contingent; and (5) the use of weapons by Japanese
forces shall be limited to the minimum necessary to protect the lives
of SDF personnel.[10] This was the path to ensuring that UN peacekeeping would be recognized as conforming to Article Nine of the
constitution, and it reflected a hard-won political compromise. In
short, the consensus that emerged in 1992 over the use of the SDF
abroad rested on principles that limited the SDF to noncombat
roles, restricted its use of weapons to individual self-defense, and
ensured that the Japanese government would be able to bring its
military home if conditions on the ground worsened.

The SDF's first peacekeeping mission to UNTAC included over
six hundred Ground Self-Defense Force (GSDF) engineers and
seventy-five Japanese police officers. The Japanese were assigned to
four tasks: observing the cease-fire, monitoring the election, civilian
policing, and rear area reconstruction activities. Japan's police officers were dispersed around Cambodia to monitor elections and to
train Cambodian police recruits. The GSDF personnel, led by
Lieutenant Colonel Watanabe Takashi, were all in Cambodia by
October 14. They departed six months later, on April 10, 1993. A
second group, led by Lieutenant Colonel Ishioroshi Yoshio, arrived
to replace them on April 8, working for another half year until their
departure on September 26. The primary responsibility of these
troops was to rebuild the roads and bridges that had been destroyed
in the protracted civil war. The GSDF forces were located in Takéo
Province and had to build their own housing in addition to repairing
roads. Some of the GSDF were sent to Kampot to complete the

reconstruction of a national highway there, and from June, the GSDF worked on building a container facility at Sihanoukville port. As UNTAC ordered, the Japanese forces also took on additional construction projects, including building much-needed sources of water, oil, food, and medical supplies, as well as housing.[11]

Japan's MSDF and Air Self-Defense Force (ASDF) also supported the work of the GSDF in Cambodia. Two MSDF transport ships and one supply ship visited Cambodia to carry supplies for the GSDF units in two trips, one in the spring and again in the fall of 1992. The ASDF provided six C-130 transport aircraft that supported the deployment, carrying vehicles and other equipment. From October 1992 through September 1993, Japan's air force flew weekly to Phnom Penh to supply the GSDF forces, for a total of forty-six trips to Cambodia. UNTAC officials in Phnom Penh also relied on the ASDF for supplies from Manila and Okinawa.

Two Japanese died in this first UN peacekeeping mission, Takada Haruyuki from the National Police Agency and Nakata Atsuhito, a UN volunteer. Neither was a member of the SDF, but their deaths were duly noted in the government report on the UNTAC mission. MOFA wanted to build on the Cambodia experience and argued that this was the basis upon which to expand Japanese PKO participation. MOFA felt this was a breakthrough for Japan in its support for the United Nations and wanted this type of international role for Japanese forces to grow.[12]

International appraisal of Japan's first PKO experience was not as positive, however. Because of Japanese government worries about domestic politics and intense media coverage, they asked for special treatment for the SDF. They were stationed in a safe area, and were given far more comfortable quarters than other peacekeepers. For those running the UN operation, managing the SDF was difficult; Japanese forces arrived late and left early. Japan's police officers, sent from October 1992 to July 1993, were also skittish. After the death of a police officer in May 1993, many Japanese police sought safety in Phnom Penh. In the midst of the mission, a Japanese cabinet minister went to Cambodia to ask Akashi to allow Japanese personnel to leave after the May elections, drawing ire from others in the UN PKO mission. Akashi turned down this request but allowed Japanese police to serve as election monitors in a relatively quiet province.[13]

In the ensuing years, Tokyo found increasing opportunity for SDF participation in UN peacekeeping. Japan's military participated in sixteen of the twenty-six missions where Japanese officials were committed, and this included missions far beyond Asia. From May 1993, the GSDF joined the UN Operation in Mozambique in three deployments of forty-eight personnel each to assist in internal stability. Again in 1996, the GSDF sent a contingent to transport UN Disengagement Observer Forces in the Golan Heights, as well as to assign two staff officers as observers. The SDF presence there lasted until January 2013. The SDF also served in East Timor in the UN transitional administration. From May 2002 through June 2004, the number of Japanese military engineers in East Timor grew to a couple of thousand. Similarly, staff officers were sent in 2010, and in early 2012, a large contingent of over two thousand SDF personnel participated in the UN Stabilization Mission in Haiti. The SDF's most recent deployment to South Sudan, a far more dangerous environment, once more raised questions about whether Tokyo was ready to allow the SDF to fully participate in maintaining the peace once on the ground.[14]

Despite its political handicaps, the SDF has become an integral part of Japan's UN policy. Alongside diplomats, medical teams, and aid workers from the Japan International Cooperation Agency, Japan's military continues to demonstrate its ability to work with civilian populations abroad in postconflict reconstruction, or "peace-building." The PKO Law passed in 1992 was amended in 1998 and again in 2001 to facilitate rapid deployment of SDF personnel to UN missions. But the restrictions on Japan's military continue to hinder its role in UN peacekeeping efforts. In a speech on January 24, 2008, Minister for Foreign Affairs Kōmura Masahiko, a longtime advocate of greater Japanese participation in peacekeeping and "peacebuilding," spoke to a symposium of international leaders and pointed out that Japan was still ranked eighty-second among nations providing personnel to the UN. He noted that Japan still could not undertake more of the "upstream" activities in peace-building, such as monitoring cease-fires. Kōmura also pointed out the limitations in Japan's decision-making on UN peacekeeping participation, noting that the government must pass special measures laws, one by one, before it can send the SDF abroad. Kōmura wanted a new law for Japan's military, a "general law" that would apply to UN PKOs as well as to Japan's defense operations. A general law for the SDF would cover operations included in the PKO Law as well as the traditional self-defense mission stipulated in the existing SDF law.[15] Yet, to date, Japan has not rewritten its SDF Law to consolidate the new international obligations of its military. Instead, the PKO Law has been revised as new missions revealed the need to clarify for the SDF what it could and could not do on the ground. Fearful of repeated opposition by the Japanese Socialist Party, the government resisted going back to the Diet to improve upon the original law until 1998, despite promising to do so within three years.[16]

MOFA continues to lead in arguing for revisions. Playing a larger role in PKOs was one means of demonstrating Tokyo's ability to play a responsible role in UN activities and was initially seen as one way Japan could strengthen its bid to become a permanent member of the UN Security Council. Refining Japan's PKO participation has now become MOFA's focus. Over time, as Japan's PKO experience grew and as the SDF took on new missions in new settings, the government suggested several improvements. Lifting the freeze on SDF participation in missions where conflict was ongoing, for example, would have allowed the SDF to participate in UN missions in Yugoslavia and Somalia. Another idea was to up the number of SDF personnel that could participate in PKO missions from the original cap at two thousand. This would allow Japan to participate in multiple missions simultaneously.

Additional impetus to reconsidering the original PKO Law came from those who had served in Cambodia. Japanese media interviews with returning SDF personnel revealed some dilemmas on the ground. For example, an *Asahi Shimbun* interview with Matsubara Ken'ichi, the commander of the GSDF Twelfth Division involved in peacekeeping in Cambodia, revealed that his forces had been deployed close to the Japanese election monitors in Takéo for protection. But the PKO Law had only specified that personnel could use their weapons for their own self-defense or for rescue. What would happen if other Japanese working nearby came under fire? As written, Matsubara felt, the law would prevent the GSDF from helping other Japanese working on the ground.[17]

Once the Cambodia mission was over, the Japanese government and the LDP began to review the PKO experience. Three themes emerged. First, the SDF needed to gain access to UN information on the overall peacekeeping mission, even if SDF personnel were not allowed to participate in keeping the peace. Second, Japan needed to rethink its insistence that the SDF remain under Tokyo's command. The PKO Law stipulated that the Japanese government could withdraw its forces when the situation got dangerous, but those in the field felt Japanese forces could not leave if other countries' forces were ordered to stay. Finally, PKO missions were treated as an added responsibility, and not as the SDF's primary mission, which remained the defense of Japan. The government thought this should change if the military were ordered abroad. Tokyo needed to consider what the SDF would need in terms of weapons and training for its PKO mission, and thus this mission needed to be elevated to the same level of responsibility under the law.[18]

On March 13, 1998, the government's proposal for revising the PKO Law was approved by cabinet resolution. Both houses of the Diet reviewed the bill and passed it into law in June. The SDF had learned new lessons, not only in Cambodia, but also in Rwanda and the Golan Heights. The new PKO Law allowed the use of weapons for self-defense based on the orders of unit commanders; it allowed the SDF to conduct election monitoring at the request of international organizations other than the United Nations; and it permitted the SDF to supply materials for humanitarian purposes even when there was no cease-fire agreement in place.[19]

Japan's PKO Law would be revised again and again as the challenges of UN peacekeeping grew in the face of global terrorism and as the SDF gained greater insight into the way in which its mission requirements could change during deployment. Prime Minister Koizumi ordered a review of Japan's PKO experiences in 2002, with an eye to expanding future international peace cooperation. In May of that year, Koizumi promised to analyze how Japan could strengthen its ability to help bring peace (*heiwa no teichaku*) and build governance (*kunizukuri*) for those societies torn apart by conflict. As one of the sixteen experts deliberating the future of Japan's international engagement, General Nishimoto Tetsuya represented the SDF's perspective on how to implement Koizumi's ambition.

In the decades since the Gulf War, the SDF had been slowly integrated into Tokyo's policy-making on international efforts to build and sustain global peace.[20] But Japan's participation in international peacekeeping has been advocated by diplomats rather than by generals. Japan's Ground and Air SDF, along with civilian officials, have represented Japan in UN operations and have done so in increasingly dangerous settings. To be sure, the SDF had reservations about the constraints on their participation. Japan's MSDF has largely focused on missions with the United States, and has participated in U.S.-led military coalitions. The navy has had fewer constraints, and has felt more at ease with its growing experience in international cooperation.

## The Self-Defense Force in the Antiterror Coalition

The 9/11 attacks on the United States by al-Qaeda produced a UN Security Council Resolution that called for a collective response to the terrorist attack. A decade after the first Gulf War, Tokyo's response to the Iraq War was far different. Prime Minister Koizumi and his cabinet promptly drafted legislation to allow the SDF to support the U.S.-led antiterror coalition in Afghanistan. In a speech to the 153rd Diet, just weeks after the terrorist attacks, the prime minister argued that Japan must participate in collective action against terrorism based on "the laws of political morality."

Instead of referencing Article Nine and its limits on the use of force, Koizumi instead drew attention to the broader intent of the Japanese constitution's preamble. Paragraph 3 of that preamble, he argued, was the basis for considering Japan's responsibility to contribute to international peace and stability. Koizumi continued, "We believe that no nation is responsible to itself alone, but that laws of political morality are universal; and that obedience to such laws is incumbent upon all nations who would sustain their own sovereignty and justify their sovereign relationship with other nations. We, the Japanese people, pledge our national honor to accomplish these high ideals and purposes with all our resources."[21] The question was not whether Japan would participate in response to the terrorist attacks on the United States, but rather how.

The bureaucracies responsible for foreign and security policies were also primed for a rapid Japanese response, and even the ruling party's main opposition, the DPJ, supported a strong military response to the attacks against the United States. There was no veto to the dispatch of Japan's ASDF to help with the anticipated refugees that would result from a U.S. offensive strike against Iraq. In sum, as Jeffrey Hornung points out in his in-depth analysis of this period, "because decision makers throughout government shared the same belief, unlike the Gulf Crisis, implementation also encountered no problems." The consensus within the government and among the newly realigned political parties in Japan on playing a role in international response to the terrorist attacks, and on the legitimacy of using the SDF in such a coalition response, was in stark contrast to the disarray that characterized Japanese decision-making in the immediate aftermath of the Cold War. The SDF had proven itself a reliable partner to MOFA and the Japan International Cooperation Agency, as well as to Japan's increasingly pragmatic opposition party, the DPJ.[22]

Japan's MSDF again played a prominent role in the international military coalition organized by the United States in the wake of the 9/11 attacks. The Special Measures Law for Preventing Terrorism at Sea, presented to the Diet on October 5, 2001, passed into law on November 2, 2001, and allowed Japan to participate in refueling operations for one year, with an option for extension. Under Article

Four of that law, the cabinet was required to approve a basic implementation plan, and then the director general of the Defense Agency would determine the mission requirements. A final go-ahead from the prime minister would then be needed. The implementation plan and the mission parameters were revisited every six months as deployments rotated. Overall, Japan's refueling mission involved fourteen ships and about 2,400 MSDF personnel. With the combined missions set under the initial Antiterror Law and the new maritime Special Measures Law, the MSDF participated in refueling missions for eight years. Under the earlier law, the MSDF largely supplied U.S. ships, but this gradually shifted over time until around 76 percent of the ships refueled by Japan were from countries other than the United States. Pakistan and France became the primary recipients, along with less frequent supply to the United Kingdom, Germany, Canada, New Zealand, and Denmark (see figure 2.2).[23]

But the U.S. invasion of Iraq tested Japan's political tolerance far more. The discussion in the UN over Iraqi weapons of mass destruction made it clear that Washington was preparing military action against Iraq. Gaining UN approval would facilitate the formation of a supporting coalition; the Japanese government strongly advocated that the United States remain committed to a multilateral effort and tried to support U.S. efforts at gaining a UN resolution against Iraq.[24]

There could be no direct Japanese combat role, of course. Nonetheless, Koizumi turned yet again to the Japanese constitution's preamble to make the case for providing humanitarian assistance to Iraq after Saddam Hussein's government had been toppled. At a summit meeting with President George W. Bush in May 2003, Koizumi told the U.S. president, "Japan wished to make a contribution [to the reconstruction of Iraq] commensurate with its national power and standing." He had already ordered the dispatch of

FIG. 2.2    The crew of the MSDF's *JS Ikazuchi* says farewell to its
Pakistani counterparts after participating in a refueling mission to support
the U.S. antiterrorism coalition formed after 9/11. © *Asahi Shimbun*

ASDF C-130s to help those fleeing from the war, but the scope
and scale of Japan's aid to Iraq's reconstruction required new legislation—and again a debate over what latitude the SDF would have
for working in an international coalition.[25]

As expected, there were critics in the Diet, but the UN Security Resolution 1483 calling on member states to provide assistance
in the reconstruction of Iraq offered a way forward. Adopted on
May 22, 2003, Resolution 1483 called upon member states "to
assist the people of Iraq in their efforts to reform their institutions and rebuild their country, and to contribute to conditions
of stability and security in Iraq." Iraq needed help in restoring
most of its basic social needs, including medicine and education,
as well as rebuilding roads, ports, and other vital infrastructure.

Coalition militaries were asked to provide transport and supplies and to stabilize local communities.[26]

The Koizumi cabinet began to consider Japan's response and came up with a plan that would include civilian aid workers and the military to help with reconstruction. But the Iraq mission was not a UN PKO, and the conditions there did not meet the principles set for SDF participation under the PKO Law. On June 13, 2003, the government presented new legislation, the Law Concerning the Special Measures on Humanitarian and Reconstruction Assistance in Iraq (or the Iraq Special Measures Law), to the Diet for approval. Deliberations were lengthy, but on November 29, 2003, two Japanese diplomats—Counsellor Oku Katsuhiko of the Embassy of Japan in the United Kingdom and Third Secretary Inoue Masamori of the Embassy of Japan in Iraq—were shot and killed on their way to attend an aid conference for the reconstruction of Iraq. In only a couple of weeks, the bill was approved in the Lower House and sent to the Upper House. On July 26, it was passed into law.[27]

## The Ground Self-Defense Force in Samawah, Iraq

GSDF commanders struggled to envision how they would perform their new mission on the ground in Samawah, Iraq. In January 2004, a fact-finding mission was sent to Iraq, and it identified the southern region in Muthanna Province, under British military control, to be a safe place for the SDF to operate. The commander of that early mission, GSDF Colonel Satō Masahisa, had served in two previous PKO missions, first as a member of the MOFA group sent to Cambodia and then as a unit commander in the Golan Heights. His work in Iraq, however, was under the scrutiny of live television, as journalists sought to follow his every step. This live coverage had an unanticipated benefit, however, for government officials seeking a larger role for the SDF in UN peacekeeping. For the first time, the Japanese watched SDF officers in the field as they navigated the cultural and political complexities of post-Hussein Iraq alongside a host of other world militaries. Many seemed to take pride in watching the charismatic "Colonel Satō with the mustache" think about how Japan could aid the Iraqi people (see figure 2.3).[28]

Despite this national gaze, Satō related some of the odd policy disconnects experienced by Japan's military as it prepared for its mission in Iraq. His unit comprised only thirty people and thus was too small for military transport, but Japan's civilian airliners were reluctant to allow them to fly together or to allow them to wear their uniforms, due to the antiwar sensitivities of Narita Airport officials. With the help of the British, Satō and three others went into Iraq quietly ahead of the rest of the unit to get a feel for what was happening there. Ultimately, the Japanese fact-finding mission had to wait for the Dutch in Kuwait, who were late to arrive because the Kuwaiti government did not want the Americans to transport forces in the middle of rush hour traffic. The Dutch had been assigned to police the Muthanna Province and thus provided briefings to the Japanese team. Later, British and Australian forces moved in, and when the GSDF assumed its mission in Samawah, the Australian prime minister stated that his forces would protect the SDF working in the province.

Satō's main concern, however, was the rapidly changing power dynamics on the ground in Iraq, and he worried about the growing frustrations of the Iraqi people. No private companies or nongovernmental organizations were allowed on the ground in Iraq to meet local demands for services. Thus, Satō tried to fill that gap. He described his approach as being like the "chief executive officer

FIG. 2.3   Ground Self-Defense Force Colonel Satō Masahisa talks to the press in Samawah, Iraq, on January 19, 2004. © *Asahi Shimbun*

of the Satō Trading Company" as the GSDF tried to help Iraqis rebuild. To try to meet local demands, he reorganized the SDF unit by the functions it needed to perform, at least until the larger GSDF unit, commanded by Colonel Banshō Koichirō, could arrive at the end of the year. In the end, officials from MOFA were sent to join him, bringing with them help in securing funding for what needed to be done in Samawah.

The Iraq Reconstruction Assistance Force was ultimately to serve in Iraq for two and a half years. Six hundred GSDF personnel were assigned to the force, with five hundred composing the main force, which rotated every three months. The remaining one hundred personnel would provide support and rotate every six months. Command was divided between the GSDF regional commander and the chief of staff. Members of the cabinet secretariat were also assigned to the unit as policy advisers.

Preparations took some time, but in 2004, the first GSDF unit was deployed to Iraq. In an internal report, the GSDF characterized its operations in Samawah this way: "First and foremost, the Japanese forces worked to restore access to healthcare, water, and public facilities to the Iraqi people. But when these basic services were interrupted by unrest, the GSDF had to support other nations' efforts to reestablish peace and stability." No matter how safe Samawah was initially thought to be, the SDF was working in an increasingly unstable Iraq.[29]

In its internal assessment of the mission, the GSDF noted some of the unforeseen difficulties it faced in Samawah. This was the first time that Japan's military was asked to work outside the UN framework on postconflict reconstruction. U.S.-led coalition forces had overthrown the Iraqi government, and control of the country remained contested. Moreover, Iraqi reconstruction of the country proved an enormous task. While Japan's SDF had experience with

UN-led transitions from conflict to peace, there was no blueprint for the type of situation it faced in Iraq.

Originally, Japanese aid workers were also expected to work closely with the GSDF—a new endeavor for both. The Japanese government had committed up to 5 billion dollars in funding for reconstruction, of which 1.5 billion dollars would be grants. Yet only 200 million dollars of this grant aid was dedicated to Muthanna Province, the poorest province in Iraq, with a high unemployment rate.[30]

And when Japanese aid workers were taken hostage in April 2004, the Japanese government prohibited civilians from traveling to Iraq, complicating the Samawah reconstruction effort. Three Japanese had been taken hostage and shown on Al Jazeera television as being the captives of the Mujahadeen Squadron, which issued a threat that the captives would be executed if Japan's military forces did not leave the country immediately. The hostages were eventually released, but no more aid workers were allowed to travel to an increasingly unsettled Iraq.[31]

Thus, the GSDF had to step in to play a larger role than initially anticipated in implementing projects designated as official development assistance. Expectations of the Samawah residents for Japanese aid were very high, especially given Japan's overall largesse in Iraq, and so while it did not have access to funding decisions, the GSDF worked hard to satisfy those expectations by delivering much-needed services. The SDF not only provided initial humanitarian assistance and reestablished basic services but also became involved in constructing major public facilities, including large-scale power plants, rebuilding the Samawah General Hospital, and building roads and bridges as well as irrigation systems. Japanese official development assistance funded all of these projects.[32]

A second issue for the SDF unit in Samawah was ensuring its own safety. Rockets and other weapons fired at, and hit, the Japanese barracks. The GSDF took steps to reinforce its buildings and brought in unmanned surveillance helicopters to provide warning. Back in Japan, new training facilities imitating conditions on the ground were built at the Kita Fuji Maneuvering Ground near Mount Fuji to give the soldiers heading to Samawah a chance to experience what it might be like once they got there. In fact, the training ground was often called "mini-Samawah." Although ostensibly sent to a noncombat zone, the GSDF nonetheless came under fire and accordingly had to undertake extraordinary training to learn how to defend against it.[33]

## THE SDF USE OF WEAPONS ABROAD

Perhaps more than any other overseas deployment to date, the Iraq mission highlighted the contradiction of sending the SDF abroad but limiting its use of weapons. For lawmakers in Tokyo, the Iraq mission was permissible only if it was strictly for reconstruction, and keeping Japanese forces far away from the regions in Iraq that were still dangerously unsettled was paramount to ensuring they would not be involved in any conflict. But for many in the SDF, this was an uncomfortable situation; the fact that Japan's troops had to ask for protection by other militaries—first the Dutch and then the British and the Australians—rankled.[34] To be sure, the SDF was not ready for the unsettled situation in Iraq and had no authority to help keep the peace there.

As the SDF was increasingly sent abroad on more complex and potentially more dangerous missions, the limits imposed by political leaders on how Japanese forces used their weapons became a problem. Japan's legislators sought to minimize the situations in which the Japanese forces would use weapons, but they also restricted their rules of engagement once they were abroad. The forces could not escape history's shadow when they went overseas, and Japan's military adventurism in the 1930s on the Asian continent had not been forgotten. Deploying the SDF in coalitions alongside other military commanders ensured a degree of restraint. Nonetheless, Japan's political leaders wanted strict limitations on how their military used its weapons. The original PKO Law allowed individuals to use their weapons in self-defense; the law was later amended to allow an SDF commander to order the use of weapons to defend all members of his unit.

The Antiterrorism Special Measures Law pushed this further, allowing those who deployed abroad in coalition forces to use their weapons on behalf of anyone working alongside the SDF. In Iraq, a new scenario arose, one that then head of the Defense Agency Ishiba Shigeru had anticipated during deliberations over the Iraq Special Measures Law: what if GSDF personnel were to face a situation where a Japanese member of their unit was taken hostage? This was a real possibility for those in Samawah, who were not permitted to use their weapons to find and rescue hostages, even if they were SDF personnel. This problem would not be addressed until the Abe Shinzō cabinet reinterpreted the constitution in July 2014.[35]

Another consideration for the Japanese military was the receptivity of the local population to its presence. The Japanese were very sensitive to how their forces were seen, and the *Asahi Shimbun* teamed up with local Iraqi newspapers, *Al Samawa* in June and *Uruk* in November 2004, to survey local views on the GSDF's activities and presence. Both surveys found many residents in Iraq were positive about the SDF presence. As time went on, Iraqis grew more critical of the occupation of their country, and this was true too of the residents of Samawah, but the SDF seemed to be spared the brunt of this resentment. One GSDF analyst suggested that Samawah residents seemed to view the Japanese military more favorably than other forces because there was high local interest in the work of the GSDF. Perhaps the Japanese government's continuous aid to Iraq, including projects in Samawah even after the GSDF returned home, eased some of these frictions.[36]

Once home in 2006, the GSDF reviewed its Iraqi mission with an eye to future policy reform. Five thousand five hundred members of the GSDF had served in Iraq with no loss of life—a remarkable achievement given the experiences of other forces there. The deployment raised critical questions back in Tokyo. Within the GSDF, the role of reconstruction drew fire as some questioned whether this was the proper mission for a military. In his foreword to the official GSDF report on the mission, its first commander, Banshō, responded to these concerns head on. Titling his essay "Are we donkeys or are we lions?," Banshō included a story he shared with GSDF troops in Samawah. He addressed their ambivalence, saying it would be easy to think of this humanitarian support mission as carrying the load for other militaries—the work of a donkey—rather than fighting a war—the work of a lion and the real work of a military. But he argued it is because the GSDF is a military with all of its attributes and capabilities that this work of a donkey can get done in Iraq. Without our military capabilities, we would be unable to complete this mission, he explained. GSDF commanders set out to create a comprehensive operational plan and hold daily tactical briefings. Once again, Banshō emphasized that this was an operation that could only be achieved by a military organization. This language was turned against the GSDF later on by opposition party critics as the Japanese government considered allowing the SDF greater latitude for participation in UN PKOs.[37]

Nonetheless, the debate over SDF participation in international military coalitions continued to evolve in Tokyo. Iraq presented a new opportunity for the SDF to work with other Japanese agencies. Japan's military had little experience in working alongside its international aid experts, and, unlike the United States and the United Kingdom, it had no formal coordination processes to rely on for the Iraq mission. In his analysis of the Iraq experience commissioned by the Joint Staff College in 2013, GSDF Lieutenant Colonel Sakaemura Yoshiyuki argued that Japan could consider improving its ability to provide the dual needs of security and development through a more conscious effort at improving interagency coordination and planning in advance of these missions.[38]

At the time, however, the Japanese public remained skeptical. By the end of 2004, media polling revealed a majority of Japanese wanted their military to return home. In the Diet, Prime Minister Koizumi continued to advocate for the GSDF to extend its stay and cited popular support in Samawah as demonstration of the value of the mission. While Koizumi was right in saying the majority of Japanese supported what the SDF had done in Iraq so far, they did not support the one-year extension of the operation that the cabinet decided on December 10, 2004. The polls conducted by the *Asahi*, the *Nikkei*, and the *Yomiuri* that month all revealed that a majority of the public opposed such an extension. There was no lack of critics abroad, either. Sending a military into Iraq, where the dangers were mounting, without adequate ability to defend themselves seemed foolish. Not allowing SDF commanders to use their weapons as they saw fit could not only endanger the SDF but also place an undue burden on other nations' militaries that worked alongside the SDF to provide for its protection.[39]

## Antipiracy Cooperation in the Gulf of Aden

The debate over how the SDF could enhance Japan's contribution to global security did not end with 9/11. The conversation in the legislature over global security cooperation continued. Japan had long been involved in Southeast Asia, helping states develop the capacity to cope with piracy and other maritime threats, so when piracy against global shipping in the Gulf of Aden intensified in 2008, it offered an opportunity once again to send the SDF abroad. This time the coalition was organized to combat Somali pirates.

The International Maritime Organization reported 293 incidents of piracy in 2008, with 111 of these being off the coast of Somalia. This was a leap of 60 percent from the previous year, and the UN Security Council took up the call for action. Japan cosponsored resolutions that ultimately led to the establishment of a multinational naval force tasked with patrolling and defending shipping in the Gulf of Aden. In January 2009, the Combined Maritime Force was established to fulfill the UN mandate to prevent piracy.[40]

Interestingly, it was not the ruling party that advocated for a Japanese role in this new naval coalition; it was an up-and-coming Diet member, Nagashima Akihisa, from the DPJ. Nagashima embraced the idea of a stronger role for the SDF in international cooperation and raised this in the Upper House in the context of special committee discussion on antiterrorism and on the Iraqi reconstruction mission. In special committee deliberations on Japan's role in the international antiterror coalition, he added a new opportunity for the SDF—antipiracy cooperation. Nagashima's point was simple: shouldn't Japan be responsible for the mission of protecting its own shipping instead of relying on others? Prime Minister Asō Tarō registered some surprise: "My first thought, frankly, was that this is the kind of idea that would be proposed by someone in my own party—not from someone in the opposition!"— and then went on to say that, in principle, he approved of Nagashima's idea.[41]

Minister of Defense Hamada Yasukazu ordered a report on SDF options for antipiracy on January 28, 2009. Chief of Staff of the Joint Staff Saitō Takashi, MSDF Chief of Staff Akahoshi Keiji, and Director of the Defense Intelligence Headquarters Shimodaira Kōji began their assessment of the options, and the MSDF started to consider how it could contribute. Hamada also ordered the commander in chief of the MSDF Self-Defense Fleet, Admiral Izumi Tōru, to begin preparations. A field investigation team was dispatched to the region on February 8 to review possible bases for the SDF; the thirteen-member team visited Yemen, Djibouti, Oman, and Bahrain during its twelve-day tour. They visited regional ports as well as U.S., French, and Djiboutian military bases, and they consulted with the Combined Maritime Forces in Bahrain on what operations were under way in response to pirate activities.[42]

Not only was this a new locale for SDF operations, it also brought together Japan's two maritime agencies, the MSDF and the Japan Coast Guard (JCG). The JCG was the representative to the Regional Cooperation Agreement on Combating Piracy and Armed Robbery against Ships in Asia and thus was deeply familiar with multinational antipiracy efforts. The JCG would be deployed with the MSDF for the Gulf of Aden mission to detain and arrest Somali pirates—a role for law enforcement. On February 20, the MSDF and the JCG held their first joint exercise off the point of Kure aboard the MSDF destroyer *Takanami*, with two JCG patrol boats playing the role of pirate and their target vessel. Two hundred fifty personnel took part in the exercise, including 60 members of the JCG. Two weeks later, 155 government officials came together in a joint map exercise at the MSDF Staff College to focus on coordination for the mission.[43]

The Ministry of Defense (MOD) aimed for a new law that would define the mission and its parameters. The government's Law on the Penalization of Acts of Piracy and Measures Against Acts of Piracy was submitted to the Diet on March 13 for deliberation.

Anticipating a slow Diet deliberation process, the Asō cabinet decided to move ahead with the deployment so that Japan's MSDF would arrive as promised for duty in the coalition. In the meantime, Defense Minister Hamada issued an Order for Maritime Security Operations on the same day, deploying the *Sazanami* and *Samidare,* two Japanese destroyers, with approximately four hundred personnel on board, to the Gulf of Aden. Prime Minister Asō, Defense Minister Hamada, Joint Staff Chief of Staff Saitō, and even the DPJ's Nagashima, who initiated the Diet discussion on antipiracy, traveled to the MSDF base at Kure in Hiroshima on March 14 to send off the antipiracy mission.

Within the framework of international cooperation, Japan's political leaders had become far more at ease with sending their military abroad. To be sure, the mission needed to conform to the aims of supporting peace and providing for the security of the Japanese people. But trust in the SDF had grown, and Japanese leaders had come to appreciate the benefits of showing the flag abroad. Moreover, the SDF itself was more experienced in overseas assignments and could work easily with civilian and military counterparts abroad. The antipiracy mission also brought new learning opportunities. In 2009, Japan signed a Status of Forces Agreement with Djibouti, where it based P-3C reconnaissance aircraft to support its surface ships in the mission. Since 2009, the MSDF has participated in Combined Task Force 151, one of three task forces operated by the thirty-one-nation Combined Maritime Forces organized to protect some of the most important shipping lanes in the world. By mid-2015, the MSDF had conducted 621 escort missions, protecting over 3,500 ships transiting the Gulf of Aden.[44]

Japan's experience in multilateral military coalitions has expanded considerably since the end of the Cold War, and the SDF now sees its role in international peace operations as one of its primary missions. As Japan's military operated overseas with other militaries, however, the restraints over how it used its weapons remained a critical focus of Diet deliberations. Legislators wanted to strictly limit the opportunity for the SDF to use force. For those who had been on the ground in these missions, however, it was clear that in certain situations, the SDF needed to be able to apply force more effectively in order to do its job. In particular, the difficult situation in South Sudan raised new questions for Tokyo policy makers. MOFA, under the PKO Law, sent observers to the new nation's national referendum. But as the situation on the ground deteriorated, it was clear that a larger role for Japan that included the SDF could emerge and prompt yet another round of debate over just how much danger the SDF could be exposed to without amending the PKO Law.[45]

## New Asian Partners

Just as many in Japan grew increasingly comfortable with the idea of their military operating abroad to restore peace, many of Japan's neighbors also began to welcome the SDF as partners in humanitarian and disaster relief as well as in helping to build capacity in maritime defenses. Three generations after World War II, the SDF has created strong partnerships with the militaries of many Asian neighbors.

Asia's growing concerns over maritime security have partly prompted the development of these ties, but Japan's SDF has also proven its value, providing critical humanitarian and disaster relief in the wake of natural disasters in the Philippines, Indonesia, and even in China. The SDF also began to build closer ties with the militaries of other U.S. allies and partners. Perhaps most conspicuous have been the growing strategic ties between Japan and Australia. Tokyo and Canberra began their strategic dialogue in 2006, in a trilateral initiative with Washington. Cooperation in the Western Pacific has blossomed to include intelligence, surveillance, and reconnaissance as well as maritime activities.[46]

Maritime capacity building is a new avenue for military cooperation in the region. With Southeast Asian nations such as the Philippines and Vietnam, Japan is providing assistance in building maritime defense capacity. Japan expanded its support for Philippine maritime defenses, leasing ten coast guard vessels. In 2015, the MSDF conducted bilateral maritime defense training with the Philippine Navy as the U.S. Navy conducted a similar exercise. The following year, the MSDF sent two destroyers and a submarine to observe the annual U.S.-Philippine Balikatan exercise. The MSDF ships then went on to visit Vietnam. Prime Minister Abe has invited the leaders of Vietnam and the Philippines to Tokyo to discuss shared maritime security concerns in the Asia Pacific. When Abe first met with newly elected Philippine President Rodrigo Duterte in Tokyo in September 2016, the prime minister announced an additional two coast guard cutters would be made available to Manila. Similarly, Japan has expanded its strategic dialogue with India. Beginning in 2009, the two navies consulted on maritime concerns, followed by discussions between Japan and India's respective air and ground forces. In 2015, the MSDF joined in the bilateral Malabar exercises between the U.S. and Indian navies, and the following year, the three navies exercised closer to the East and South China Seas in the seas north of the Philippines.[47]

The MOD has also begun to share military technology with its security partners. In 2014, the Abe cabinet relaxed restrictions on defense exports, adopted in 1967, to allow the ministry to explore military sales. In an ambitious early foray into the competitive weapons trade, Japan bid alongside the French and the Germans on providing Australia with a new fleet of conventional submarines. While many in Washington and Tokyo saw the sale as a good strategic investment, Canberra did not choose the Japanese subs and went with the French instead. The Ministry of Defense had little experience in competing for military contracts and was unprepared for the politics within Australia that shaped decision-making. The MOD is also exploring possible defense sales to India after the Indian government expressed interest in a Japanese search and rescue airplane.[48]

. . .

The decision to send Japan's SDF overseas was incremental and largely ad hoc. It not only took time to build a political consensus at home on the benefits of international security cooperation, but it was an ongoing learning experience for Japan's military. To some extent, the SDF's involvement in military coalitions abroad was driven by the U.S. desire for Japan to take on a greater military role internationally. As time went on, however, the benefits to Japan of sending its military abroad to work alongside the militaries of other partners became more apparent. Japan's longstanding commitment to the United Nations as the preferred framework for global security cooperation made UN Peacekeeping Operations a natural focus for expanding Japanese military cooperation.

The UN Transitional Authority in Cambodia gave the SDF its first taste of what many in Japan refer to as peacebuilding, and in many missions since, the SDF has been assigned across the globe, working side by side with other national militaries as well as civilian populations in need of assistance. While public opinion in Japan has gradually come to embrace this new role for the military, legislators remain focused on ensuring limits on how the SDF uses force. Avoiding scenarios where the SDF would be called upon to impose the peace, in other words, has been an important goal in Tokyo's decision making.

Over time, the SDF slowly developed a larger voice in government policy deliberations over international security cooperation. SDF leaders reviewed their own performance, reflecting on the lessons learned in each mission, and their analysis revealed the divergent expectations they face. However, only a small percentage of SDF personnel have had this international exposure, and the learning that accrued has been mission specific. According to the *Defense of Japan 2018*, roughly 11,000 of Japan's over 200,000 SDF personnel participated in UN peacekeeping operations. For missions in support of U.S.-led military coalitions, the number is far smaller. For example, the activities included under the Iraq Special Measures Law included only 1,240 SDF personnel, and under the Antiterror Law, only 320 MSDF personnel were dispatched. Similarly, for the antipiracy mission only 1,380 SDF have had that experience.[49]

Nonetheless, whether under UN auspices or led by the United States, Japan's military has gained experience in a variety of international coalition operations, including peacekeeping, postconflict reconstruction, disaster relief, and maritime coalition operations. This has had some unintended benefits. For example, MSDF participation in the multinational antipiracy effort in the Gulf of Aden brought Japanese and Chinese naval personnel together to work toward a shared goal—a valuable opportunity given the rising maritime tensions between Asia's two largest navies in waters closer to home. The SDF now assists other militaries in developing the capacity for UN peacekeeping and disaster relief missions. Moreover, Japan's military has become fully incorporated in civil-military cooperation on international peacebuilding. The SDF now works alongside aid workers, NGOs, and the civilian communities it has been assigned to assist. As a result, Japan's military has come out of the domestic shadows and into the international spotlight, making it an increasingly cosmopolitan arm of the Japanese state.

# THREE

# Mobilizing the Military

CLOSER TO HOME, Japanese leaders began to face growing pressure on their nation's defenses as the military balance in Northeast Asia grew far more challenging. With increasing frequency, Japan's security planners were forced to reassess some of their most basic assumptions about how to defend their country and to remedy gaps in military planning that had largely gone unnoticed during the Cold War. The Japanese military had to increase its defense operations and add new missions and capabilities to keep pace with the growing military might of its neighbors.

These gaps were obvious when Kim Jong-il announced North Korea's withdrawal from the Treaty on the Nonproliferation of Nuclear Weapons, commonly known as the Nuclear Nonproliferation Treaty, in 1993 and signaled his intention to build a nuclear arsenal. The Clinton administration sought out its Japanese ally, asking for assistance should the use of force become necessary.[1] However, Japan's politics were in flux in the early 1990s, as internal strife within the Liberal Democratic Party (LDP) had led a group of Diet members to leave the party. In 1993, Prime Minister Hosokawa Morihiro led a liberal coalition of smaller parties and wrested power from the conservatives for the first time since 1955. The Hosokawa cabinet interpreted Japan's constitution strictly and opposed allowing the Self-Defense Force (SDF) to respond to regional contingencies with U.S. forces. In the end, the Clinton administration chose not to go to war on the Korean Peninsula, but the U.S.-Japan alliance now confronted a new dilemma. Should a conflict break out in Japan's vicinity, what were Japan's leaders willing to allow their military to do with U.S. forces?

Not long after the crisis with North Korea, growing cross-strait tensions between Beijing and Taipei led to another military showdown for the United States in Northeast Asia. By 1996, the LDP was back in power in Japan, albeit now in a coalition government, but the Taiwan Strait crisis was equally sensitive for Tokyo decision makers. U.S. bases in Japan would undoubtedly be needed should military conflict erupt across the Taiwan Strait. Washington continued to press Tokyo to clarify what it could—and could not— do in the case of a regional contingency. But more to the point, it was increasingly apparent that the danger of some sort of military conflict in the region had grown in the Cold War's wake.[2]

Japanese civilian leaders were ill prepared to answer Washington's queries largely because they had yet to come to a consensus on the use of their own military in case of a crisis. The SDF had been organized to defend Japanese territory, and yet the practices and policies for mobilizing Japan's military for national defense still had to be codified. As North Korea and Chinese forces intruded into Japanese airspace and surrounding waters, Japan's civilian decision makers had to consider how they might respond if force was used against Japan. To keep pace with the growing military power of its neighbors, the Ministry of Defense revisited the premises of its military planning. While Japanese leaders had seen diplomatic advantage in sending the SDF abroad on global missions, it became increasingly clear that by the early 2000s, Japanese leaders needed their military to deter aggression at home.

## Repeated Crises, Abroad and at Home

In the first decade after the Berlin Wall came down, Japan's security planners were repeatedly overwhelmed by the demands of crisis management. Multiple crises shook Japan's security policy-making in the 1990s, raising important questions about the role of the postwar military. Japan's neighbors in Northeast Asia began to behave in ways that shook the U.S.-Japan alliance, and thus the premises of Japan's security planning. Most jarring was North Korea's announcement to exit from the Nuclear Nonproliferation Treaty and the prospect of Kim Jong-il's pursuit of a nuclear arsenal. While the Korean Peninsula was always Asia's flashpoint throughout the Cold War, this was the first time Tokyo confronted a U.S. request for clarity on what its military could and could not do in support of U.S. forces in a regional contingency. The answer was very little, under existing Japanese laws.

The Taiwan crisis came soon thereafter. In 1996, China conducted missile tests near Taiwan in the run-up to its first direct presidential election. Again, this prompted a conversation in the alliance over how Japan might contribute, should it become necessary. In a Taiwan contingency, the SDF would have no direct role, but U.S. forces in Japan would be needed and the Japanese government would need to approve their use. But it was Beijing's attempt to coerce Taipei that most alarmed Tokyo. Japan's security planners were already sensitive to China's nuclear modernization, and the growing signs that Beijing intended to use its military power to assert its interests in the region signaled a potentially serious threat to Japan's own security. By the mid-1990s, it became clear in Tokyo that Japan was faced with a militarily powerful neighbor that seemed increasingly willing to use that capability to alter the regional balance of power.

Adaptation to the new realities of Northeast Asia was slow. The SDF had a good working relationship with U.S. forces in Japan, and U.S. strategic planners found Japan's military to be a more comfortable partner than most Japanese politicians. While Japanese bureaucrats and politicians hesitated to turn to the SDF for policy ideas, U.S. civilian counterparts saw the strategic potential of Japan's military and had pressed Japan's political leaders to use it more effectively alongside U.S. forces.

Japanese leaders did not embrace the full military integration that characterized the NATO and the U.S.-Republic of Korea alliances, and in the aftermath of the Cold War, the question of how the Japanese and U.S. militaries would operate together in Northeast Asia became far more pressing. As the North Korean crisis revealed, the lack of formal contingency planning in the U.S.-Japan alliance meant that the two governments had no idea how they would work together in a conflict. Even whether the U.S. military could count on the use of bases in Japan and how many might be available in a conflict was not clear. With no combined command between U.S. and Japanese forces, the two militaries could only explore some of these issues through their exercises. U.S. war planners did not know how Tokyo decision makers would deploy their military in a crisis or if Japan's military could play a role beyond logistical support for U.S. forces in Japan if war broke out. Japan's reluctance to allow the SDF to use force alongside the U.S. military would shape alliance deliberations for decades, even as North Korean and Chinese forces increasingly tested Japan's military readiness.[3] The United States and Japan did not, in fact, announce shared strategic goals for the alliance until 2005.[4]

But it was two crises within Japan that instigated far greater attention to the weaknesses in the Japanese government's approach to mobilizing its military. In 1995, the Japanese government faced two critical national emergencies: the Aum Shinrikyō terrorist attacks on Tokyo's subways and the Kōbe earthquake. Both of these crises laid bare the deficiencies in the government's ability to manage serious threats to public safety. Policy makers and citizens both saw the glaring contradictions in the Japanese government's ability to protect its people and the unresolved questions within the government over the appropriate role for Japan's military in crisis management.

The first crisis involved a chemical weapons attack on civilian targets by a religious sect, the Aum Shinrikyō. On June 27, 1994, seven people were killed and six hundred injured in Matsumoto City in Nagano Prefecture, poisoned by sarin gas. An eighth victim died in 2008 after being in and out of hospital for years.[5] Sarin is an odorless, colorless organophosphate, which can be used as a pesticide but can also be an extremely potent nerve agent, and thus it is outlawed under the Chemical Weapons Convention of 1993. The following spring, Aum conducted a similar sarin gas attack on the Tokyo subway, killing eleven and injuring five thousand five hundred. The National Police Agency began an investigation of the Aum group at all of its facilities. The SDF was asked for assistance in the investigation, and chemical units from the Ground Self-Defense Force (GSDF) were put on alert across Japan. However, by law, SDF personnel were not allowed to participate in a law enforcement investigation, so the fourteen GSDF chemical experts had to be temporarily assigned to the Police Agency as technical advisers. On March 23, 1995, the police chased a car owned by Aum for two hours, prompting the governor to request SDF support in capturing the potential terrorists. Seven GSDF personnel were sent directly from their Imazu base to support the chase.

The investigation of Aum Shinrikyō continued through the summer. Cyanide fumigators were found in subway stations again in May and July, although no one was harmed. Meanwhile, Asahara Shoko, Aum's leader, was arrested. Some suspicious connections between the religious cult and individual members of the SDF were found. One member of the SDF was arrested for working with Aum, and he claimed during his interrogation that Asahara met with four SDF personnel and discussed a coming war between Japan and the United States. The courts ordered Aum Shinrikyō to disband in late October 1995, and in December, the Japanese government, under the Anti-Subversive Activities Law, prohibited members of the group from reassembling.[6]

The terrorist attack prompted greater attention to the relationship between the SDF and local first responders. Across Japan, the SDF and local police and fire departments began to conduct drills together in case of further incidents. This helped to remove some of the bureaucratic barriers that had impeded the government's ability to help the victims and capture those who had planned and executed the attack. Moreover, after anthrax attacks in Washington were made in the months after the 9/11 terrorist attacks, the Ministry of Defense ordered further efforts to improve the ability of SDF and law enforcement agencies to respond to biological as well as chemical weapons.

The second crisis to confront the Japanese people in 1995 was a natural disaster. The Great Hanshin Earthquake of January 17, 1995, registered at a magnitude of 7.3 and resulted in massive fires across Kōbe and its suburbs. Once again, this crisis exposed the government's inability to respond rapidly to a national emergency. The human toll was high: in addition to 6,434 deaths and 43,792 injuries, almost 105,000 homes were completely destroyed and another 144,000 were damaged. Of the homes destroyed, 7,132 were lost to fire. Japan's seismologists had focused on the potential for a major earthquake south of Tokyo and in the Tokai region where fault lines had been clearly established, but the Kinki region, which includes Kōbe and its surroundings, was not thought to be at risk.

The prime minister's office was slow to respond. The earthquake struck at 5:56 A.M., but the Murayama cabinet did not set up a disaster relief operation until one o'clock in the afternoon. Meanwhile, the GSDF units stationed nearby at Itami in Hyōgo Prefecture convened an emergency call at 6:30 A.M., and within the hour, they had helicopters in the air above Kōbe. Two hundred forty GSDF personnel were mobilized from the Thirty-Sixth Infantry Regiment under the SDF Law's Article 83 (clause 3), which allows commanding officers to make the decision to mobilize if a natural disaster strikes nearby. A little after 8:00 A.M., the Maritime Self-Defense Force (MSDF) also began to mobilize in response. Meanwhile, the GSDF sent liaison officers to let municipal leaders know they were ready to assist. Governor Kaihara of Hyōgo Prefecture formally requested SDF assistance at 10:00 A.M., four hours after the quake had struck, and the Defense Agency established a disaster response headquarters. The region had no plan for large-scale disaster response, and municipal leaders in Kōbe and its surroundings had little to no experience in disaster preparedness.

The SDF disaster relief mission in Kōbe concluded more than four months later. At its peak, 25,900 personnel were actively involved. Japan's emergency response had suffered from two problems. First, the delay was largely a consequence of the disconnect between municipalities and agencies of the central government, particularly the SDF. Despite Governor Kaihara's willingness to reach out to the SDF, the mayors of Kōbe and Ōsaka cities never requested the assistance of the SDF, and under the SDF Law, the Japanese military could not provide assistance to municipalities without a mayor's request for their help. Second, the number of SDF personnel dispatched seemed far too few given the scale of the disaster. The SDF hesitated to assert authority where no explicit permission had been given and thus sent forces only to locations that it knew had been approved. Other factors unrelated to the bureaucratic logjam were also important. Roads were badly damaged, and those that were passable were clogged with civilian traffic. GSDF helicopters had no place to land, making airborne transport difficult in the densely populated city. Nonetheless, everyone agreed that, had the city government and the SDF conducted training drills in advance, they would have been able to manage the disaster far better.

On December 1, 1995, Japan's Disaster Countermeasures Law was revised to reflect these lessons learned. The SDF was given greater latitude for operations, including the authority to use private land and buildings temporarily for relief operations. The law allowed mayors, in addition to prefectural governors, to request SDF assistance. There was some debate over revising the SDF Law to allow the SDF to make its own determination about when to deploy in a natural disaster (*jishu haken*), but this was seen as unnecessary. The consensus within the government was that the SDF could already do that under the existing law; the problem in Kōbe was that commanders on the scene had been too hesitant to assert their authority for fear of political repercussions.[7] Thus, it was SDF operations—not the SDF Law itself—that needed to be improved. The long-standing fear of the SDF that it would be criticized for encroaching on the authority of locally elected leaders was also a legacy of the difficult debate over the role of the military in postwar Japan.

Both the sarin gas attacks and the Kōbe earthquake revealed that the Japanese government was woefully unprepared to cope with public security threats. Moreover, it revealed the cost of civilian hesitancy in using the SDF as an instrument in crisis response. The barriers to civil-military cooperation in a crisis stemmed from a long-standing concern over the military's influence at home in the prewar era and the strong ideological differences in the postwar era over the SDF role in Japanese society. No party was more opposed to the SDF and their role in civil affairs than the Japan Socialist Party (JSP), the LDP's nemesis.[8] And yet in the mid-1990s, as political reforms had prompted significant realignment among parties in Tokyo, the coalition government formed in 1994 included the JSP and the LDP. Thus, the prime minister who confronted the 1995 crises was the JSP's leader, Murayama Tomiichi. Conservatives blamed Prime Minister Murayama for his hesitant response to the two crises, yet the problem was far more complex. Sensitivity over the SDF as an instrument of the state, even one that could aid in national emergencies, had a long history. While a convenient scapegoat, the JSP was not the only political party that had opposed greater reliance on Japan's military. Many in the LDP had also resisted the idea of deploying their military as first responders in a domestic crisis. Japan's law enforcement agencies seemed far more appropriate. To be sure, bureaucratic rivalries also played a part. The National Police Agency saw the Japanese military as a potential rival and jealously guarded its right to protect Japanese citizens at home. This institutional tug of war between domestic law enforcement and the military would surface yet again in thinking about the country's maritime defenses.

The inability of the Japanese government to respond rapidly and effectively to both the Aum attacks and the earthquake in Kōbe demonstrated just how isolated the SDF had been from domestic emergency management planning. Sensitivities within the SDF about overstepping its authority slowed its response; local authorities were ill-prepared for crisis and were uninformed or unwilling to call the SDF for help. Local law enforcement and first responders did not work naturally with their country's military, and this too had to be remedied so that Japan could more effectively integrate its military into national crisis management.

## Upgrading Japan's Defenses

Pyongyang's nuclear proliferation might not have initially prompted greater contingency planning for Washington and Tokyo, but it did set in motion an array of improvements to Japan's military planning. North Korea's impact on Japan was twofold: first, it raised questions about how Japan would defend itself from the growing arsenal of missiles aimed its way, and second, it raised concerns about nuclear proliferation in Northeast Asia. Would Japan need to match Pyongyang's capabilities or find another way of deterring potential aggression?

Few in Tokyo have advocated the nuclear option. But it was realism rather than pacifism that informed the thinking of Japan's security planners. In the postwar period, Japanese leaders had periodically ordered a review of the decision to remain a nonnuclear state. The last time Tokyo planners had to consider nuclear acquisition by a neighbor was in 1964 when China declared itself a nuclear power. In the 1970s, as Japanese policy makers considered ratifying the Nuclear Nonproliferation Treaty, the government once again took a look at the nuclear option but determined that the choice would lead to greater insecurity. In the mid-1990s, as the Cold War began to recede into the past, the Japanese government considered again whether the country's security could be adequately defended in the nuclear era without nuclear weapons.

While the motivations for these policy reviews differed, the conclusions reached each time did not. Japan has little strategic depth and thus is badly suited to the deployment of land-based nuclear forces. Submarine-based nuclear forces could be an effective deterrent, as the French and British had found, but Japanese planners inevitably reached the conclusion that the nuclear option would only exacerbate regional fears of a return of Japanese military ambition, which would likely stimulate an arms race in response. However, the public's strong antipathy to nuclear weapons trumped this strategic assessment.

Japanese planners were thus far more comfortable relying on the United States for extended deterrence. So long as the United States remained committed to deploying forces in the region and upholding its treaty commitment to defend Japan against aggression, Tokyo could be assured of a sufficient deterrent against Chinese and Russian nuclear forces. North Korea's nuclear program only deepened the conviction that keeping the United States engaged in Japan's defense was by far the better deterrent option.[9]

## TOKYO'S MISSILE GAP

Yet Pyongyang's missiles were a problem for Tokyo as it had no capability of its own to contend with a ballistic missile threat. The Taepodong missile launch in 1998 shaped Japan's defense debate in several ways. First, the launch rattled the Japanese public and compelled the Japanese government to prove that it was taking steps to ensure the country was adequately defended. The Defense Agency was inundated by requests from the media for information about the SDF's response—and about what Japan's ally the United States was doing to safeguard Japan. Unaccustomed to briefing the public on what it was doing to defend Japan, the Defense Agency did not respond for over a day, and when it did, a midlevel career bureaucrat was sent to brief the press rather than the agency's director-general.

Second, the launch of an intermediate-range ballistic missile compounded an already difficult discussion within the U.S.-Japan alliance. A successful North Korean ballistic missile program reopened questions about the U.S. extended deterrent. Japan did not have a similar weapons system, and while the government had not ruled out the possibility of acquiring the ability to develop missiles of its own, there was still considerable resistance to the idea of arming the SDF to be able to strike the territory of other nations. The SDF was limited to defense and had no authority for offensive capability. Instead, the Japanese government relied on the offensive strike capability of the U.S. military to deter against aggression. Finally, the Taepodong launch over Japanese territory raised the prospect of future missile tests. The SDF had to prepare to respond in the case of a failed launch, or worse yet, to consider how to contend with a deliberate attack.[10]

North Korea's ambitions did not change Japan's commitment to remaining a nonnuclear state, but they did prompt a rethinking of how best to shape Pyongyang's choices and, if need be, deter a hostile government armed with nuclear missiles. Negotiated disarmament remained Tokyo's preferred choice, and in 2002, Prime Minister Koizumi Junichirō approved bilateral talks with Kim Jong-il. There were other reasons for outreach. Seoul and Washington had tried their hand at talks with Kim Jong-il, and Koizumi believed there was no reason Tokyo should sit on the sidelines when its interests were at stake. In addition, North Korea's abduction of Japanese citizens in the 1970s remained an unresolved problem for

Japan-North Korea relations. Add to this the rising concern about Pyongyang's proliferation, and there was plenty of reason to try to find a path to negotiations.

The Koizumi cabinet was largely successful. After a secret round of talks that culminated in a visit to Pyongyang by Prime Minister Koizumi in September 2002, Koizumi and Kim issued the Japan-Democratic People's Republic of Korea (DPRK) Pyongyang Declaration. Included was a moratorium on ballistic missile testing by North Korea. The declaration read, "The DPRK side expressed its intention that, pursuant to the spirit of this Declaration, it would further maintain the moratorium on missile launching in and after 2003."[11] The Pyongyang Declaration was quickly overshadowed in Japan by the more stunning revelation: North Korea took responsibility for the abduction of thirteen Japanese citizens during the 1970s and 1980s. In October 2002, North Korea released five of these abductees to the Japanese government, and Koizumi would return again to Pyongyang in 2004 to bring home their families, but the Japanese public was outraged at the knowledge that the Kim regime had systematically abducted young Japanese from Japanese territory. The backlash against the Japanese government was intense, as was the antipathy against North Korea. Whereas Japan had in the past promised economic aid should Pyongyang abandon its nuclear ambitions, public sentiment made it virtually impossible for the government to reward a regime that continued to forcibly detain Japanese citizens. For years afterwards, the domestically sensitive issue of the abductees would dominate Japan's position in the multilateral Six Party Talks, begun in 2003, that sought to persuade North Korea to abandon its nuclear weapons.[12]

Meanwhile, the threat to Japan from North Korea's missiles did not diminish. In addition to testing a new intermediate-range missile, North Korea also accelerated its production of shorter-range missiles that could cross the Sea of Japan. These Nodong missiles were increasingly deployed along the eastern coast of North Korea, raising concerns in Tokyo that Japanese targets, including U.S. bases on Japanese soil, would be vulnerable. In response, Tokyo and Washington intensified deliberation on ballistic missile defense cooperation. Japanese planners had reached three conclusions about their missile defense needs. First, a sea-based system seemed most likely to provide Japan with adequate flexibility to track, identify, and ultimately shoot down incoming ballistic missiles. Second, the Patriot system for managing aerial threats needed to be upgraded to include ballistic missiles, and the Patriot Advanced Capability-3 (PAC-3) system was introduced to Japan (see figure 3.1). Finally, the BADGE air defense system operated by Japan also needed to be upgraded to accommodate the mission of missile defense. All three combined were initially estimated to be an 800 billion to 1 trillion yen (7.6 billion to 9.5 billion USD) investment in upgrading Japan's capabilities.[13] These three comprised Japan's integrated ballistic missile defense system.

## NEW CONTINGENCY LAWS

While North Korea focused Japanese attention on enhancing SDF capabilities, the more politically difficult challenge was addressing critical institutional weaknesses in Japanese defense policy making. Civilian and uniformed leaders had worked closely on developing Japan's military capability, but they had not yet come to a common understanding of how they would cooperate should Japan need to respond to aggression. In other words, there was little clarity on how and when Japan's civilian leaders would mobilize their military to defend the country. The discussion of a law that would stipulate the conditions and the procedures for managing the mobilization of

FIG. 3.1   Ground Self-Defense Force personnel perform a PAC-3 ballistic missile defense exercise at GSDF Camp Asaka on June 21, 2017. © *Asahi Shimbun*

Japan's military in a crisis—what the Japanese government referred to as *yūji hō* (emergency legislation)—was perhaps the most delicate of all discussions on Japanese military planning. Given Japan's prewar history, allowing the military to take control during a crisis was seen as far too risky in the early postwar years. The legacy of war and defeat was still strong, and the democratic constitution of 1947, which stipulated civilian control over the military, was still young. Imagining a crisis—and allowing the military to take charge during that crisis—was still seen as dangerous. But without these laws, as General Kurisu Hiroomi had warned years earlier, the SDF would be forced to act without legal sanction should a conflict erupt. Laws stipulating the conditions of sharing authority between civilian and military authorities in the case of an attack on Japan were long overdue.

By the end of the 1990s, it was clear that the Japanese government needed to prepare more carefully for crisis management and, if needed, for a full mobilization of the military to defend the nation. Civilian and military planners had been studying what to do in an "emergency" (*yūji*) for over a decade. Putting legislation together for cabinet consideration was only the first step. Submitting it to the Diet for approval required a steady prime minister ready and willing to counter the inevitable resistance from opposition parties and the Japanese public. After a decade of repeated crises and increasing reason to worry about North Korea's intentions, the Japanese public had begun to shift away from seeing the SDF as a threat to democracy. Instead, there was growing evidence that the public was concerned about whether the SDF was adequately prepared to defend Japan. Civilian leaders too faced criticism for not ensuring public safety.

The September 11 attacks on the United States further eroded the Japanese sense of complacency. In 2002, the Koizumi cabinet brought the results of the Ministry of Defense's *yūji hō* study to the Diet in the form of new legislation that elevated crisis planning to the prime minister's office for a coordinated government response to a national crisis, including armed attack. For over a year, the Diet deliberated on the government's bill, with critics focusing on how civilian authority would be organized during a crisis as well as how the constitutional protections afforded to Japanese citizens would be maintained. The largest opposition party, the Democratic Party of Japan (DPJ), was concerned with ensuring that the government would be required to report to the Diet on any crisis it thought would trigger the law, as well as seek Diet approval for mobilizing the SDF to defend the nation. On May 13, 2003, the DPJ concluded an agreement with the LDP and its coalition partner, the Kōmeitō, which agreed to the legislative oversight the DPJ required. The package of laws, passed on June 6, 2003, fundamentally changed the institutional relationship between Japan's military and a broad array of national bureaucracies and local governments.[14]

This legislation took fifty years to realize, but it solved a critical gap in Japan's crisis planning, creating regular opportunities for civil-military cooperation in managing public safety. First, it established a set of priorities and responsibilities for various agencies, including the SDF, as the Japanese government transitioned to emergency management. Second, it brought the SDF into regular communication with a host of Japan's first responders and local governments. In contrast to the muddled response to the 1995 Kōbe earthquake, this interface between the SDF and civil authorities at all levels of government not only led to smooth and rapid crisis response during the 2011 crisis but also began to build trust between Japan's military and local communities. This would be invaluable seven years later, when Japan confronted its worst disaster since World War II, the "triple disasters" of the Great East Japan Earthquake.

A final piece of this new legal framework for crisis management was passed in July 2005. Japan's ballistic missile defenses depended on the rapid delegation of authority from civilian to military leaders to deal with an incoming missile attack. The 2005 law gave the defense minister authority to order the SDF to be on alert and to destroy any incoming missiles. The commander in chief of the Air Defense Command, an Air Self-Defense Force (ASDF) general, was in charge of determining when to initiate missile defenses. The new law governing Japan's ballistic missile defense (BMD) response had been passed just in time for another round of North Korean Taepodong tests and a nuclear detonation in 2006. Tokyo upgraded and deployed ever more capable PAC-III batteries and equipped its Aegis ships with more advanced interceptor missiles. Japan's BMD system was fully operational by 2009, as sea-based and land-based components were deployed, and the new BMD Integrated Missions Command was created under an air defense commander. Attention was then given to alerting the Japanese public of the dangers of potential incoming missiles. A new nationwide system for issuing civil defense alerts was developed, and in 2012, when Pyongyang launched longer-range missiles from its western coast, residents of Okinawa received alerts of the possible dangers associated with the missiles' trajectories.[15]

## DYNAMIC DETERRENCE AND SELF-DEFENSE FORCE MISSION PRIORITIES

Japan's long-term defense plans reflected the increasing pace of change in the military balance of Northeast Asia. Only one long-term defense plan had been needed during the Cold War, and this National Defense Program Outline (NDPO) was not undertaken until 1976. Almost two decades later, the Defense Agency announced a new NDPO in 1995 that reflected growing concerns about North Korean proliferation and the need to develop an alliance response to the end of the Cold War in Asia. Both of these plans rested on the assumption that Japan would maintain a basic force posture in peacetime and plan for bolstering its capabilities in case of a crisis.

By the early 2000s, however, it was clear that the SDF needed to adapt to the growing presence of foreign military forces in and around Japanese waters and airspace. A third NDPO was announced in 2004—the first reflection of how much Northeast Asia had changed since the end of the Cold War. Accordingly, this new defense plan came with new mission priorities for Japan's military. Three SDF missions reflected Japan's new defense priorities. At the top of that list was ballistic missile defense, followed by countering guerrilla and special operations attacks, and third, responding to an invasion of Japan's offshore islands. The SDF also regrouped to improve Japan's defenses in its southwestern region—a direct response to the deepening concern over China's growing military power. Moreover, Japan's three services needed to plan together. Since 1954, the three services of the SDF had been represented in a Joint Staff Council, but each service reported directly to the head of the Defense Agency. The Staff Offices of the Air, Maritime, and Ground SDF provided intelligence support to the SDF. The SDF Law was amended to reorganize Japan's military leadership so that joint operational planning could be improved and to streamline the transfer of military expertise to the minister. A Joint Staff Office (JSO) replaced the Council, and the chief of staff had sole responsibility for conveying military advice to civilian decision makers and the Defense Intelligence Headquarters was put under the command of the civilian head of the Defense Agency (later the Ministry of Defense). This new structure was aimed at streamlining the flow of information as well as improving the SDF's ability to jointly imagine the operational requirements for Japan's defense. It was also expected to improve significantly the SDF's ability to train and operate with the U.S. military.[16]

The 2004 NDPG was the first to clearly identify the source of military threats to Japan. Noting that the Russian threat had been significantly reduced, the defense plan instead named North Korea as "a major destabilizing factor to regional and international security, and a serious challenge to international non-proliferation efforts." The Ministry of Defense argued also that Japan should remain attentive to the future actions of China, as it "has a major impact on regional security." Of particular note were Beijing's efforts to modernize the People's Liberation Army (PLA), including nuclear and missile forces as well as its naval and air forces, and to expand its area of operations at sea.

The 2004 defense plan was revised yet again in 2010 after a new political party took power in Tokyo. The 2010 NDPG put the priority on defenses, and while noting that a large-scale war between major powers was less likely than ever, it cited a growing number of "gray zone" disputes: confrontations over territory, sovereignty, and economic interests that stopped short of war. Particularly noteworthy in this updated plan was the assessment that the global balance of power was shifting in favor of China, India, and Russia, diminishing the influence of the United States.

In terms of Japan's threat perception, the 2010 NDPG held the same view of North Korea's threat as its predecessor. But its description of China had changed: "China is steadily increasing its defense expenditures. China is widely and rapidly modernizing its military force, mainly its nuclear and missile forces as well as its navy and air force, and is strengthening its capability for extended range power projection. In addition, China has been expanding and intensifying its maritime activities in Japan's surrounding waters. These trends, together with insufficient transparency over China's military forces and its security policy, are of concern for the regional and global community." Moreover, it noted that Russian military activities in East Asia remained "robust."

Interestingly, the Ministry of Defense also reordered SDF mission priorities in the 2010 plan. Ensuring the security of the sea and air space surrounding Japan emerged at the top of the list; second was the need to respond to attacks on offshore islands; and third was the need to respond to cyber-attacks. In addition, the plan included a new section on how to improve Japan's military force posture. Three goals were identified for the SDF: improved readiness, an emphasis on joint operations, and the continuation of international peace cooperation activities. BMD received far less attention.

Finally, the 2010 NDPO abandoned the basic force posture concept that had been the central premise of Japan's defense planning since the 1970s. No longer would the model be to maintain a given level of capability that could be expanded as tensions rose. A new concept of dynamic deterrence was put forward as a better response to Japan's changing military environment. Dynamic deterrence depended instead on an assessment of threat in Japan's security environment. As the capabilities of Japan's neighbors were growing, the SDF would need to upgrade its own capabilities in kind. The focus was on deterrence, however, rather than warfighting as the primary motivation behind Japanese planning.

Three years later, this NDPO would be replaced yet again as the DPJ left office and the LDP and Kōmeitō returned to govern Japan. The 2013 plan was not in fact that much different, but it placed even greater emphasis on maritime security and identified outer space as an arena for strategic competition. It included the lessons learned from the SDF response to the Great East Japan Earthquake of

March 11, 2011, and it recognized the growing threat from Chinese ambitions for the Senkaku Islands in the East China Sea. In response to the latter concern, the plan called for the development of an amphibious force capable of securing and, if necessary, retaking islands.

Threat assessment continued to highlight both North Korea and China. SDF priorities remained similar to those of 2004, but BMD climbed back up to third place. Dynamic deterrence was refined even further. Japan's military was to emphasize "both soft and hard aspects of readiness, sustainability, resiliency and connectivity, reinforced by advanced technology and the capability for C3I (command, control, communications and intelligence)." In addition, the SDF was still to make a proactive contribution to peace through bilateral and multilateral military cooperation.[17]

## Ordering Defense Operations

Japan's prime ministers and defense ministers ordered the military to defend Japanese territory against foreign intrusions ever more frequently as foreign military forces operated in and around Japanese territory. By the early 2000s, the SDF was regularly confronting Chinese, North Korean and Russia militaries in ever-closer proximity to the Japanese home islands. The military's readiness was tested, as was the ability of Japan's civilian and military decision makers, to cope with a far more difficult security environment.

### MARITIME SECURITY OPERATIONS

North Korean activities in and around Japanese waters in the late 1990s necessitated action from Japan's military, and while the Japan Coast Guard (JCG) responded to these clandestine activities off

Japan's west coast, ultimately the MSDF was called in to help. "Suspicious ships" from North Korea repeatedly challenged the JCG. In 1999, two North Korean ships—the *Daiichi Taiseimaru* and *Daini Daiwamaru*—outran JCG vessels, and Kawasaki Jiro, the head of the Ministry of Land, Infrastructure, Transport, and Tourism, which is responsible for JCG operations, informed Minister of Defense Norota Hosei of their need for support. Norota then asked Prime Minister Obuchi Keizo to issue for the first time an Order for Maritime Security Operations. This experience prompted the government to decide that any foreign ship which outran the JCG would be automatically pursued by the MSDF.

Despite this arrangement, it was the JCG that fired on a North Korean intruder in December 2001. The JCG confronted the vessel in Japanese waters and then pursued it at high speed, exchanging fire with the sailors onboard. Ultimately, the JCG sank the North Korean ship in China's exclusive economic zone (EEZ). Nine months later, after negotiations with China, the Japanese government brought the North Korean vessel to the surface, transported it to Tokyo, and put it on display in the Japan Coast Guard Museum in Yokohama as a warning to all ships that Japan would not tolerate intrusions into its territorial waters. Later, Japan would sign on to a multilateral effort to monitor and, if necessary, interdict North Korean ships suspected of carrying missile parts or fissile material as part of the Proliferation Security Initiative.[18]

In addition to grappling with North Korean ships, the JCG had long managed maritime law enforcement near the Senkaku Islands. In the 1990s, fishing boats and activists became bolder in approaching the disputed waters. For years, Japanese and Taiwanese activists had been most active, but in 2004, mainland Chinese activists landed on the islands and succeeded in raising the flag of the People's Republic of China. And in 2008, Tokyo became worried after a Chinese government survey ship approached the Senkaku Islands. Since then, Chinese vessels have increasingly operated in and around Japanese waters across its southwestern region, prompting diplomatic protests to Beijing and warnings to the vessels apprehended by the JCG.

A PLA incursion in 2004 spurred the Japanese government to go further than protests and law enforcement vessels and involve the SDF. A second Order for Maritime Security Operations was issued, and Japan's MSDF tracked a Chinese submarine trying to pass submerged through the Miyako Strait. While Japan's straits are classified as open waters for passage, submarines must surface under international law. The MSDF confronted the sub, demanding that it surface. Above the confrontation on the surface, media helicopters filmed the encounter, and Japan's military operation against the wayward Chinese sub made headlines. Chinese officials later explained that their sub commander had simply lost his way, but one U.S. analyst interpreted the visit to Japan's southern straits as a test of SDF readiness, suggesting that the PLA Navy had deliberately sought to see how quickly, and with how much force, the MSDF would respond to the incursion. A Japanese submarine expert at the MSDF War College, in his analysis, was more inclined to discount the danger of the incident and to accept the possibility that the Chinese commander was not expert enough to navigate the shallow waters near the Okinawa islands and may indeed have lost his way.[19] Whatever the sub commander's motivation, the incident would not be the last. Chinese submarine activity in the East China Sea noticeably increased thereafter, and by 2018, Chinese submarines were confident enough to surface and reveal their presence off of the Senkaku Islands, drawing sharp protests from the Japanese government.[20] The MSDF today conducts far more intelligence gathering and surveillance operations across the East

China Sea. Japan's submarine fleet has also grown by six subs in an effort to keep up with China's increasing presence there.

## MISSILE DESTRUCTION ORDERS

Ballistic missile defense operations are also a new and visible effort by Japan to strengthen its defenses. In March 2009, Pyongyang issued notification of its intention to launch an experimental satellite. Minister of Defense Hamada Yasukazu issued the first "order for the destruction of ballistic missiles," deployed MSDF destroyers to the Sea of Japan, and put Patriot missile units in Tōhoku and Tokyo on alert. Again, twice in 2012, Hamada's successors, Tanaka Naoki and Morimoto Satoshi, issued similar orders, but this time because the North Korean missiles launched from its western coast, MSDF Aegis destroyers were deployed in the East China Sea and the Patriot missile units in Okinawa and Tokyo were put on alert. In February 2016, the SDF was put on extended alert and deployed in both the Sea of Japan and the East China Sea, and Patriot missiles deployed forward in Ishigaki and the Miyakojima Islands as well as on the main island of Okinawa were on alert as Kim Jong-un accelerated his missile testing. The SDF and the Ministry of Defense received information from U.S. forces through a Shared Early Warning system. Since then, the U.S. and Japanese militaries have vastly improved their cooperation through exercises and intelligence sharing on North Korean missile activities. In June 2016, trilateral exercises between Japanese, Korean, and U.S. forces on joint missile defenses were organized in Hawaii.[21]

Japan has increasingly exercised its BMD abilities in response to Pyongyang's missiles. In 2017 alone, North Korea sent a barrage of short- and medium-range missiles in Japan's direction, with some falling in Japan's EEZ and others with longer trajectories flying over

Japanese territory. The BMD system Japan has in place can track North Korea's missiles, but whether it can handle a large-scale attack against Japan is unclear. Planned improvements include adding the Standard Missile-3 (SM-3) Block IIA missile to the MSDF's Aegis destroyers as well deploying land-based Patriot Advanced Capability-3 (PAC-3) batteries across Japan to protect critical command centers and military bases.[22] But this is not sufficient to guard against the large-scale attack that Kim Jong-un can order with the arsenal now at his disposal. By 2021, Japan is scheduled to deploy eight BMD-equipped Aegis destroyers.[23] In 2018, Japanese planners will finalize the next five-year defense buildup plan and are expected to introduce a far more sophisticated land-based ballistic missile system, similar to the Aegis Ashore system deployed by the United States in Romania.

With Japan's embrace of BMD, command decisions made by Japan's civilian and military leaders have become more regular. By 2016, civilian leaders had issued ten missile destruction orders, giving the ASDF commander in charge of BMD the authority to shoot down any debris or incoming missile. To ensure readiness, this ASDF command has been on alert status for increasingly longer durations. The first three times a destruction order was issued by Japan's minister of defense, once in 2009 and twice in 2012, North Korea informed international agencies of its intention to launch. The Japanese government therefore made its destruction order public. As Pyongyang's missile launches became more frequent and its intentions less clear, the Japanese government stopped publicizing destruction orders. In a May 2016 press briefing, Defense Minister Onodera Itsunori noted that he had no obligation to make destruction orders public. Senior ministry officials explained that with no North Korean announcement of their launch, it would be provocative for Japan to issue a missile destruction order.

The destruction order issued in August 2016 remained in place into 2017 as North Korea accelerated its missile testing and increased the number of missiles capable of reaching Japan. This intense effort to coordinate Japan's BMD readiness provided the opportunity for civilian and uniformed commanders to execute their shared role in responding to military threats.[24]

## AIR DEFENSE OPERATIONS

Chinese aircraft are increasingly testing Japan's air defenses, especially in the East China Sea. In December 2012, as tensions over the Senkaku Islands dispute mounted, a small surveillance plane operated by China's State Oceanic Agency entered Japan's airspace over the contested islands for the first time.[25] This small plane went undetected by ASDF radar on the main island of Okinawa Prefecture. But the JCG, on patrol around the islands, informed the ASDF of the intrusion, and it scrambled fighter jets from Naha. By the time the Japanese fighters reached the islands, the Chinese aircraft had moved on. Prime Minister Abe Shinzō's cabinet, formed just a few weeks later, took the opportunity to publicly restate how the ASDF responds to intrusions into Japanese airspace so as to deter any further flights over the Senkaku Islands. The following year, the Chinese sent a drone to the islands, and Japan announced new rules of engagement specifically for drones.[26]

Beyond the vicinity of the Senkaku Islands, Chinese challenges to Japan's airspace have also grown apace. ASDF scrambles against Chinese aircraft increased from fewer than 100 in 2010 to 851 in 2016. The ASDF had considerable experience in air defense operations against the Soviet Union. Even after the Cold War ended, Russian air forces continued to patrol the skies on the border with Japan. Indeed, the ASDF has had two fronts to cover—one against a steady stream of Russian aircraft to the north and another against the increasingly active Chinese PLA Air Force to the southwest across the East China Sea.

As Chinese aircraft increasingly test Japan's air defenses, the Russian Air Force also continues its regular flights in and around Japanese airspace. Scrambles to meet Russian fighters have ranged from 200 to 300 per year over the last decade, reaching a height of 301 in 2016. Russian bombers occasionally circumnavigate Japanese islands. In fact, a week before U.S. President Donald Trump visited Tokyo in November 2017, Japanese fighters intercepted two Russian bombers as they transited around the northern coasts of Japan. Russia also sends its navy through the East China Sea and has at times conducted exercises with the Chinese there. In June 2016, a Russian destroyer approached the Senkaku Islands, only to be followed by a Chinese PLA Navy frigate, raising red flags in Tokyo as to the extent of Russo-Chinese military coordination in testing Japan's military readiness.

## The Senkakus and Japanese Military Planning

The territorial dispute between Japan and China over eight small, uninhabited islands in the East China Sea long had lain dormant, managed quietly by both governments since 1978 so as to avoid damage to the overall bilateral relationship. In the first decades of the 2000s, however, Chinese military capability was on the rise, and activities by Chinese government ships in and around Japan increased substantially. The clash between Tokyo and Beijing that erupted first in 2010 and far more ominously in 2012 changed Japan's outlook on the possibility of China's use of force. The Senkaku Islands dispute also fundamentally altered Japanese thinking about the dynamics of the U.S.-Japan alliance. Preventing the escalation of a crisis involving Japanese and Chinese citizens into a conflict between their two governments became a more pressing priority.

Initially, tensions erupted in 2010 over a Chinese fishing trawler whose captain refused to obey the JCG's injunction to leave Japanese waters. Despite the intensity of the diplomatic confrontation that ensued, both governments sought to repair the damage and develop crisis communications links to avoid any future incidents. Within two years, however, the militaries of China and Japan became involved. China deployed maritime law enforcement vessels to Senkaku waters to patrol what it saw as Chinese islands, effectively leading to a government standoff on the high seas. The status quo had changed, and the militaries of both countries, operating regularly in the East China Sea by this time, waited just over the horizon, backing Japanese and Chinese coast guard vessels. What Tokyo had long treated as a law enforcement mission turned into a serious challenge to Japan's island defenses.

Japan's defense planners had already identified the Chinese maritime presence as a problem. Since the 2004 National Defense Program Outline, the Ministry of Defense had made island defenses one of Japan's top military priorities. The SDF began to redeploy in greater numbers to the southwestern region of Japan, moving away from its heavy concentration in the north near Russia in what was once the front line of the Cold War. Because of China, Japan's military needed to attend to the areas of the country that lay exposed to continental Asia, where both North Korean and Chinese forces were growing. Defending the hundreds of small offshore islands that compose the Japanese archipelago requires not only the presence of Japan's coast guard and navy but also its air and ground forces. Even the GSDF expanded its presence and intelligence-gathering capabilities in the outer Ryūkyū Islands and began to develop amphibious landing capabilities (see figure 3.2). General

FIG. 3.2 A GSDF amphibious unit trains alongside U.S. Marines at USMC Camp Pendleton in California as part of the Iron Fist 2018 exercise on February 6, 2018. © *Asahi Shimbun*

Banshō Koichirō, commander of the GSDF Western Army from 2013 to 2015, dubbed this as building Japan's "southwestern wall." During his time there, Banshō organized joint exercises between the GSDF, the MSDF, and the ASDF to coordinate on the island defense mission across the many islands strewn between southern Kyūshū and Okinawa. The ASDF also relocated assets closer to the East China Sea and announced it would bring a second F-15 fighter squadron to its Naha Air Base in Okinawa. The MSDF enhanced its ability to deter and defend against potential aggression, planning for increased submarines and greater intelligence, surveillance, and reconnaissance capability for the East China Sea.[27] Both the GSDF and the ASDF strengthened their ability to respond to crises in the Senkaku Islands and across the East China Sea by building small bases in the smaller islands of the Ryūkyū chain.

Military preparedness was combined with an upsurge of popular Japanese antagonism toward the Chinese. The growing presence of Chinese ships in Japanese waters, especially near the Senkaku Islands, angered many. The island dispute with China unleashed dangerous nationalist politics in Tokyo, as well as in Beijing. Preparing to defend the islands militarily against a Chinese attempt to land there was one thing, but escalating a skirmish to a full military clash between the Japanese and Chinese militaries was another.

In Tokyo, the cabinet of Prime Minister Noda Yoshihiko sought to restrain one of the main advocates of Senkaku nationalism, Governor of Tokyo Ishihara Shintarō. Ishihara was a self-proclaimed nationalist with decidedly anti-China views who had long advocated for a strong Japanese defense of its sovereignty in the Senkakus. Ishihara brought this sentiment to his public campaign to acquire the islands in 2012. Tokyo taxpayers were not so enamored with Ishihara's crusade, however, and this gave Prime Minister Noda some advantage. Nonetheless, the national government arranged to purchase the islands in order to take them off the market and out of Ishihara's hands. Just as worrisome for the Japanese government was the possibility that a Taiwanese or Chinese buyer might purchase them and declare sovereignty for either nation. The Noda cabinet purchased the islands in September, and it set off a cascade of protests within China and prompted the Chinese government to send maritime forces to assert its sovereignty over the islands. For the first time, Chinese government ships were patrolling the Senkaku Islands, joining the Japanese Coast Guard and MSDF who had long been patrolling their waters.[28] Equally worrisome were the demonstrations that took place in both countries, but the scale of popular protest in China was far greater. In 2012, as tempers flared between Tokyo and Beijing, the destruction of Japanese property in China was widespread. Protests in Japan were largely peaceful.

As tensions over the Senkaku Islands dispute grew, so too did the interactions between Japanese and Chinese military forces. In 2013, China announced a new Air Defense Identification Zone that overlapped with Japan's across the East China Sea. Tokyo did not recognize the demarcation for either civilian or military flights. ASDF radar facilities were upgraded on the outer Ryūkyū Islands, and an additional fighter squadron was relocated from Tsukui Base in Fukuoka to Naha in 2016, reflecting a reorientation of ASDF air defense capabilities to cope with Chinese activities.[29]

As the Japanese and Chinese militaries came into closer contact, and as tensions continued to raise fears of a miscalculation or accidental collision, Prime Minister Abe and Chinese President Xi Jinping instructed their governments to begin discussions on a risk reduction agreement. The differences over the islands, however, continued to stall its progress, despite the fact that incidents between military aircraft were increasing. In 2015, Japan reported two incidents of Chinese air force pilots operating close to MSDF surveillance aircraft in international airspace. In 2016, China complained of Japanese fighter aggressiveness when it flew its long-range H-6K bomber, accompanied by jet fighter escorts, through the southern Ryūkyū Islands.

China's challenge to Japan's administrative control over the Senkaku Islands presented a new dilemma for the U.S.-Japan alliance also. Washington and Tokyo once again revised the Guidelines for U.S.-Japan Defense Cooperation, this time taking into account the new assertiveness of Chinese forces near Japan. Tokyo's concern about "gray zone" contingencies prompted the request for this update to the military division of labor in the alliance. The United States was also interested in helping Japan avoid escalating to a use-of-force incident. The danger of miscalculation was real, and with the breakdown in communication between Beijing and Tokyo, the alliance became the primary channel for crisis management. Tokyo and Washington agreed to establish the Alliance Coordination Mechanism to allow for a full bilateral discussion of behaviors in Japan's vicinity that could escalate to military force.[30]

But the challenge went far deeper than crisis management. Many in the planning community in Tokyo understood that Washington might not be willing to go to war with Beijing over small, uninhabited islands; therefore, Japan's military had to be prepared first and foremost to defend the islands should Chinese forces seek to control them. In the inevitable military escalation that would then be expected to follow, however, the U.S. response would be decisive. For the first time, Japanese leaders had to consider how to prevent the United States from abandoning them in the face of Chinese military pressure. By 2014, President Obama clearly addressed Japanese concerns and publicly stated that the U.S. considered the Senkaku Islands were covered by the bilateral security treaty.

## A Defensive Military No More?

The decades after the Cold War were far from quiet in Northeast Asia, and for Japan's leaders, the growing tensions in the region revealed some alarming gaps in their national security planning. Crisis after crisis demonstrated the need for a more sustained look at the decision-making procedures and practices that would improve the military's role in responding to a threat to public safety. From a terrorist attack by a homegrown cult to massive natural disasters, Japan's leaders needed their military's organizational capacity and technical skills to cope with domestic emergencies. Successive prime ministers, even those who had come from Japan's opposition parties, recognized that their military was not a threat to the nation but rather was Japan's most powerful first responder. Since 1954, the SDF has been organized and equipped for the mission of "exclusive self-defense," and during the Cold War, the SDF was only tasked with defending Japanese territory. After the Cold War, however, this changed to allow for the SDF to participate in select international military coalitions as Japan's contribution to global security challenges. Now, with foreign military power growing in the region and Pyongyang and Beijing willing to press closer and closer to Japanese territory, Japan's leaders are worried about their ability to dispel doubts about their willingness to use military force to defend their country.

The increasing sophistication of North Korean missiles has created a severe dilemma for Japan, making it more reliant on the United States to deter aggression—even at the conventional level. BMD was a new defense requirement, one that remained incomplete. Japan's political leaders also worried that without the ability to retaliate, Tokyo would be unable to deter Pyongyang—and potentially Beijing. In 2003, two politicians—one from the ruling party and another from the opposition party—brought this capability debate to light in the Diet. Ishiba Shigeru was at the time Japan's defense minister, leading the Diet discussion of Japan's response to the Bush administration's coalition building in Iraq and Afghanistan. He was also a well-known defense wonk, well read on strategic debates and with a penchant for studying the details of weapons systems. In the newly emerging Democratic Party of Japan, Maehara Seiji was seen within Japan as a hawk, part of a small but growing group of liberal legislators with interests in security and foreign policy. Ishiba and Maehara faced off in the

Diet over the effectiveness of Japan's deterrent posture, with Maehara arguing that the time had come to consider an offensive strike option that would give Tokyo more teeth should North Korea ever consider using its growing missile arsenal against Japan. Ishiba, without hesitation, agreed.[31]

Equipping the SDF with the capabilities it needed to defend Japan seemed uncontroversial, but using that capability to strike another country clearly suggested a departure from the accepted understanding that Japan would only use force if it was attacked. The idea that Japan would launch a preemptive strike countered the long-standing notion that the constitution prohibits the use of force offensively by Japan. Yet the logic of a retaliatory capability as a means of deterring an ever more aggressive North Korea was also persuasive to many, both inside and outside of government. After the North Korean missile and nuclear tests of 2006, the Ministry of Defense began to consider what else it could do to strengthen Japan's defenses. In addition to BMD, the ministry considered a longer-range missile that could destroy North Korean missiles on their launch pads to enhance deterrence. For many in the SDF, the ability to attack enemy bases and launch pads seemed an obvious next step for reducing Japan's vulnerability to missiles.

By the mid-2010s, as the Senkaku dispute with China escalated, the addition of an offensive strike to Japanese capabilities was also appealing to some who thought that the United States was less than enthusiastic about defending Japan if it risked a war with China.[32] China too had missiles that could reach Japan and was an established nuclear power. Moreover, the clash over the Senkaku Islands had raised the prospect that Beijing just might attempt to take the islands from Japan by force, and thus having the ability to strike back could be useful to deter that kind of opportunism. Prime Minister Abe testified in the Upper House that the time had come to consider seriously whether Japan could always ask the United States to cope with the missile threat and argued that the Japanese should consider how best to deter adversaries who threatened to attack Japan's territory and citizens.[33]

There were also misgivings about how an offensive strike option could be achieved under the government's interpretation of the Japanese constitution. Yet, like nuclear weapons, missiles had never been ruled out as an option even under the exclusive self-defense mission. The Ministry of Defense began to consider its next procurement plan for 2019–2023, and the LDP National Security Subcommittee issued a proposal for acquiring strike capability. Pyongyang was conducting a far more aggressive test of its ballistic missiles in 2016 and 2017, including an attempted ballistic missile launch from a submarine, and it aimed multiple salvos of shorter-range missiles to fall within Japan's Air Defense Identification Zone (ADIZ) in the Sea of Japan. Tokyo's readiness to cope with a barrage of missile launches became an even more pressing concern, and while LDP politicians argued that this new strike capability would only be used to retaliate against a direct attack on Japan, it was the first time that Japanese leaders justified the need for offensive capability. Deterrence, they suggested, required it.

• • •

External pressures on the SDF grew as regional forces increasingly challenged Japan's waters and airspace. A new sense of foreboding came from the sense of hostility from North Korea, both from missile launches and from intrusions by "suspicious" vessels into Japanese waters. China too challenged Japan's defense preparedness as it sent its maritime forces into Japanese territorial waters and into its EEZ and its air force into Japan's ADIZ. By the end of the first decade of the twenty-first century, Chinese ships were challenging

Japanese sovereignty over the isolated and uninhabited islands that Tokyo and Beijing had agreed to disagree on, ending a decades old bilateral understanding that the broader diplomatic relationship ought to be given priority. Pyongyang's increasingly numerous and technologically advanced missiles may have awoken Japanese to their complacency over their nation's defenses, but it was China's larger shadow that shook the foundations of Japanese confidence in their postwar strategic bargain with the United States.

Readying the country for a far more unpredictable and worrisome strategic environment took some time. Japan's leaders were not prepared to cope with national crises, and this was made painfully apparent when Japanese citizens were endangered first by the terrorist attacks conducted by the Aum Shinrikyō and then by the Kōbe earthquake disaster. Reforming government emergency planning was overdue, and the first and most important changes were those made to ensuring the SDF was adequately brought into civilian crisis management planning. By the end of the 1990s, as regional tensions lingered, legislators agreed to consider the legal framework for considering how Japan would manage an attack on its security. For the first time, the steps needed to mobilize the military and to give it the authority it needed to defend Japan were clarified. Civilians were ready to allow the SDF to do the job it was organized to do and were confident that the SDF was ready to assume that role.

The SDF too needed to adapt itself to Japan's more unpredictable environment. The long-standing rivalries between the three services had to be overcome so that joint operations among the maritime, air, and ground services could be improved. Japan's prime ministers ordered the SDF to conduct defense operations more often, and new weapons systems—including a sophisticated BMD system—demanded cooperation between civilian leaders and their military commanders. The growing military pressures on Japan prompted a series of policy reforms to improve the government's ability to cope with a crisis or potentially with an attack, but it also raised some sensitive questions about when and how the SDF would be allowed to use force.

# FOUR

# The Constitution Revisited

A<small>RTICLE</small> N<small>INE</small> of Japan's constitution declares, "The Japanese people forever renounce war as a sovereign right of the nation and the threat or use of force as means of settling international disputes." The military would no longer be an instrument of power used to assert Japan's interests abroad. Nonetheless, Japan's leaders interpreted the 1947 constitution to allow for self-defense, a principle consistent with international law and with the Charter of the United Nations, the newly formed organization designed to ensure the collective security of all nations. This premise of the right of self-defense was codified in the law that set forth the mission and organizing principles of Japan's postwar military, the Self-Defense Force (SDF), in 1954.

For seventy years, successive Japanese governments sought to interpret the intent of Article Nine as they built the military capacity to provide for the nation's defenses.[1] Defense policy changes have been pursued through reinterpreting—rather than revising—Japan's constitution, and to ensure the government's interpretation was constitutional, the bureaucrats of the Cabinet Legislative Bureau scrutinized legislation with particular care when it came to the Japanese military.[2]

Constitutional debate over Article Nine was perhaps richest in the early postwar debates when the SDF was brand new and when Japanese politics were far more fluid. The constraints that Article Nine implied had yet to be defined in practice. The Cold War had hardened major-power relations as Japan emerged from occupation, however, and the competition between the United States and the Communist powers was deeply militarized. With U.S. forces remaining on Japanese soil, the import of Article Nine for Japanese citizens was tested more by the U.S. military's operations than by questions about the nascent new force tasked with defending Japan. In the Diet, the 1950s proved to be a rich moment of deliberation as Japan's leaders confronted this new geopolitics. Most of the questions revolved around what the second paragraph of the constitution meant for Japanese military capabilities. Paragraph 2 has some odd language that to this day prompts many to think that any military forces acquired by Japan would be unconstitutional: "in order to accomplish the aim of the preceding paragraph, land, sea, and air forces, as well as other war potential [*senryoku*], will never be maintained." The government had decided that self-defense was acceptable. But what kinds of weapons would be defensive and what would constitute *senryoku?* Could Japan acquire nuclear weapons? Could it acquire missiles?

A second attempt to clarify Article Nine's meaning for Japan's military grew out of concern for alliance dynamics in the early 1970s. A defining court case in Japan also put pressure on the Japanese government to clarify that it would not allow the SDF to be drawn into any future conflict alongside American forces, and in 1972, the government announced that Article Nine prohibited what it called the right of collective self-defense. Japan's military could not fight with others, or on behalf of others. But limited in purpose as Japan's military was, Washington still wanted to see Tokyo take on a bigger military role in the region, especially in the wake of the Vietnam War.

Japan's political leaders today are once again revisiting their interpretation of the constitution as it pertains to using military force. Two evolving operations for the SDF have prompted renewed focus on Article Nine. The first is the decision made in the 1990s to allow the SDF to deploy in coalition with others abroad. Second, rising pressure from North Korea and China has raised new questions about Japan's ability to defend itself and on the efficacy of military cooperation with the United States.

Beyond Article Nine, Japan's constitution also reshaped civil-military relations. Article Sixty-Six expressly prohibits uniformed officers from governing the country, a concern in the initial years after World War II because of the prewar military's control over decision-making under the Meiji Constitution. Under the 1947 constitution, Japan's legislators have jealously guarded their discretion over the use of force and have been particularly sensitive to alliance military planning. Even as civilian leaders became more comfortable with the idea that the SDF could be deployed abroad, they were anxious to avoid any risk that the SDF would engage in war.


## New Missions, New Laws

The constitution has been front and center in the Diet deliberations over all the new missions assigned to the SDF since the end of the Cold War. The government's policy options were based on drafting laws consistent with the intent of the constitution, but at times, Article Nine has seemed infinitely elastic. As noted in Chapter 2, sending Japan's military abroad was a significant break from the past and one that occasioned considerable Diet debate. When the Peacekeeping Operations (PKO) Law was passed in 1992, the legislative balance pitted the conservatives in the Liberal Democratic Party (LDP) against their progressive critics in the Japan Socialist and Communist Parties, reflecting the differences that had characterized debate over the meaning of Article Nine since the mid-1950s.

The decision to send Maritime Self-Defense Force (MSDF) minesweepers to the Persian Gulf in 1991 was widely seen in Japan as violating the spirit of Article Nine. And even after long and careful debate, many also saw the dispatch of the SDF to Cambodia to participate in a UN PKO as contradicting the spirit of the postwar constitution. Yet the PKO Law that the Diet passed did not allow the SDF to use force under the UN flag and instead attempted to set out a role for the SDF in the peace-building process that would preclude the use of force. Japan's military, in other words, became an instrument of diplomacy and a much-needed demonstration of Japan's contribution to global peace.

Concern that the SDF would be drawn into America's wars had long motivated Diet members from the liberal opposition parties to call for greater accountability by Japan's civilian decision makers. There was also little desire among LDP lawmakers and the bureaucrats in the Defense Agency to allow the Japanese military to enter into combat with U.S. forces. Despite this, Washington continued to urge Tokyo to expand its military role, and this did not change in the years after the Cold War ended. Japan's refusal to participate in the 1991 Gulf War reflected the idea that the United States was urging the Japanese military to use force as a means of settling an international dispute in direct violation of Japan's constitution. While some in the LDP were beginning to see that Japan's position was losing viability given its economic stature, most legislators still hewed to a literal interpretation of what the military could and could not do.[3]

A decade later, Prime Minister Koizumi Junichirō reframed Japan's debate over its military. In the wake of the September 11 terrorist attack on the United States, Prime Minister Koizumi argued that the Japanese should focus less on interpreting Article Nine's limitations on the military and more on Japan's responsibility as "a member of the international community." Sending the SDF to contribute to international efforts to ensure global security was not only in Japan's interests, but it also aligned with the spirit of the constitution's preamble. The Japanese people called for peace but seemed unwilling to act in support of it. For Koizumi, employing military force to confront terrorism in pursuit of peace was the translation of words into action: "Merely arguing is not enough to realize peace. Peace is something that can only be built by the combined capabilities of the international community. Understanding that Japan's security and prosperity is intertwined with world peace and stability; (sic) we must fulfill our responsibilities as a member of the international community through action."[4] Koizumi wanted to reorient Japanese thinking away for the limits of Article Nine to the responsibilities Japan had to contribute to international security.

The legal framework for Japan's military decisions was, and remains, paramount. Two laws were passed under the Koizumi cabinet that provided SDF support. The Antiterrorism Special Measures Law (Antiterror Law) of 2001 enabled the SDF to participate in "cooperative and supportive activities" for Operation Enduring Freedom, the U.S. military campaign in Afghanistan. The Antiterror Law stipulated the SDF could provide an array of services, such as supplying water, oil, food, and related goods, transporting personnel and goods, providing maintenance, medical, hygiene, and communications services or equipment, and supporting infrastructure such as airfields, ports, bases, and lodging. In addition, the SDF could conduct search and rescue operations, but it would not assume any direct role in combat activities or in supporting them. For example, Japan's military could not supply or transport weapons and ammunition, nor could it provide fuel for or maintenance on aircraft preparing for combat sorties.[5] Deploying military forces but not allowing them to transport weapons reveals the contradictions still at work in Japan's military policy.

The Antiterror Law made it through the Diet in record time compared to the PKO Law of 1992, which took months to deliberate. After only sixty-two hours of debate, the Diet passed the law by a vote of 240 to 100. It limited Japan's mission to only two years and required Diet approval for any operations beyond that time. The Koizumi cabinet did extend the duration of the SDF mission, and the Diet approved the government plan in 2003, albeit with far greater deliberation than for passage of the initial law.[6]

A second law drafted by the Koizumi cabinet would take much longer to deliberate than the Antiterror Law as it brought Tokyo uncomfortably close to the U.S. decision to invade Iraq. Japan could not order its military to join in the coalition forces, but it did decide to provide support in the aftermath of the invasion. The 2003 Special Measures on Humanitarian and Reconstruction Assistance in Iraq (Iraq Special Measures Law) created a legal basis for SDF participation in humanitarian support missions in Iraq. Tokyo committed funding for the UN High Commissioner for Refugees, as well as financial assistance to countries surrounding Iraq to support refugee resettlement. Also, both the Ministry of Foreign Affairs and the Defense Agency agreed that, under the PKO Law, the government had the ability to send Air Self-Defense Force (ASDF) aircraft to neighboring countries for humanitarian support. There seemed to be more political support for sending the SDF abroad than during the first Gulf War a decade earlier, as even some of Japan's opposition political parties supported the prime minister's initial decision to send ASDF cargo planes to assist those fleeing Iraq.[7]

But Japan's contribution to the Iraq War faced far more political scrutiny than the initial antiterror response, and critics argued once more that SDF participation should be severely limited by Article Nine. The U.S. invasion of Iraq was highly controversial in Japan, as it was in many other countries, and even Koizumi's formulation of the constitution's call for Japan to contribute to global security could not overcome Japanese suspicions that their military would be involved in direct support of U.S. offensive operations. The law therefore had to specify missions that would conform to the SDF's limits.

Japanese planners in the Defense Agency sought indirect ways to support the U.S. military's operations in Iraq. Rear area support was deemed the best compromise. The agency presented options of SDF refueling of U.S. vessels in the Indian Ocean and revising the Antiterror Law so that the SDF could provide rear area support elsewhere, perhaps even in Afghanistan. Because a combat role in Iraq was deemed impossible under the constitution, the missions open to the SDF had to be limited to reconstruction or humanitarian support. Mission planning referenced three time frames: before the U.S. attack on Iraq, during the war, and in the aftermath of war. Japanese planners also had to consider the possibility of two scenarios—the first was that the United Nations would sanction the attack based on the Bush administration's claim that Iraqi President Saddam Hussein maintained weapons of mass destruction (WMD), and a second presumed that the United States acted unilaterally.[8]

For Tokyo, only a UN-sanctioned conflict would offer Japan the opportunity for participation. Morimoto Satoshi, who later went on to become defense minister, wrote of this planning effort in 2004 and outlined three possible legal bases for SDF participation in the Iraq War: another antiterror law, a new version of the existing Iraq law, or a law that focused instead on how to support postwar security in Iraq. Few wanted to revisit the debate over the U.S. antiterrorism campaign, and there was deep skepticism about the constitutionality of a direct Japanese military role in postwar Iraq. A new Iraq law seemed most likely to succeed, both in demonstrating Japan's willingness to make a significant contribution to U.S. operations and in gaining political support at home in Tokyo.[9]

This law was tied to a UN resolution for Iraqi reconstruction—without which Japan could not have sent its forces. Many in Japan opposed the Koizumi cabinet's support for the U.S.-initiated war in Iraq and argued instead for a UN-brokered peace. About forty thousand protesters took to the streets in Tokyo. Similar protests were held across the country as students, citizens' groups, and labor unions took to the streets while the deadline for Hussein drew to a close. Another complication for the Koizumi cabinet was that the legislation for Japanese mobilization in case of war, the *yūji hōsei*, was making its way through committee in the Upper House. Chief Cabinet Secretary Fukuda Yasuo did not want this long-awaited law to be derailed by the Iraq deliberations, especially as public opinion was so antagonistic to SDF participation in the U.S. war.[10]

Again the Diet imposed a sunset clause on the law that approved the mission. The Iraq Special Measures Law, like the Antiterror Law, provided a beginning and end date for the SDF deployment to Iraq. It also stipulated the conditions under which the government could implement the deployment. The government had four years to implement its plan, although if need be, there was a provision for an extension in the law. The SDF could only be sent to areas in Iraq where no fighting was taking place and where none was expected to take place. The SDF could not use its weapons beyond the purpose of individual self-defense or the defense of its units. Moreover, the SDF deployment was explicitly linked to the plan for transitioning to a sovereign Iraqi government. Japan's military would not become part of an extended occupation.

Even the ruling coalition had its misgivings about the SDF deployment to Iraq. The initial bill drafted and presented to ruling party legislators outlined three tasks: humanitarian and reconstruction support, rear-area logistics support, and the disposal of WMD. The Kōmeitō, the LDP's coalition partner, continued to worry about oversight of the SDF in the field, especially the possibility that Japan's military would transport weapons or critical war material. Some in the LDP argued that the bill was too vague about central parts of the mission. For example, the distinction between combat and noncombat areas in Iraq seemed artificial, so there was concern that SDF personnel could easily find themselves in trouble, especially given the restrictions on their use of weapons. In its final form, the bill contained no reference to the SDF's role in disposing of WMD, given that there was no proof that they in fact existed in Iraq, and the Iraq Special Measures Law required Diet approval of any dispatch of SDF personnel within twenty days.[11]

Diet deliberations over the Iraq Special Measures Law revealed the continued fault lines over using the military as an instrument of policy among Japanese politicians. The Democratic Party of Japan (DPJ), while sharing Koizumi's sentiment that Japan should demonstrate its global responsibilities, was unable to continue to support the bill once it reached the Diet. Party unity frayed, and divisions erupted between former Japan Socialist Party members and younger, more pragmatic legislators who supported a more forward-leaning approach to Japan's foreign policy. But these cleavages were not that dissimilar to those found within the LDP. Some believed Article Nine should prevent Japan from offering military support for the United States because it had initiated the use of force against another country. Some in the party wanted a civilian reconstruction plan organized under the United Nations, and others thought that the Iraq mission was simply too dangerous for the SDF, especially as its ability to operate there would be severely handicapped compared to other militaries.[12]

The debate over sending the SDF to Iraq revealed some new trends in public opinion also. Since the PKO deployments began, the Japanese people had supported limiting the SDF's use of weapons abroad, and yet polling on the Iraq decision from 2003 to 2005 also reflected concern over the dangers the military would face because of those constraints. Despite these concerns, however, major media polling revealed a lessening of opposition as the debate in the Diet progressed. The liberal *Asahi Shimbun*'s polls offered the most consistent tracking of public sentiment. As Jeffrey Hornung has pointed out, *Asahi*'s numbers reflected support and opposition for deployment slowly converging between July 2003 and March 2004. By then, those against SDF deployment to Iraq had dropped from 55 percent to 41 percent, while 42 percent supported sending the military, up from 33 percent initially. The *Yomiuri Shimbun*, whose readers tend to be more supportive of a larger role for Japan's military, revealed a similar trend in its polling, although the numbers showed a sharper rise in support than *Asahi*'s. The *Nikkei Shimbun*, read widely in the business community, showed similar growth in support for Koizumi's plan, but the trend line moved up and down each month during the debate, suggesting that Japan's business elite were more ambivalent.

While short-term polling revealed changes in opinion over the dispatch to Iraq, it is also important to note that by this time, the Japanese public had a very favorable view of their military. Polling conducted by the cabinet secretariat showed no decline in public support for the SDF even during these years of intense debate over Iraq. Indeed, by 2006, almost 85 percent of those polled saw the SDF in a favorable light. Thus public concern about the dispatch of the military abroad did not reflect the public's distrust of the SDF but rather skepticism about the way the government was using it.[13]

Japan's legislators were increasingly willing to deploy the SDF abroad, but they wanted to approve each mission. What sort of conditions prevailed on the ground and the mission assigned to the SDF had to be approved each time. No one, not even Japan's conservatives, supported giving the SDF carte blanche to operate abroad, and the legislative and executive branches of government carefully calibrated their understanding of how accountability for these overseas missions would be defined. Each mission had its own law. Each law stipulated the tasks and the duration of the mission and when the government had to consult with the legislature over the use of the military instrument. But it is also evident that the Diet was becoming more comfortable in its role of overseeing Japan's military choices. Each law required Diet approval for extension, and both the Antiterror Law and the Iraq Special Measures Law were returned successfully to the Diet for extension. Legislative oversight of the use of Japanese military force abroad was thus assured, and both branches of government accepted responsibility for the policy decision.

There continued to be a national consensus that Japan's military could be sent abroad without violating Article Nine. So long as the SDF was not faced with combat, it could represent Japanese interests and still stay true to its purpose. The SDF worked with an array of new partners during Operation Enduring Freedom's Maritime Interdiction Operation and Operation Iraqi Freedom. In the Indian Ocean, the MSDF undertook refueling operations for eight nations. In Iraq, the Ground Self-Defense Force (GSDF) worked with Dutch, British, and Australian troops. The ASDF also worked hand in hand with a host of UN partners in humanitarian relief operations from Kuwait, Jordan, and Pakistan. The Japanese government went out of its way to find operations that could be defined as noncombat operations, so that the military would not be faced with the need to fight.[14]

## Civilian Choices

Japan's constitution has not changed since 1947, but the government's interpretation of Article Nine has. Two issues of interpretation are central to understanding Japan's evolving debate over the use of force. The first has to do with the military and what missions it would be allowed and what level of force it would be able to muster. The call for *hadome*, or restraints, remains an inescapable refrain in policy discussions about the SDF, but these restraints have evolved. Early on, it was the SDF's weaponry that had to be restricted, as well as its missions. Today, SDF weaponry is top of the line and increasingly interoperable with that used by U.S. military forces in the region. Japan's armed forces travel around the globe and have served under UN command and in U.S.-led military coalitions in some of the most dangerous spots in the Middle East and Africa. Japan's forces also meet regularly with their counterparts in Asia to train and to exercise. The constitution has been reinterpreted to allow the SDF to use force on behalf of others should it be necessary to Japan's security, opening up considerable latitude for the Japanese government to allow Japanese forces to work closely with other security partners, especially the United States. And yet, the SDF remains closely monitored when it comes to using force abroad. Only slowly have Japanese legislators allowed the military to use its weapons as other militaries use theirs.

The second interpretation issue concerns responsibility for making decisions about the use of force and monitoring SDF compliance. Article Sixty-Six of Japan's constitution stipulates that only civilians can lead the Japanese government.[15] In outlining a cabinet structure, consisting of the prime minister and other ministers of state, this article removes the military from the highest level of Japanese government. More broadly, the 1947 constitution introduced popular sovereignty and with it the idea that democratically elected representatives of the Japanese people would be responsible for making national policy decisions. This framework elevated the Diet as the venue for representing the will of Japanese citizens, and yet Japan's bureaucrats also claimed they were responsible for exercising civilian control over the SDF. The tug and pull over military policy was often less evident between the SDF and the members of the Diet than it was among different civilians. Bureaucratic politics certainly played a part in Japan's defense policy making, with various bureaucracies vying for control over the defense budget (the Ministry of Finance), the procurement of military equipment (the Ministry of International Trade and Industry) and the role of the SDF in UN peacekeeping (the Ministry of Foreign Affairs).[16]

In addition, as Japan's military became better equipped and operationally more proficient, Japan's civilians also needed to become more fluent in the more advanced technology of SDF weaponry and in the tactics and logic of its operations. Just as Japan's military was expected to work more effectively within a policy-making process where civilians dominated decision-making, Japan's civilian decision makers were increasingly required to develop deeper competency in military affairs. Even Japan's Diet members had to develop greater understanding of what they were asking the SDF to do and develop the capacity to judge how well they were able to do it. The new missions assigned to Japan's military in the years after the Cold War demanded an ever greater scrutiny by the Diet. Legislators sought to ensure they had oversight over the military, but in creating an ad hoc legal structure to govern each mission, they in turn created new dilemmas for Japan's military.

ARTICLE NINE AND THE USE OF FORCE

While Japanese leaders have interpreted Article Nine to allow Japan to defend itself, they have not given the SDF full latitude to use force nor to determine how best to respond to an attack. Three principles govern the use of force by Japan's postwar military:

(1) There is an imminent threat to Japan.
(2) No other means are available to defend Japan.
(3) The use of force is limited to the minimal extent necessary.

Thus, the SDF can only use its weapons in cases where Japan's own security is threatened. Moreover, Japan's military commanders do not have complete discretion as to how much force they can use in any particular situation. Even when attacked, Japan's SDF is expected to use minimal force.[17] Interpreting the defensive mission literally, the SDF must use weapons largely as the police do—only as a last resort and with the minimum level of force necessary. When abroad, the restriction on the SDF's use of its weapons has been defined even more narrowly. And whether at home or abroad, Japan's military has yet to test these principles in combat.[18]

As civilian policy makers wrangle with how to translate Article Nine into policy, Japan's military commanders must consider how this basic admonition to use force minimally translates into military operations. For example, does the SDF need to wait for another country to strike the first blow before it initiates the use of force? What should it do to respond to incidents below the level of war—the so-called gray zone scenario of an uncertain missile launch or a paramilitary landing on Japanese islands? When sent abroad for peacekeeping or other coalition operations, whom can the SDF protect?

These ambiguities mattered in the execution of UN peace-keeping missions, and they mattered even more when the SDF joined the United States and other partners in the antiterrorism co-alition. The deployment to Iraq exposed the contradiction between the growing expectations of the SDF in international military co-alitions and the particular constraints on its use of force that had been interpreted as necessary according to Article Nine. Can the SDF operate effectively in coalition with other military partners if it cannot use force to protect others? The U.S. and Japanese mili-taries have long struggled with managing this uncertainty in imag-ining when and how they would use force in combined operations. The Abe Shinzō cabinet's decision in 2014 to reinterpret the con-stitution to allow the SDF to use force with other militaries was in part an effort to clarify the legal questions that had arisen over time. Yet even this policy change was not open-ended; only in limited cases where Japan's security was at stake would the SDF be allowed to exercise this right.

For the SDF, however, the new security legislation that imple-mented this reinterpretation finally allowed Japan's defense laws to catch up with the missions it was asked to perform. The Self-Defense Law was significantly revised. Article Three, which defined the duty of the SDF, became more expansive. Instead of defining the SDF's mission as responding to a direct or indirect invasion, the law described the duty of Japan's armed forces as "the defense of Japan." Furthermore, a new context for SDF operations was included, a "situation that threatens Japan's survival" [*sonritsu kiki jitai*]. Article Seventy-Six, which covers when Japan's armed forces can be mobilized, also included reference to this type of crisis. Thus, Japanese leaders could order the SDF to mobilize in situations that did not necessarily include an invasion. There was no change, however, to when the SDF could use force (*buryoku koshi*). The SDF could only use armed force defensively.[19]

Multilateral military cooperation had revealed serious contradictions in Japan's position on the right of collective self-defense. For example, the dispatch of the SDF to Iraq in support of reconstruction activities required other militaries to provide perimeter defenses, as GSDF members were unable to use their weapons beyond the narrow mandate of defending themselves. When Japan decided to send its MSDF to participate in the antipiracy effort in the Gulf of Aden, ships were initially discouraged from using force on behalf of other coalition partners. Coalition partners found this a severe limitation on the SDF's ability to contribute but ultimately found ways of accommodating this legal constraint on their operations.

Some legislators, particularly those supportive of a new international role for the SDF, advocated for a new general law to consolidate the growing number of laws governing SDF missions and to rationalize all of these policy changes.[20] Opposition party legislators, on the other hand, deeply resisted legitimizing the overseas dispatch of Japan's military, claiming such an act remained inconsistent with the spirit of Article Nine and would open the way for a dangerous expansion of military operations abroad. Implicit in this fear was that the military abroad would undermine civilian control in Tokyo. Even in Iraq, the SDF was not allowed to engage in combat or act to defend any other military deployed alongside them.

But the limited value of permitting Japan's military to use force only to protect itself was felt acutely by those who had been deployed overseas. Even in UN PKOs, the SDF confronted danger and was expected to be able to respond to aid others.

## THE EXERCISE OF CIVILIAN CONTROL

Correctives to the vast influence of Japan's military prior to World War II were also embedded elsewhere in the constitution.[21] The constitution's Article Sixty-Six removed the military from the highest levels of government, but the civilian bureaucracy also wanted to assert its authority over the uniformed services. The Defense Agency was initially placed directly under the prime minister's office to ensure it was compliant to the wishes of Japan's top civilian leader. Additionally, Japan's Defense Agency was staffed largely with personnel from other, more powerful Japanese ministries, including the National Police Agency, the Ministry of Foreign Affairs, the Ministry of Finance, and the Ministry of International Trade and Industry.

More than fifty years later, the Ministry of Defense (MOD) was established, putting the bureaucracy responsible for defense planning back on an equal footing with other major ministries. Today, the civilians in the MOD are no longer borrowed from other Japanese ministries. The defense ministry is growing in popularity for newly incoming Japanese civil servants, and most of the top bureaucrats in the MOD have spent their full careers working on Japan's defense plans.

Within the Ministry of Defense, civilian and uniformed policy makers now work in tandem to manage defense policy. Initially, only civilians populated the policy bureaus, with little formal need for consultations with Japan's uniformed services. Likewise, the bureau that handles Japan's military operations, once seen as the rightful domain of SDF planners, did not include civilians. As Japan's military capabilities became more sophisticated, civilians needed greater input from their uniformed colleagues. In budgetary negotiations with the MOF over major weapons systems, for example, SDF officers are better positioned to brief on the rationale for investing in new capabilities. Similarly, as Japan's SDF began to take on a bigger role in implementing Japan's foreign policy goals, political decision makers needed greater understanding of their operational concerns and requirements. Uniformed leaders speak out more often now about the problems they face, and civilians take their concerns into account more readily.[22]

The new missions undertaken over the past two decades have also brought civilian and uniformed policy makers into closer coordination. Civilians and SDF who have participated in UN missions and in a growing number of international military coalitions, have brought Japan's civilian and military policy makers closer as they consider the concrete conditions facing the SDF abroad. For the most part, this increased interaction has brought deeper trust and respect between civilian and military policy makers, and they have forged personal as well as institutional partnerships, which has made for a smoother policy making process within the government. Japan's SDF has become more capable and more cosmopolitan. Within the MOD, new mechanisms for sharing civilian and uniformed expertise have been put in place as policy makers face greater opportunity for using the military as an instrument of statecraft.

But it is the structural changes in the way civilians and military craft and implement policy that have been the most significant. In addition to the elevation of the defense policy bureaucracy to a ministry, several more recent organizational changes have brought greater uniformed voice into the policy-making process. First,

Japan's three services, the GSDF, the ASDF, and the MSDF, have been notoriously competitive, making joint operations difficult at best. In March 2006, a new Joint Staff Office was created, led alternatively by senior members of each service. The idea of the Joint Staff was to begin to forge a defense strategy that brought all three services to bear on Japan's defense needs but to amplify the SDF voice in long-term defense planning. While to date the Joint Staff Office remains largely an administrative body, there is considerable potential that this new arrangement might also translate into greater joint operational training and shared command.[23]

In a second organizational change, in 2016, the MOD announced that it would integrate all of its major bureaus to include civilian and uniformed personnel. In the past, the Defense Policy Bureau had been staffed largely by civilians, while the Operational Bureau had been the turf of uniformed personnel. Increasingly, personnel assignments have brought uniformed expertise to the policy-planning realm, and civilians have been incorporated more fully into the operational aspects of Japan's military planning. This recent announcement now opens up the possibility that leadership of various policy areas will be interchangeable, and no one aspect of Japanese defense policy making will belong solely to civilians or to the SDF.[24]

Finally, the creation of a new National Security Secretariat by the Abe cabinet will undoubtedly go a long way in bringing uniformed and civilian security planners together to shape Japan's strategic orientation. Composed largely of personnel from the Ministry of Foreign Affairs, the MOD, and the SDF, this staff serves Japan's prime minister directly. While its main task is to ensure efficient response to ongoing events and to implement the National Security Strategy, the National Security Secretariat is now taking a central role in the formulation of long-term military planning. In

2018, Japan will rewrite its National Defense Program Guidelines and prepare its five-year Midterm Defense Plan setting forth its commitments for defense spending and procurement goals. For the first time, this process will be run from the National Security Secretariat, a reflection of the need to put strategic planning at the top of the government's agenda. Once more, the integration of SDF expertise at the highest level of government is a significant reform for Japan.

For all of these steps to integrate and unify Japanese civilian and uniformed expertise, there are still moments when Japan's military creates concern about its role in politics and shakes public confidence. In 2008, ASDF Chief of Staff Tamogami Toshio wrote an essay rationalizing Japan's prewar advance into Asia. He submitted the essay to a contest organized by a rightist publisher, the APA Group, and he also encouraged his subordinates in the ASDF to contribute their own essays. Under MOD regulations, employees must gain approval before speaking or writing in public events or media. Tamogami reportedly told his colleagues he was not going to follow this procedure because the essay was based on his "personal research." The incident was widely reported in the Japanese media, and after a formal review, Defense Minister Hamada Yasukazu fired him for contravening national policy.[25]

The 2010 Chinese fishing trawler incident in the Senkaku Islands also created a furor in the Diet, and a clash between the DPJ-led government and conservatives who were now in opposition. It did not involve Japan's SDF but rather the Japan Coast Guard, and a coast guard video of the Chinese fishing trawler's collision with two coast guard ships near the Senkaku Islands was leaked by a coast guard officer, Isshiki Masaharu, after the Kan Naoto cabinet refused to release the tape publicly. Ignoring the prime minister's decision, Isshiki put the video up on YouTube, instigating a government inquiry and ultimately costing Isshiki his job. The civil servant who led the Japan Coast Guard, Suzuki Hisayasu, as well as the Diet member serving as minister of the Ministry of Land, Infrastructure, Transport and Tourism, Mabuchi Sumio, were called to testify in the Diet. The ruling DPJ suggested that Suzuki bore responsibility for the leak, but the LDP charged instead that it was the Kan cabinet that was at fault for its mismanagement of the bureaucracy. The LDP turned its rival party's penchant for arguing for civilian control against it, claiming that under the principle of civilian control, it should be the elected politicians, not the bureaucrats, who should take responsibility for policy failure. Tempers flared and accusations flew as the two parties sparred over Japan's longstanding sensitivity to the use of armed force and the exercise of civilian control.[26]

More recently, the MOD was once more in the crosshairs of Diet controversy. In 2016, the government's decision to dispatch the SDF to South Sudan drew considerable opposition criticism, and the minister of defense, Inada Tomomi, did not weather the criticism well. Although the SDF had deployed an engineering unit there in 2011, the 2016 deployment was for peacekeeping operations. The argument in the Diet revolved around the longstanding question of whether Japan was sending troops to a war zone. Once the GSDF was pulled back from its mission, considerable criticism of the handling of the dispatch resumed. The dangers in South Sudan were real, and apparently the GSDF in discussing how to fulfill its mission had acknowledged this. When word of this was leaked, legislators demanded to see the logs and a journalist demanded to see the SDF logs via a freedom of information request. Minister Inada was told by both her civilian vice minister and by the Joint Staff that no such documents existed. But apparently she was not told the truth. The political scandal resulted in

Inada's dismissal, as well as the removal of both the vice minister and the head of the GSDF. A year later, the scandal returned when other reports were found that exposed the GSDF colonel who had hidden the truth.[27]

Article Sixty-Six of the constitution gives no further guidance on how to exercise civilian control beyond stipulating that the cabinet should be composed of civilians. Japan's legislators, however, have interpreted it to mean that the military should remain far from the legislative process, and controversy over appointments has from time to time arisen. The SDF has been restricted from testifying in Japan's parliamentary proceedings, and to date, no active duty SDF personnel have been called to testify before the Japanese parliament. Recently, however, the Diet has invited retired military leaders to testify on issues related to their expertise. Moreover, Japan has now had two cabinet ministers with military experience. In 2011, Morimoto Satoshi, a professor of Takushoku University and a former ASDF officer, was appointed to the Noda Yoshihiko cabinet, and in 2014, Nakatani Gen, a former GSDF officer, was appointed to the Abe cabinet. Nakatani had served as head of the Defense Agency in the Koizumi cabinet.[28]

Former members of the SDF are increasingly turning to politics. Two members of the Lower House (Nakatani Gen and Nakatani Shin'ichi) and two members of the Upper House (Uto Takashi and Satō Masahisa) have served in the SDF. Even the disgraced Tamogami tried his hand at running for political office. In 2014, he threw his hat in the ring to run for the Tokyo governorship and drew national attention once again. He was unsuccessful, coming in fourth out of sixteen candidates and garnering over 600,000 votes. Those with SDF experience have been welcome in government, however. According to former ASDF member Watanabe Kōhei of the Sugakawa City Council, there are currently about

190 former SDF officers working in municipal and central government.

Japan's civilian leaders have become more aware of the challenges that confront their military as they ask more of it. Deliberations over the laws that allow the SDF to be deployed abroad have become far more focused on the operational requirements of the military, and far more specific about when and how legislative oversight would be needed. Evident too over time has been a growing confidence in Japan's military and in the ability of civilian bureaucracies to work with the SDF. Even more important, Japan's legislators—while still defining when it is legitimate to use force—are increasingly able to find common ground on defense policy.

## The Right of Collective Self-Defense

Legislating policy change for the military has had its downside, however. The SDF Law has been subjected to five major policy revisions since Japan's small minesweepers were dispatched to the Persian Gulf in 1991, but, if minor adjustments are included, the law has had to be updated ninety-six times. New laws were drafted and redrafted to allow for UN PKO participation, as well as for SDF participation in ad hoc multinational coalitions.[29] The tangle of laws that spelled out these various SDF responsibilities began to create a new problem. Uniformed leaders, overseeing deployments abroad, sought clarity for what they could do in scenarios that had not yet been considered by the Diet.

Perhaps the most pressing problem was the need to consider when and how the SDF could work alongside other militaries. Since the Vietnam War ended and the opening to China changed the region's geopolitics, successive Japanese governments have interpreted their constitution to prohibit the use of force by the SDF on behalf of others. In 1972, few imagined a scenario when Japan's defense needs would require cooperation with other militaries, even the U.S. forces still stationed in Japan. Japanese planners were thinking of how to develop what they would eventually conceive of as a "peacetime" defense posture as they saw regional tensions decrease. To be sure, a conflict could erupt elsewhere and that might spill over to affect Japan or U.S. forces stationed in Japan. The Korean Peninsula and the Taiwan Strait continued to be East Asia's flashpoints even as normalization of relations with the People's Republic of China became a reality. Politically, in the wake of the Vietnam War, few Japanese wanted the SDF to become engaged in fighting elsewhere, and one way to prevent that was through a narrow interpretation of Article Nine, preventing the right of collective self-defense. Japan's military could not use force to defend other militaries, even if they were defending Japan. Combined operations with the United States, for many of the government's critics, violated the intent of Article Nine and threatened the loss of Japan's sovereign discretion over its military.[30]

As East Asia became more fraught with potential conflict at the turn of the century, Japan reconsidered its defenses. Encounters between the Japanese and Chinese militaries increased, and North Korea improved its missile capabilities, making it clear that the SDF could not defend Japan alone. Further operational integration between the SDF and U.S. regional military forces would be needed to protect the Japanese home islands. After consultations, the U.S. and Japanese governments announced in 2005 a new set of strategic objectives for the alliance, identifying a shared alliance agenda for the first time. Following this development, in 2006, they announced a new alliance force posture—a U.S.-Japan deterrent force posture—to cope with the changing military balance in Northeast Asia.

This prompted Japanese planners to seek greater clarity on how the existing interpretation on the right of collective self-defense might affect a new emphasis on alliance military cooperation. Prime Minister Abe Shinzō called for an advisory panel to consider Japan's defense requirements and the right of collective self-defense in May 2007. Four specific scenarios guided their thinking: the defense of U.S. vessels on the high seas, the interception of ballistic missiles that might be heading to the United States, the use of weapons in international PKOs, and the provision of logistic support for other militaries in UN PKOs. In June 2008, the panel had recommended new legislation that would permit the SDF to undertake all four of these activities, but Abe was no longer in office to implement their recommendations.[31]

Abe returned to office in December 2012 and reconstituted the Advisory Panel on Reconstruction of the Legal Basis for Security in February 2013. This time, the advisory panel was given a broader mandate. Much had changed in Japan's security environment in the five years Abe was out of power, and China's challenge to Japan's control of the Senkakus had rattled military planners. As one of his top priorities, Abe ordered a comprehensive assessment of the legal barriers to SDF operations and asked his new panel to consider Japan's changing defense needs. Many of the core members of the advisory group had served in the earlier effort, including Kitaoka Shin'ichi, one of Japan's leading security and foreign policy scholars. A little over a year later in May 2014, the panel issued its final report. Both this panel and the 2008 panel agreed that, under the government's existing interpretation of Article Nine, Japan would find it difficult to cope with the changing demands on its military. Nothing less than constitutional reinterpretation would be necessary to adapt to Japan's harsh, new security environment.[32]

Several aspects of this report stood out. First, it sanctioned the SDF to work closely with not only U.S. military forces but also with other potential military partners. Second, the report addressed the overall needs of the SDF and weighed the impact of constraining its ability to use force in coalition with other forces as well as on its own. Finally, the report considered whether Japan could adequately defend itself without integrating the command structures of U.S. and Japanese forces.[33] The advisory panel had taken its assignment to heart. The report revealed a sweeping review of how Japan could best use its military to support its global interests and concluded with the recommendation that Japanese military power should be available in support of collective security, the very principle embodied in the Charter of the United Nations. Instead of looking simply at specific missions, the advisory panel took a hard look at the changes under way since the end of the Cold War and advocated a proactive Japanese role in shaping global security institutions, such as the United Nations, at a time when they were more and more necessary.[34]

Two months after the report's release, the Abe cabinet announced it would draft legislation to implement the advisory panel's recommendations. Abe did not embrace all of them and did not embrace the expansive approach to collective security. But in a Ministry of Foreign Affairs report, "Cabinet Decision to Development of Seamless Security Legislation to Ensure Japan's Survival and Protect its People," the Abe cabinet put forward three specific scenarios under which the Japanese government thought Japan's SDF needed to have greater latitude to operate. It specified that the right of collective self-defense should be exercised in order to (1) respond to a security challenge below the level of armed force, (2) provide greater contributions to global peace and security, and (3) defend Japan. None of these involved missions the SDF had not already confronted. The first scenario clearly reflected the run-in with China over the Senkaku Islands, whereas the second and third were missions that the SDF was already fulfilling.

The Abe cabinet's reinterpretation on collective self-defense was limited and reflected the LDP's desire to navigate the considerable domestic opposition to this reinterpretation of Article Nine. It reflected also the LDP's effort to gain the support of its coalition partner, the Kōmeitō. While the LDP has supported constitutional revision since its formation in 1955, Kōmeitō supporters strongly opposed revision of Article Nine, yet over the course of their coalition with the LDP, they found ways to compromise on national security policy. Constitutional reinterpretation, however, was a difficult hurdle for the junior coalition partner.

The Kōmeitō sought to limit Abe's latitude on reinterpretation, and its president, Yamaguchi Natsuo, publicly stated that his party's role was to act as a *hadome* (restraint) in order to protect the spirit of Article Nine. Discussions were held between LDP Vice President Kōmura Masahiko and Kōmeitō Vice President Kitagawa Kazuo to determine how the Abe cabinet would draft the new legislation. Kōmura and Kitagawa met eleven times as part of their consultative committee on security legislation and agreed on three criteria under which Japan could exercise the right of collective self-defense: "1) When an armed attack against Japan has occurred, or when an armed attack against a foreign country that is in a close relationship with Japan occurs and as a result threatens Japan's survival and poses a clear danger to fundamentally overturn people's right to life, liberty, and pursuit of happiness; 2) When there is no other appropriate means available to repel the attack and ensure Japan's survival and protect its people; and 3) Use of force to the minimum extent necessary." Yamaguchi of the Kōmeitō noted that any further changes in Japan's constitution would require a formal

FIG. 4.1  Demonstrators gather in front of the National Diet on August 30, 2015, to protest the Abe Cabinet's 2015 security bills. © *Asahi Shimbun*

process of revision, "putting the government decision in front of the Japanese people." Kōmura concurred: "So long as we have Article Nine, this will be as far as we can go." If more significant legal changes are needed for Japan's military, the constitution will need to be revised (see figure 4.1).[35]

Persuading the Japanese people of the necessity of constitutional reinterpretation was not an easy task. The Japanese were deeply divided over Abe's reinterpretation of Article Nine. According to the *Yomiuri Shimbun*, the cabinet's approval rating dropped by nine points after the reinterpretation to allow for collective self-defense in July 2014. Diet deliberations over the legislation to implement this constitutional reinterpretation in the following year drew protests on a scale unprecedented since the 1960 demonstrations against the revision of the U.S.-Japan security treaty.[36]

The government's two-thirds majority in the Lower House and simple majority in the Upper House meant that there was no doubt the new security laws would pass, despite the public outcry. The government argued that Japan's military readiness depended on eradicating the legal barriers that prevented the SDF from working effectively with others. Building a national consensus on allowing the SDF to use force alongside other militaries proved difficult, however. As the bills passed into law, all of Japan's major media polls showed that the vast majority of the Japanese public felt their government had not adequately explained this change in policy.[37]

The Abe cabinet's decision to reinterpret the constitution to allow the right of collective self-defense was also seen as a means to improving the U.S.-Japan alliance at a time when Tokyo most needed Washington's support. The confrontation with China over the Senkaku Islands had worried Japanese leaders who thought that the limits imposed on the SDF would hurt Japan's own security as it handicapped alliance cooperation. On a visit to Washington, DC, in May 2014, Ishiba Shigeru, former defense minister and then secretary-general of the LDP, put it this way: "If Japan chooses *not* to exercise the right of collective self-defense, it will be unable to maintain deterrence and independence, and it will be unable to contribute to the peace and stability of the region. Alternatively, as the United States is attempting to transform its bilateral alliance relationships in Asia from the old hub-and-spokes model to a networked set of alliance relations, Japan could become a source of instability if it insists on remaining in an unreciprocated military partnership with Washington."[38] Ishiba's preference was to move the U.S.-Japan alliance further in the direction of other U.S. alliances, where both partners agree to defend each other.

Few in the government argued for a full integration of Japanese and U.S. military forces, however. And even within the LDP, there was disagreement over whether a significant policy change was needed. Ishiba did not represent a majority view. The LDP's coalition partner initially thought that the existing constitutional interpretation might be sufficient to meet most of the government's concerns in the Senkakus, and also thought Japan could expand SDF participation in UN PKOs without reinterpreting Article Nine. The Kōmeitō contended that "gray zone" contingencies, such as a landing on one of Japan's many islands, could best be handled by the Japan Coast Guard and should be considered police missions rather than military ones. Deliberations over the SDF role in a "gray zone" contingency revealed the continuing sensitivity to situations that involved nonmilitary actors. A strict separation between law enforcement an military operations had been one way of limiting access by the military to any role that could threaten democratic practice. Many in the LDP shared this concern. After announcing the cabinet decision, the LDP Vice President Kōmura stated, "This hundred-year war between the military and the police has been reduced to a fifty-year war."[39]

Not all of the debate surrounding collective self-defense was about the bilateral alliance with the United States, however. For much of the postwar era, there have been strategic advantages for Japan to keep a low military profile. First, military self-restraint reassures Japan's neighbors that its intentions remain limited when it comes to the use of force. Sensitivities to Japanese military power run high in South Korea and China, where memory of colonization and military conquest continues to shape popular and strategic thinking. Even though the U.S., Japanese, and South Korean militaries train together to respond to the threat of ballistic missiles from North Korea, Seoul continues to reject any Japanese military role on the peninsula.

Second, integrating military operations with the United States also requires rethinking the use of force by allied commanders. To date, the two militaries have largely considered use-of-force questions separately, with U.S. forces tasked with offensive strike operations and Japan's SDF tasked with operations necessary to the defense of Japan. This distinction was often seen as similar to the relationship between a sword and a shield, but as weapons systems have become increasingly interoperable, and as deployments and exercises of U.S. forces within Japan have become increasingly integrated into Japanese military bases, the responsibility for the use of force has seemed to blur.

Third, many in Japan still believe that Tokyo can contribute to international efforts to keep the peace without changing its basic military stance. The SDF had already demonstrated its ability to perform UN peacekeeping and regional humanitarian and disaster relief missions without changing the government interpretation of Article Nine. Moreover, opposition party critics to the 2015 security legislation argued that the SDF could still defend Japan under the principle of the right of self-defense. In other words, Japan had all the military capability it needed to assist in coalition efforts without pursuing a broader military role with the United States in Asia. *Ittaika,* or military integration between Japanese and U.S. forces, would only undermine Japanese control over the use of force. Finally, Japan's reliance on the U.S. strike capability even for its own defenses has ensured that its planning is integrated with Washington's regional military planning. This strategic bargain binds the United States to Japan as much as the other way around. A purely defensive military strategy by Japan, in fact, strengthened the likelihood that the United States would help Japan in case of attack.[40]

Yet the advantages to Japan of limiting its military forces may diminish in the years ahead. Some defense policy makers in Japan worry that its restraint will be misinterpreted by Pyongyang or even Beijing. Ishiba, for example, has long argued that the ambiguity in Japan's approach to military force simply invites miscalculation by its neighbors. By reinterpreting the constitution each time there is a need for policy change, he argues, Japan is creating the impression that there are no real restraints at all. In addition, as weapons systems have become more complex, it is harder to separate defensive from offensive capability. The Ballistic Missile Defense system Japan has developed and deployed alongside the United States could be interpreted as an effort to build its first-strike capability.

While the Japanese public may find a missile defense system preferable to deploying offensive weapons, Japan may yet decide to build a longer-range strike capability as North Korea advances its arsenal of short-, medium-, and intermediate-range ballistic missiles. South Korea has always had aircraft that could reach the North and has also introduced missiles capable of attack. As its neighbors continue to build their ability to strike Japan, Tokyo is finding this option difficult to resist.[41] In the spring of 2017, the Defense Division of the LDP's Policy Research Council began deliberations in preparation for the next five-year defense plan, scheduled for completion by the end of 2018. Heading the team on ballistic missile defenses was Onodera Itsunori, who had just finished a term as Japan's defense minister from 2012 to 2014. The report, announced in April 2017, recommended significant strengthening of Japan's Ballistic Missile Defense capability, including adding a land-based system that would provide far better early warning and coverage for tracking and, if needed, destroying incoming missiles. In addition, the LDP committee recommended consideration for the first time of a conventional strike capability. No longer is this seen as a violation of Article Nine.[42]

By 2018, Tokyo had ordered the SDF to participate in two missions where the right of collective self-defense had been needed. The first was the UN peacekeeping mission in South Sudan. Japan had been participating in the PKO since 2011, but in November 2016, it sent SDF to South Sudan to operate under the new security laws. For the first time, SDF personnel were allowed to protect civilians under assault or attack (*kaketsuke keigo*), regardless of nationality. But the cabinet decision to send the SDF to South Sudan included a new condition for overseas dispatch during UN PKOs—a condition that the SDF had already faced in the Golan Heights: If the situation worsened to the point where the SDF could no longer perform its mission safely and effectively, it would be withdrawn.

Even Japan's opposition Diet members questioned this insistence on national control during a UN PKO. Gotō Yūichi, then head of the Democratic Party's security policy committee, pointed out that Japan needed to be able to respond to the situation on the ground when the SDF was sent abroad and raised this as a new consideration for Diet oversight. The deterioration of security in South Sudan, largely a result of the disarray in the South Sudanese army, meant that the Japanese sent to assist, including members of the Japan International Cooperation Agency, needed to be evacuated. The United Nations Mission in South Sudan took time to respond to the growing violence, and Japan's SDF clearly reached the limits of its ability to operate. Deployed at the airport, it was unable to offer assistance to anyone—not even the Japanese aid workers trapped in a nearby hotel.[43]

In Tokyo, fears that the SDF would be overrun or unable to perform its duties adequately prompted Tokyo to end the mission. In the Diet discussions that followed, Minister of Defense Inada Tomomi struggled to defend the decision to send the SDF to a region that clearly required greater exercise of the use of force, and when details of an internal SDF discussion of the dangers there were revealed, the minister was caught off guard. These memos showed that the GSDF in July 2016 had described the situation in South Sudan as a combat zone (*sentō*), implying that the government willfully ignored the five principles for PKO deployment that conditioned the Japanese military's participation. Despite the new security laws, this South Sudan mission yet again revealed the difficulties of trying to impose limitations on the use of force for Japan's military in situations that could deteriorate into armed conflict.[44]

A second example of the implementation of the new security laws was in response to a U.S. request for SDF assistance in providing "asset protection" for the Carl Vinson strike group operating in the Asian theater. In other words, the MSDF was part of the U.S. Seventh Fleet when deployed, and this carrier battle group conducted a tour of Asian capitals and conducted exercises in the South China Sea. The Abe cabinet sent the Japanese destroyer *Izumo,* the largest of the MSDF's helicopter-capable ships, to join the U.S. strike force. The MSDF also used this opportunity to visit Singapore, Vietnam, Indonesia, the Philippines, and Sri Lanka to strengthen cooperation with its partners from the Association of Southeast Asian Nations (see figure 4.2).

Looking ahead, decisions on when and how the SDF will use force will continue to evolve. While the 2015 security laws were seen as the last effort at reinterpreting Article Nine of the 1947 constitution, it is unlikely that this will be the last test of Japan's policy of military self-restraint. New capabilities will require another look at protocols for using force. Should a conflict erupt in Northeast Asia, Japan's military will undoubtedly need to consider new operations that will test the boundaries of the current interpretation of the constitution.

Yet the political consensus, based on the legal position taken by the Cabinet Legislative Bureau, is that Article Nine can no longer be reinterpreted when it comes to the use of force. Ruling and opposition Diet members alike believe Japan has stretched its

FIG. 4.2   The USS *Ronald Reagan* and the JS *Izumo* sail together in the waters south of Japan for an exercise on October 18, 2015. U.S. Navy, photo by Mass Communication Specialist 3rd Class Nathan Burke / Released.

interpretation of the current constitution to its fullest, and future decision makers will need to revise Article Nine if they want to alter the parameters of the use of force by their military.

## Revising Article Nine

As Abe moved forward with his agenda of security reforms, he also tried to move the national debate over the constitution forward. The LDP had long supported constitutional revision, but by 2017, more political parties in Japan had come to share that position. Yet Japan's political parties do not all agree on what to revise. The new Japan Innovation Party advocates constitutional revision to rebalance national and local authority in Japan. The Kōmeitō seeks more environmental protections and prefers adding amendments to the existing constitution rather than revising the existing document. Article Nine, however, is broadly supported in Japan. Even the LDP wants to maintain the "no war" clause, although its revision draft from 2012 renames the military from the Self-Defense Force to the National Defense Force. The purpose of Japan's military, however, remains self-defense, and the rejection of the use of force as a means of settling international disputes is still at the heart of Japanese thinking about their military. Koizumi was the first Japanese prime minister to redirect attention away from Article Nine to argue for Japan's international responsibility, a refrain that continues to be used today in national policy. By emphasizing the aspirations of the Japanese people outlined in its preamble, he avoided squabbling over the meaning of Article Nine and looked toward defining how Japan would fulfill its responsibility to contribute to peace and security. Nonetheless, Koizumi saw the need to embed his decisions within the language of Japan's constitution.

In contrast, Abe has reinterpreted the constitution to allow Japan to deploy its military more effectively and has actively advocated revision. Public opinion polls by Japan's major media outlets have revealed serious concerns over Abe's effort to reinterpret the constitution. Worries over the government's approach were twofold. Many, including the Kōmeitō, argued that this discussion deserved more careful deliberation to build a consensus within Japan. Others, including those polled by the *Nikkei Shimbun*, worried about the concerns of Japan's neighbors and suggested that the Abe cabinet needs to provide greater consultations and transparency about its ultimate objectives for those outside Japan. While the wide differences in the ways these polls asked questions made it difficult to gauge popular sentiment, it was clear that for many Japanese, the

Abe cabinet's reinterpretation came dangerously close to overturning Article Nine.

At times, Abe seems unable to separate his goal of reforming Japan's defenses from his more deeply felt ambition of revising the postwar constitution. In his writings during his time out of office and even after he returned to office in 2012, Abe unabashedly argued that the Japanese themselves did not author the constitution, and its origins as a product of the U.S. occupation compromise its ability to represent Japan's contemporary identity. In Abe's New Year's address in 2014, he argued that the constitution "expresses the form of the nation," and thus after sixty-eight years, the time had come to "deepen our national discussions, with a view to introducing amendments" that reflect how Japan has changed over time.

Those anxious about Abe's intentions criticized the way he approached revision and impugned his revisionist motives. Hovering over the debate over collective self-defense, for example, was the accusation that the new legislation was not necessary for Japan's defense and should be understood as "Abe's war bills." The legislation easily garnered a majority, as the LDP-Kōmeitō coalition held two-thirds of the seats in the Lower House. Yet the public seemed ambivalent about the way he had won the debate. In a May 2014 opinion poll by the *Asahi Shimbun,* many Japanese were concerned that the constitution was being changed without any public deliberations or support. As Japan's security goals change, more and more attention is paid to the way in which its elected leaders understand the instrument of military power and to what extent their ambitions reflect the will of the Japanese people. Even within the SDF, there are concerns that too much political enthusiasm for a strong Japan will temper the need for a realistic assessment of Japan's defense needs and operational requirements.[45]

While changing public attitudes toward Japan's military have accompanied a rising interest in the constitutional debate, these two trends do not yet add up to a public majority wishing to rid the Japanese constitution of Article Nine. Yet there is a sense that the taboos associated with the Japanese military have not served the public interest. In the 1990s, deep misgivings about deploying the SDF led to conspicuous policy failures, such as the inability to act during the first Gulf War and the initial response to the Kōbe earthquake.

The Great East Japan Earthquake and accompanying tsunami in March 2011 proved to be a critical turning point in the Japanese public's views of their military. As first responders on March 11, 2011, the SDF was quickly dispatched to the Tōhoku region, with none of the confusion that had complicated policy two decades earlier in the Kōbe City disaster. The Nīgata earthquake in 2004 had already begun to reveal changes in the SDF's disaster response. But the scale of the devastation in 2011 proved too great for any municipality to consider alone. A wall of water over thirty meters high had wiped out most of the cities, towns, and villages along the northeastern coast. SDF personnel combed the coastlines for survivors and set up basic services for the 450,000 survivors, most of whom were in temporary shelters with no access to food, water, or other daily supplies. The cabinet secretariat's survey after the Great East Japan Earthquake revealed a ten-point jump in the percentage of people with favorable views toward the SDF, from 80.9 percent in 2009 to 91.7 percent in 2012.[46]

A growing number of Japanese seem willing to discuss revision of their postwar constitution. The *Yomiuri Shimbun* has tracked attitudes toward constitutional revision, and particularly Article Nine, for decades and presents the most detailed polling on the public's views on the topic. For those who tend to support revising Article

Nine, the concern is largely about the ambiguous language of the second paragraph, which implies Japan does not have the right to have military forces at all. Postwar governments, of course, have interpreted this as not applicable to the right of self-defense, but much of the debate in the Diet has focused on limiting the "war potential" [*senryoku*] referred to in that paragraph.

The first paragraph of Article Nine, which stipulates that Japan shall not use military force as a means of settling international disputes, is widely supported, and even the pro-revisionist LDP has not sought to change it.[47] Under former Prime Minister Mori Yoshirō, an LDP commission produced the first LDP draft that offered new wording for Article Nine. Outside of government, the *Yomiuri Shimbun* and the *Sankei Shimbun* also produced drafts of what a new constitution might look like, with a similarly rephrased version of Article Nine. When Koizumi led the LDP to a massive victory in the Lower House in 2005, the conditions for Diet deliberation on revising the constitution seemed closer at hand. Electing a majority of pro-revision legislators to the Upper House was the next step.[48]

Japan's political parties have had widely different ideas on what ought to be revised but, since the late 1990s, have begun to discuss the possibility of revision. They have come together to put in place the mechanisms by which a national debate could be held. In the 1990s, a cross-party conversation in the Diet explored a broad array of issues that political leaders thought required revision. The next step was to put in place the procedures by which revision could be accomplished. According to Article Ninety-Six, a two-thirds majority in both houses of the parliament is the necessary prerequisite to a national referendum on constitutional revision. In December 2000, a cross-party research commission on the constitution was formed in both houses to study processes for constitutional revision in other countries, and it produced its final report in April 2005.[49] In September 2005, another special research commission on the constitution—this time mandated specifically with drafting a national referendum bill—was established in the Lower House. The Diet began discussions on a national referendum law in May 2006.[50] In May of the following year, the Constitutional Revision Procedures Act, or so-called National Referendum Law, was passed in the Diet by a vote of 122 to 99.[51]

However, this process was largely championed by the LDP, and when the LDP lost in the Lower House election of 2009, Diet discussions on constitutional revision came to a halt. Three years later, when the LDP recaptured power with another two-thirds majority in the Lower House election, Abe returned as prime minister, and the effort to revise Japan's constitution resumed. For a time, Abe's LDP tested support for amending Article Ninety-Six to make it easier to revise the constitution, but this was unpopular with the LDP's coalition partner, the Kōmeitō, and with the Japanese public. Nonetheless, with Abe's return to power, the political momentum for constitutional revision increased.

The LDP's Upper House victory in 2016 produced the opening for revision that the party had long worked for. The LDP won 56 seats, giving it a total of 121 seats, and its coalition partner, the Kōmeitō, won 14, bringing their total to 25. This gave the ruling coalition that supported the Abe cabinet a solid majority in the 242-seat Upper House. The more historic outcome of the election, however, was the tally of legislators who identified themselves as supporting constitutional revision. The LDP, of course, had long been an advocate, and the prime minister was a strong force for moving forward with revision. One of the newer opposition parties, the pro-revision *Ōsaka Ishin no Kai,* or Initiatives from Ōsaka party, picked up seven seats, five more than before. Smaller parties and some independents also supported revision. Just as important, however, was the defeat of parties that had strenuously opposed revision. The Social Democratic Party, which had long ardently defended the 1947 constitution, lost a crucial anti-revision leader in the Upper House. A new party, led by constitutional scholar Kobayashi Setsu, who had testified against the Abe cabinet's new security legislation in the Diet, had no luck at all with Japanese voters. With two-thirds of the Upper House now also willing to consider revision, meetings of the Diet constitutional committee began in earnest.[52]

Prime Minister Abe surprised many by making Article Nine the target of revision less than a year later. On the seventieth anniversary of the promulgation of Japan's constitution on May 3, 2017, Abe made his goals concrete. In a video prepared for a public symposium of pro-revision groups, he linked constitutional revision with the upcoming 2020 Tokyo Olympics, arguing that, just as the 1964 Olympics had been a new beginning for postwar Japan, so too would the 2020 Olympics be a moment of rebirth for the nation. Abe thus set a date for revision only a few years in the future. Even more surprising, he argued that Article Nine should be amended to include language that would remove all doubt as to the constitutionality of Japan's SDF. Coming just as his party's National Defense Division was arguing for the SDF to acquire a conventional strike force, Abe's agenda on the constitution caused a sensation. Some within the party wondered aloud if his remarks truly represented the LDP's priorities. The LDP's coalition partner, the Kōmeitō, largely supported Abe's statement of keeping both clauses of Article Nine intact while clarifying the legality of the SDF, but some, such as Vice President Kitagawa, questioned if this should be the top priority by 2020.[53] Even within the LDP, many wondered if this push for constitutional revision was wise, given the simultaneous push by the Abe cabinet for increased military preparedness.

Abe's role in the debate was crucial.[54] On March 25, 2018, the LDP approved a new draft at its annual party convention. Rather than change the nature of Japan's military, this first revision proposal sought instead to end the long-standing debate within Japan over the constitutionality of the SDF. The draft preserved the existing two paragraphs of Article Nine but appended additional language to explicitly recognize the SDF. In his address to the conference, Abe stated, "The time has finally come for us to work on constitutional revision, the goal of our party since its formation" (see figure 4.3).

Revision of Japan's postwar constitution, long a distant aspiration of Japan's conservatives, now seems much closer at hand. Practically speaking, however, managing to keep two-thirds of the Lower and Upper Houses of the Diet in coalition could prove difficult, even for the prime minister. Lately, Abe and others have preferred to speak of amending the document rather than fully revising it, perhaps in an effort to keep the Kōmeitō on board and to make it more palatable to the Japanese public. Abe's leadership of his party was endorsed once more in the LDP's presidential election in 2018. How much others in the LDP are willing to champion the revision of Article Nine remains to be seen, but even more important, the LDP will need to forge a consensus with other parties in the Diet before its proposal can be presented to the public in a national referendum.

• • •

At one time, the Japanese public overwhelmingly believed that their security would best be served without military power, but today, public polling reveals a shift in attitudes toward the SDF and toward

FIG. 4.3   Prime Minister Abe Shinzō speaks at the March 2018
Liberal Democratic Party convention, where the party approved a new
proposal for revising the constitution. © *Asahi Shimbun*

the idea of constitutional revision. Japan's SDF is highly respected
within the country as well as abroad. At home, the SDF earned
popular support after the Great East Japan Earthquake struck in
2011. The Japanese public also has come to value the SDF contribution to UN PKOs and to other international coalitions. Perhaps
most important, the Japanese public now see the rising military tensions in Northeast Asia as a challenge to their security and value
their military's role in defending their country. There is now far less
fear attached to the notion of giving the military a larger voice in
deliberations over how to defend Japan.

Civilian and uniformed military planners in Japan today rarely
talk about the need for civilian control. Instead, the MOD has recently passed institutional reforms that call for a shared policy re-

sponsibility between those in and those out of uniform. Outside the corridors of the ministry, other bureaucracies have developed closer and more equal relations with their counterparts responsible for managing Japan's defenses. In the Diet, the exercise of civilian control has taken on a more professional tone. Just as Japan's military has become more accepted as a professional force, the civilians that shape military policy have also become less polarized and more knowledgeable on military issues.

Military policy aside, however, there is a growing interest in Japan in debating what—if anything—needs to change in the document that has shaped Japanese governance for over seventy years. Prime Minister Abe has advocated for shedding the "postwar regime," an era he associates with looking backward at the mistakes of the past and of continued apology. He has written of his desire to build a "beautiful country," one in which younger Japanese can take pride in their nation. Constitutional revision has been a part of this vision and remains a high priority for him. The LDP may want to tweak the language of Article Nine, but few call for erasing it completely. Yet Abe has put constitutional revision on the agenda. It remains to be seen whether he has the support of the Japanese people.[55]

Moreover, Japan's domestic debate over its military and over the 1947 constitution does not exist in a vacuum. As important as the conversation in Tokyo over the legalities of constitutional interpretation is the political viability of the strategic bargain with Washington. After the Cold War, Japan's prime ministers have sought to ensure that the alliance continues to work for Japan, and in doing so, have moved slowly toward revising the constitution. Interpreting the 1947 document no longer seems politically legitimate, and yet revision of Article Nine promises to be divisive. Ironically, the argument for revision Abe has put forward has less to do with

Japan's contemporary military needs and significantly more to do with his discomfort with the U.S. role in drafting the document that limits Japan's military power to this day. Fusing a realist call for greater military power with a revisionist desire to free Japan from American influence, Abe has often confused the Japanese public on his real ambitions.

Yet, as the past decade or more of Japan's security planning makes clear, Japanese leaders are no longer convinced that restricting their military to territorial defense alone will be sufficient to provide for their country's security. Reinterpretation of the constitution has already made possible significant changes in the missions and the capabilities of the SDF. Whether revision is the next step or not remains to be seen. However, the military self-restraint implied by Article Nine of Japan's constitution remains tied to Tokyo's interpretation of its security environment. While there is no argument yet in Japan for a return to embracing the use of force as a means of pursuing the nation's interests, there is far greater interest in ensuring that Japan's military is ready and able to defend the country—and actively deter aggression by Japan's neighbors.

# FIVE

# Relying on Borrowed Power

W HEREAS JAPANESE LEADERS adapted slowly to their growing need for military power, they realized quickly that Japan would have to work much harder to harness U.S. military power in the wake of the Cold War. Japan had relied on the United States to deter aggression, but the presence of U.S. forces on Japanese soil seemed all that was really needed to ensure Japan's security in the global military competition between the former Soviet Union and the United States. Japanese leaders avoided public discussion of extended deterrence out of deference to the sensitivities of their citizens to nuclear weapons. For Washington, Japan's growing military capabilities were a welcome addition to the U.S.-led effort to contain the Soviet Union, and by the 1980s, Japan's Self-Defense Force (SDF) demonstrated it was quite capable of contributing to the U.S. strategy to contain Soviet naval forces in the Western Pacific.

Unlike other U.S. Cold War alliances, the U.S.-Japan alliance did not rest on the assumption of military reciprocity. Japan was not obligated to defend the United States as part of the strategic bargain. Article Nine of Japan's constitution was interpreted narrowly to preclude the use of force by the SDF on behalf of the United States or any other nation. In 1960, the United States and Japan revised their bilateral security treaty to include an explicit guarantee of U.S. military assistance in case Japan was threatened or attacked. In return, Japan offered the United States access to military bases and facilities on Japanese soil—bases that would support U.S. strategy in the "Far East." Trading bases for defense assistance seemed a good bargain for Tokyo and Washington in the early Cold War years, but by the end of the Vietnam conflict, the United States had had enough of waging ground wars in Asia and brought many of its military forces home. Moreover, as Japan's economy grew to become the second largest in the world, U.S. legislators turned their gaze on Japan's low defense spending. As it had done with NATO allies decades earlier, the U.S. Congress began to call for greater burden sharing in the U.S.-Japan alliance. Fearful of acquiring greater military power, Japanese leaders instead sought to offset the costs of U.S. forces operating in Japan.

The SDF's role in the U.S.-Japan alliance had been far more restrained than in other U.S. alliances, and Japan's political leaders were reluctant to allow their military to imagine combat alongside U.S. forces. Not until 1978 did the two allies formally discuss how their militaries might cooperate in the event of a conflict, and even then there was no combined contingency planning, although the United States and Japan did coordinate plans to repel Soviet aggression. As the military balance in Northeast Asia began to shift to Japan's disadvantage by the beginning of the new century, however, this restraint on Japan's military became more troubling. In addition, Japanese diplomats and security planners alike recognized that Tokyo and Washington seemed to be drifting apart. The U.S. focus on the Middle East after 9/11 also alarmed some in Tokyo who saw their own security concerns diverging from those in Washington.[1]

Throughout the 1990s and into the 2000s, Japan's leaders grappled with myriad challenges to the alliance with the United States. Managing a foreign military on Japanese soil had long been difficult, particularly given the postwar sensitivities of the Japanese to nuclear weapons and to the inevitable strains on local communities that host U.S. bases. The basic strategic bargain made by Tokyo long ago was to trade U.S. bases on Japanese soil for U.S. assistance in defending Japan. For the United States, Japan was an indispensable partner in its Cold War strategy, and as Asia's balance of power began to tilt in favor of China in the Cold War's wake, Japan became even more valuable. Japan's military played an ever greater role in regional security cooperation with the United States, and yet the alliance capabilities were pressed to keep pace with the growing military threat to Japan from North Korea and China.

As North Korea developed a larger arsenal of missiles capable of threatening Japan and as China's military began to expand into Japan's EEZ and ADIZ, Japanese planners faced a new and chilling reality: would the treaty with Washington work in a military crisis? As both North Korea and China gained greater military capability, they were increasingly able to threaten U.S. forces in the region or to threaten the U.S. homeland. Tokyo's leaders had to consider if they could really count on Washington to use force on their behalf if the risk to the United States became too great. For much of the postwar era, the Japanese had counted on the military power of the United States to keep their nation safe and to deter aggression. Changes in Asia's military balance suggested that Japan needed to reconsider that premise, especially after Americans elected a president who openly questioned the value of alliances to the United States.

## The U.S.-Japan Strategic Bargain

The limitations on Japan's use of its own military created a strategic dependency on the United States.[2] As Sakamoto Kazuya argued in his seminal work on the alliance, the lack of military reciprocity in treaty obligations informed Tokyo's approach to alliance management from the start.[3] The trade-off between a U.S. commitment to assist in Japan's defenses and a Japanese commitment to sponsoring U.S. strategic forces in the region was manageable for most of the Cold War. Attending the treaty was a memorandum of understanding that committed the United States to consultations with the Japanese government on how U.S. forces stationed in Japan might be deployed.[4]

To be sure, each government wanted the other to do more. The United States wanted Japan to build a bigger military and to allow it to contribute more to regional security. Japan wanted the U.S. to manage its military forces on Japanese soil better so as to reduce tensions with the Japanese public. Many in Japan found hosting U.S. forces burdensome, and Tokyo was anxious to reduce the number of U.S. forces on Japanese soil. Popular opposition to U.S. forces peaked during the Vietnam War, and a nationwide antiwar movement brought calls for the U.S. military to leave Japan. This reached residents in Okinawa, who were still under U.S. administration, and fed into local desires for a return to Japanese sovereignty. With the security treaty coming up for renewal in 1970, the intense domestic activism against the treaty prompted the Japanese government to assert its interests with Washington. The Satō-Nixon communiqué of 1969 announced the return of the Ryūkyū and Bonin Islands to Japan. The drawdown of U.S. forces in the wake of the Vietnam War was thus done in tandem with the reversion of Okinawa. The consequence was a consolidation and reduction of U.S. bases on the main Japanese islands while the U.S. military concentrated its forces in Okinawa Prefecture—an outcome that would come back to haunt Japanese leaders in the wake of the Cold War.[5]

Reciprocity in the alliance came under greater scrutiny in the United States once Japan became one of the world's richest nations. The U.S. government's frustration with the slow pace of Japanese rearmament had been part and parcel of the alliance dynamic since the alliance began, but as trade frictions with Japan grew in the 1980s, congressional interest in the equities of the U.S.-Japan alliance intensified. The NATO alliance had long discussed greater burden sharing, and the United States and its European allies had agreed on defense spending targets.[6] This proved to be an ineffective approach with Japan, given concerns over Article Nine in Tokyo and lingering unease across East Asia about Japanese military power. But the mood in the United States toward Japan was becoming increasingly fraught, and demands from Congress for greater burden sharing prompted the ruling Liberal Democratic Party (LDP) to action.

Kanemaru Shin, a former Defense Agency head and the secretary general of the LDP from 1984–1986, argued for thinking more compassionately about the U.S. forces that helped provide for Japan's defense. He persuaded Diet members across party lines that greater financial generosity would be deeply appreciated by the U.S. government, and new laws were passed that reflected the growing consensus within Japan on the need for the U.S. military presence. Kanemaru posited that a wealthy Japan needed to offer a helping hand to the United States, and the government set aside funds that became known as the *omoiyari yosan,* or compassion budget. A series of bilateral agreements allowed Tokyo and Washington to share the costs of U.S. forces in Japan, and Tokyo gradually assumed more and more of the direct costs associated with the U.S. presence. The Japanese government paid the salaries of Japanese workers on the bases, including those who provided critical maintenance for U.S. ships and aircraft, built new facilities and housing for U.S. forces, and even paid the utilities bill for all U.S. forces.[7] Yet Tokyo did not assume any legal obligation for these funds, pointing out that the provision of financial support for U.S. forces was at the discretion of the Diet.

A new approach to defining allied burden sharing emerged—one that demanded more of Japan's military. By the end of the 1980s, the U.S. government had begun to argue that its Cold War allies ought also to provide military assistance in "out of area" operations. The Iran-Iraq War was the first example of this attempt to extend defensive alliances to broader global security challenges. Iranian attacks on oil tankers passing through the Strait of Hormuz prompted the United States to begin escorting merchant vessels. The Reagan administration reached out to Japan and its European allies for help. The Nakasone cabinet quietly reviewed its military options. The prime minister reportedly favored sending minesweepers from the Maritime Self-Defense Force (MSDF) to contribute to the coalition effort. Britain and France had agreed to send their minesweepers, but members of Nakasone's own cabinet argued strenuously against sending the SDF out of the country. Nakasone relented, and on October 7, 1987, his cabinet announced financial support for the Gulf States affected by the conflict. Also included in Japan's contribution was an increase in funding for U.S. forces stationed in Japan, acknowledging that Japan recognized the toll on the U.S. military but also revealing that it felt ill at ease with using its military as an instrument of foreign policy.[8]

Paying for U.S. forces stationed in Japan seemed consistent with the bargain outlined in the security treaty. Japan could help the United States maintain its forces in its country while the United States helped Japan defend itself. By the end of the 1980s, however, this struck a nerve with the publics in both countries. In the United States, even on Capitol Hill, the idea that Japan was paying for U.S. forces began to look as though the United States was being paid for providing military protection. In a classic statement of the era, Paul Kennedy of Yale University testified at the Senate Budget Committee in Congress in 1988, "I feel somewhat perturbed, Senator, at the notion that burden sharing, as between the United States and its allies in the Pacific, and perhaps also in Europe, would increasingly take the form of the United States having the bases, providing the troops, providing the armed services, and those other countries paying for it. . . . It would be an ironic commentary upon the two hundred years of the American Revolution, if this country turned itself into the Hessians of the late twentieth century, for whatever good reason."[9] The U.S. military, in short, should not be treated like mercenaries. In the 1990 Gulf War, Tokyo's unwillingness to contribute military support to the U.S.-led coalition received heavier criticism. As noted earlier, the Gulf War revealed the limits of financing U.S. forces as an alternative to assuming greater international security responsibilities.

In Japan, Kanemaru's notion that Japanese financial support for U.S. forces was a symbol of Japanese gratitude also began to chafe. When the Democratic Party of Japan (DPJ) came into office in 2009, alliance equities were on the agenda. The DPJ campaigned on changing the terms of the U.S. military presence in Japan, arguing for a revision of the Status of Forces Agreement (SOFA) and an end to paying for U.S. forces. The DPJ wanted to cut government spending overall and get rid of the LDP's pork barrel projects. In its first year in office, the Hatoyama Yukio cabinet began to scrutinize the budgets of every ministry and government agency, subjecting each to a public review (*jigyō shiwake*). Sessions of DPJ legislators calling on bureaucrats to explain themselves to the taxpayers were televised across Japan and were widely popular. Defense Minister Kitazawa Toshimi argued against politicizing the alliance in this way, however. In 2011, he concluded a five-year agreement with Washington and consolidated Japanese spending under a Host Nation Support agreement. The DPJ also retired the term *omoiyari yosan* to describe Japanese spending on U.S. forces in Japan. In a press conference with U.S. Ambassador to Japan John Roos, Foreign Minister Maehara Seiji said that his government had replaced the term because Japanese support for U.S. forces in Japan was a strategic agreement that supported the national interests of both countries, and to attach a sentiment of compassion simply missed the mark.[10]

Japan's financial support for the U.S. military is not inconsequential. Between 1978 and 2016, eight bilateral agreements on Japanese government spending related to U.S. forces were concluded, for a total of 6.9 trillion yen ($65 billion)—an average increase of roughly 17 percent per year. In the five-year Host Nation Support agreement concluded in 2016, Tokyo committed to spending from $1.7 to $2 billion per year, depending on yen-to-dollar exchange rates and what was needed for facilities improvements. Thus, Japan provided both military and financial support as its contribution to the alliance and to U.S.-led military coalitions.

Whereas once financial contributions were the only means by which Japanese felt able to support security cooperation, by the early twenty-first century, Japan's military played a significant part in representing Japanese interests abroad.[11] In this regard, the 2003 war in Iraq was a significant departure for Japan, as more and more

Japanese saw the benefit of sending the SDF abroad to support the United States in fighting terrorism. Nonetheless, the war had strong opponents, and the SDF's role was limited to postwar reconstruction in Iraq. The alliance with the United States loomed large in Japanese calculations at the time. Prime Minister Koizumi Jun'ichirō put it this way: "The United States is a unique ally for Japan. Despite the great sacrifices it has made, the United States now continues to strive on in its efforts to create a stable, democratic administration in Iraq. . . . The United States is Japan's ally, and I believe that Japan must also be a trustworthy ally for the United States. It is from that perspective as well that I recognize the extreme importance of maintaining the relations of trust within the Japan-U.S. alliance."[12] Koizumi recognized that the perceptions of the U.S. public would be important should Japan ever need U.S. defense assistance. Sending the Japanese military to help in Iraq was meant to demonstrate Japan's newfound willingness to share the risks, not simply the costs, of the alliance in a world moving toward collective security practices. The 1960 treaty's strategic bargain of U.S. defense assistance for access to Japanese bases no longer reflected the complex trade-offs needed in the post–Cold War era. More than a decade after Iraq, however, this question of Japanese burden sharing resurfaced in the U.S. 2016 presidential election.

## U.S. Bases and Japanese Citizens

Japanese citizens calculated burden sharing in a very different way. Public perceptions of the equities in the alliance were a considerable source of tension between the national government and the localities within Japan that host the U.S. military. The extended presence of U.S. bases in Japan has continued to challenge the

Japanese government since the end of the Cold War. Several rounds of consolidation of U.S. forces were undertaken during the Cold War. The Korean War drew off a large number of U.S. forces, and the drawdown continued into the mid-1950s. In 1960, when the U.S.-Japan security treaty was revised, the United States maintained 46,295 troops on the main islands of Japan. But there were almost as many U.S. military personnel—37,142—in Okinawa, which remained under U.S. administration until 1972, when the Ryūkyū Islands were returned to Japan. Another round of base consolidation followed the Vietnam War, and by 1980, U.S. forces in Japan—including Okinawa Prefecture—totaled 46,004. The result of this consolidation effort was to concentrate U.S. bases on the small island of Okinawa, out of sight of metropolitan Japanese in the Kantō and Kansai regions.[13]

In 1995, just as the U.S. and Japanese governments began their first major post–Cold War strategic review, three U.S. military personnel were arrested in Okinawa for the rape of a twelve-year-old girl. When the governor appealed to Tokyo for help, Japan's Minister of Foreign Affairs Kōno Yōhei downplayed the crime, infuriating the governor and enflaming the growing outrage on the island. In September, eighty-five thousand protesters gathered in Okinawa's capital, Naha, to protest the crime, calling for the withdrawal of U.S. forces from their islands and for a revision of SOFA. Governor Ōta Masahide reacted by refusing to participate in the land expropriation process that allowed the government of Japan to offer the land to the U.S. military. When the official at the Defense Agency responsible for managing the bases traveled to Naha to discuss the standoff with the government, Ōta refused to see him. The spiraling political crisis in Okinawa led to the formation of a special committee of U.S. and Japanese officials to find ways of reducing the footprint of U.S. forces on the island.[14] Okinawa's tolerance for the concentration of U.S. bases was eroding just as Tokyo and Washington were attempting to adjust to their growing security concerns in Northeast Asia.

SOFA has long been a sore point for most communities hosting U.S. forces in Japan, as it offers extraterritorial privileges to U.S. military personnel and their families stationed in Japan. Perhaps the most sensitive aspect of this extraterritoriality is the provision for criminal jurisdiction—a point that was highlighted in Okinawa after the 1995 rape. Under SOFA, the U.S. military is permitted to try military personnel accused of criminal behavior. But in this case, Japanese authorities asked that the three U.S. military personnel accused of the rape, if indicted, be handed over for trial in a Japanese court. The crime tapped into a deeper sense of discrimination in Okinawa. Not only are the bulk of U.S. military bases concentrated on the small islands, but there is also a widespread perception in Okinawa that U.S. forces there are allowed to do things that they are not allowed to do on Japan's main islands. Because of the nature of the crime and the intensity of political protest in Okinawa, the U.S. and Japanese governments moved quickly to cooperate on the criminal investigation, and once the evidence supported the indictment of the three men accused of the rape, the U.S. government agreed to transfer them to the Japanese police to await trial in Japanese courts.[15]

The following year, the Special Action Committee on Okinawa, formed by the U.S. and Japanese governments, recommended a series of reforms in the way the U.S. and Japanese governments managed U.S. military forces. The reforms were designed to address this perception of difference between Okinawa and the main Japanese islands. First, under SOFA, U.S. military personnel indicted for "heinous crimes"—murder, rape, robbery, or arson—would be transferred expeditiously to Japanese authorities for prosecution.

Second, a series of modifications were made in U.S. military training. These included shutting down live-fire exercises across public roads and moving some large-scale exercises by the U.S. Marine Corps in Okinawa to Japanese SDF training grounds on the main islands. Finally, the land area used by the U.S. military in Okinawa was to be reduced, and U.S. facilities there would be consolidated. Included in this consolidation plan was the return of a major U.S. facility, Marine Corps Air Station Futenma, located in the heavily populated city of Ginowan in central Okinawa. Fixed-wing aircraft used by the marines were relocated to Iwakuni in Yamaguchi Prefecture. A new site for the Marine helicopters would be found in Okinawa; the less populated northern area, around Nago City, was designated as the most appropriate site.[16]

The influx of several thousand U.S. Marines worried rural residents in Nago. Others, including members of the Japan Communist Party, prefectural citizen activists, as well as sympathetic groups from Japan's main islands, converged on the small city to counter the Ministry of Defense's efforts to relocate the U.S. Marines there. A referendum was organized in December 1997 to oppose the government plan. The Japanese government offered considerable economic subsidies to the small, underdeveloped municipality, however, and the result was a divided response to the referendum. In the end, and after much campaigning by the Defense Agency and the LDP, a slim majority passed the nonbinding referendum in 1997. The newly elected mayor of Nago, Kishimoto Tateo, presided over the complex negotiations on how to design a new runway for the U.S. Marines for twelve years, or three mayoral terms in office. In 2010, Nago residents turned away from compromise with Tokyo as the relocation plan failed to progress, and they elected Inamine Susumu as mayor on a platform of opposition to the new base. In the Oura Bay, Inamine would join other Nago residents in his boat and advocate the need to protect the diversity of Nago's natural environment. Inamine went on to reelection in 2014, but in 2018, with strong support from the LDP, Nago residents voted him out of office in favor of a candidate that promised economic benefits in the form of subsidies from Tokyo.[17] Economic incentives to host U.S. bases continue to be the most important tool for the Japanese government, especially in Okinawa, where the U.S. military presence has historical roots in war and occupation.

National political change has also shaped the debate over U.S. military bases in Okinawa over the last decade. In 2009, Washington and Tokyo outlined the implementation plan for relocating the helicopter facilities at Futenma Air Station to Camp Schwab in northern Nago City and moving U.S. forces to Guam. The Guam Agreement, as it was called, attempted to commit the Japanese and U.S. governments to completing the relocation effort just as a new political party was expected to take power. The DPJ had long opposed the Futenma relocation plan, and, once in office, Prime Minister Hatoyama Yukio announced a policy review. In coalition with the Socialist Democratic Party and the smaller People's New Party, however, the Hatoyama cabinet seemed hamstrung. DPJ Secretary General Ozawa Ichirō traveled to Okinawa to dampen concerns there, while Foreign Minister Okada Katsuya began his discussions with the United States. Minister of Land, Infrastructure, Transport, and Tourism Maehara Seiji also visited Okinawa in an attempt to broker a new policy on Futenma and U.S. base consolidation. In the end, the Hatoyama cabinet decided to move the U.S. Marine airstrip off Okinawa altogether, identifying a new island as a potential spot for the marine helicopters. With the media, Washington, and its coalition partners all up in arms about what was happening on Okinawa, Hatoyama was under intense pressure to realize his plan. Local residents of Tokunoshima, an island in

Kyūshū Prefecture 124 miles north of the main island of Okinawa, refused to accept the new base. Hatoyama's initiative ended in failure and wreaked havoc within the newly elected party. Shortly thereafter, Hatoyama stepped down, and Ozawa Ichirō left his post as the DPJ secretary general.

While it would be easy to write off the tensions in Okinawa over U.S. bases as political differences between the conservative leadership in Tokyo and a more liberal or progressive political culture in Okinawa, this understates the causes of the problem. Even after Ōta left office in 1998, three Okinawan governors, all conservatives with powerful political channels to Tokyo, took up the cause of relocating Futenma and reducing the U.S. military presence in their prefecture. Governor Inamine Keiichi publicly scolded U.S. Defense Secretary Donald Rumsfeld during his visit to Naha for his lack of attention to the plight of Okinawans, yet Inamine also negotiated with Tokyo for considerable economic gains for Okinawa. Governor Nakaima Hirokazu struggled to restore ties with Tokyo. The confusion in Tokyo during the DPJ years left Nakaima with little hope for a settlement of the relocation issue, but when the LDP returned to power in 2012, he was persuaded to approve the land reclamation permit required to start construction. Nakaima was defeated at the polls as a result and was succeeded in December 2014 by a fellow conservative, Naha Mayor Onaga Takeshi—an articulate and staunch antibase voice among Okinawan conservatives.[18]

Tokyo's ability to sustain local support for the continued presence of U.S. military in Okinawa has had mixed results, even when the political parties in power in Tokyo and Naha have aligned. The LDP tried to improve its position in Okinawa but faced significant electoral setbacks. In the Upper House election of 2013, the LDP candidate, Asato Masaaki, lost, making Okinawa one of the only two prefectures that did not see LDP gains. With Onaga's win in the gubernatorial election, the LDP faced an unprecedented challenge to its alliance policy. The Abe Shinzō cabinet took a tough stance toward Governor Onaga, and initially Chief Cabinet Secretary Suga Yoshihide refused to meet with him, trying to ostracize him for his open refusal to endorse the land reclamation permit. The LDP was particularly frustrated that a member of its own party could oppose the national government so directly.

When the LDP's efforts to undermine Onaga failed, the national government then sought the help of the courts. Tokyo aimed to implement Governor Nakaima's decision to allow landfill construction to proceed in Oura Bay, and Governor Onaga endeavored to stay Tokyo's hand on the grounds that the national government had failed to abide by its own environmental impact mitigation plans. In March 2016, both Abe and Onaga accepted a court effort at mediation, and ultimately, the Supreme Court dismissed the prefecture's appeal, allowing the plan to proceed (see figure 5.1). Protest in Nago continued nonetheless. More than two decades later, many of the residents of Okinawa have yet to accept the idea that a new facility should be built for the U.S. Marine Corps, and a runway that the U.S. and Japanese governments thought would take five to seven years to complete has yet to be built. In 2018, after the unexpected death of Governor Onaga, Denny Tamaki, the heir apparent in the All Okinawa social movement that brought Onaga to power, won a decisive victory over the LDP challenger. Despite the strong campaign waged by Tokyo, Okinawans elected yet again a governor who would oppose the national government's effort to move ahead with building a new base.[19]

As the Japanese government struggled with base consolidation in Okinawa, U.S. forces on the island were reduced, largely due to rotations to the wars in Afghanistan and Iraq as well as to their

FIG. 5.1 Okinawa Governor Onaga Takeshi and Prime Minister Abe, who have been at odds over the Futenma base relocation in Itoman, Okinawa on June 23, 2016. In March 2016, the Supreme Court had dismissed the prefecture's appeal to block the move. © *Asahi Shimbun*

dispersal around Japan. After the deployment of Osprey aircraft, and as the Ground Self-Defense Force and the U.S. Marine Corps increased their amphibious landing training, Saga Prefecture in Kyūshū also absorbed some U.S. forces from Okinawa. Nonetheless, U.S. forces remain concentrated in the small southern island, where bases used by the U.S. military still occupy up to 10 percent of the prefecture's total land area and 18 percent of the densely populated main island.[20] Nonetheless, the U.S. and Japanese government relocation plan reduces the number of U.S. Marines on the small island by half.

But it is Japan's own worries in its southwestern waters that have overshadowed protests against the U.S. military presence in Okinawa. The clash between Tokyo and Beijing over the Senkaku Islands transformed the outer islands facing the East China Sea into a growing hub of coast guard and SDF operations. Challenges to the Japan Coast Guard by Chinese maritime forces in the waters surrounding the Senkaku Islands prompted the coast guard to upgrade its presence on Ishigaki Island. A new coast guard fleet is now dedicated to Senkaku patrols, and the government is reportedly considering constructing new bases for larger patrol vessels near the East China Sea. In 2017, the Japan Coast Guard reported 696 Chinese ships in the vicinity of the Senkakus, including Chinese Coast Guard vessels and PLA Navy frigates and submarines.[21]

Chinese activities in the East China Sea convinced Japan's defense planners to increase their own military presence in Okinawa. A second runway was built at Naha Airport to accommodate the transfer of an F-15 squadron from Tsuiki Air Base in Fukuoka Prefecture to bolster air defenses. Existing SDF bases in Miyakojima (air) and Ishigaki (ground) islands were upgraded. New, smaller facilities were built in Yonaguni (ground and air) in order to improve the SDF's ability to monitor Chinese air and maritime forces. MSDF surveillance aircraft and submarines are now rotated more frequently through the East China Sea from their bases in Okinawa and southern Kyūshū. Furthermore, the U.S. Marines and the GSDF began to cooperate on building Japanese amphibious landing forces capable of defending the many islands in the southwest. Trying to persuade Tokyo to withdraw all of the U.S. marines from Okinawa became far more difficult as it ran counter to the Japanese government's efforts to strengthen their defenses. Okinawan resistance to U.S. bases there ran into a far more determined national leadership than when the Futenma relocation was first discussed in the 1990s.[22]

## Japan's Military in the Alliance

The SDF has claimed a larger role in the U.S.-Japan alliance, but civilian leaders carefully scrutinize its operational integration with U.S. forces. Unlike NATO or the U.S.-South Korea alliance, the U.S.-Japan alliance has no combined command structure and no combined contingency plans.[23] The Japanese government's interpretation of Article Nine precluded that. From the late 1970s, the United States and Japan created bilateral guidelines for defense cooperation. The premise initially was to define the military roles and missions for the defense of Japan. Exercises based on these guidelines introduced the SDF to U.S. operational priorities and practices and provided the only means by which the U.S. military could understand the capabilities and command responsibilities of its Japanese counterparts.[24] The last decade of the Cold War brought the two militaries into greater cooperation in the Western Pacific, as the Reagan administration sought to mobilize the Western alliance's pressure on the Soviet Union. Declaring at the Williamsburg Summit in 1983 that the security of the West was indivisible, Prime Minister Nakasone Yasuhiro lent Japan's military and technological power to the U.S.-led coalition that sought to win the Cold War. In the northwest Pacific, Japan's military played an important role in supporting U.S. efforts to contain the Soviet Far Eastern Fleet, which operated throughout Japan's northern waters, from Vladivostok in the west to the Kamchatka peninsula due north, to protect its submarines. Japan's ASDF also faced off against Soviet fighters to the north of Hokkaido as U.S. forces conducted intelligence-gathering operations from their bases in Japan.

It did not take long after the end of the Cold War for these assumptions about the division of labor for Japanese and U.S. forces to be tested. The North Korea crisis of 1993–1994 revealed just how hesitant Japan's leaders were to allow their military to operate in combat with U.S. forces beyond Japanese territory. From Washington's vantage point, the ambiguity surrounding Japan's decision-making on the use of force needed to come to an end. Politically, the U.S.-Japan alliance would be in jeopardy if a war on the Korean Peninsula broke out and Tokyo decided it could not help. This was not the Middle East; it was Japan's own neighborhood. For the United States, the utility of the alliance was managing the emerging threats in Northeast Asia, and Japan's support in a crisis in Northeast Asia was deemed indispensable.[25]

If Japanese and U.S. military forces were to work well together in a crisis, then clarity over how and when they could operate together was indispensable. With decades of bilateral exercises under their belt, the U.S. and Japanese militaries had developed a significantly better understanding of their operational roles should conflict emerge in the region. This first review of military cooperation between the SDF and U.S. forces began shortly after the first North Korea crisis. By 1997, Washington and Tokyo had completed their review of the U.S.-Japan Defense Cooperation Guidelines and had agreed to proceed with thinking through what the SDF could do with U.S. forces in "areas surrounding Japan."[26]

Predictably, the Japanese government's decision to expand the SDF role in the alliance drew fierce criticism, especially from opposition parties in the Diet. Government officials denied that this notion of "situations surrounding Japan" was limited by geography and instead argued that U.S.-Japan military cooperation would be considered for contingencies near and far that could affect Japan's security. Tabletop planning and exercises explored the implications of this expansion of SDF responsibilities. No combat roles were envisioned; rather, U.S. and Japanese planners concentrated on how the SDF could support U.S. forces in a variety of contingencies outside of the defense-of-Japan scenario. Logistical support, refueling, and other types of operations were considered. After 9/11, military cooperation between U.S. and Japanese forces expanded noticeably, as U.S.-Japan naval cooperation moved beyond the Asia Pacific to the Indian Ocean and eventually to the Gulf of Aden. Japan's naval leaders gained considerable experience in coalition operations and deepened their familiarity with U.S. regional strategy.

Full operational integration of the two militaries was not possible, however. Japanese politicians and policy makers referred to it as *ittaika*, literally translated as "becoming a unified force." The most obvious restraint was political—the Japanese government's interpretation of its constitution prohibited the right of collective self-defense. But few Japanese leaders wanted a joint military command. U.S. military planners in the early 1950s had argued for a joint command with the Japanese military, but Prime Minister Yoshida Shigeru had rejected the idea. U.S. documents outlining this idea were declassified in the 1980s, prompting Prime Minister Nakasone to brush off opposition party charges that some sort of secret agreement had been reached with the United States. Nakasone asserted that Japan was fully in charge of its military in all aspects of alliance cooperation.[27] Opposition party critics had long been suspicious about Washington's ambitions for the Japanese military and of the conservative party's willingness to rebuild Japanese military power under the guise of alliance cooperation. Sensitivity over ensuring civilian control over the SDF was driven in part by this fear that the U.S. and Japanese militaries were operating beyond the control of Japan's elected leaders. As civilian planners in Tokyo grew more confident over time, and as a new generation of Japanese military leaders came to the fore, these worries receded somewhat.[28] But the U.S.

desire for a stronger Japanese military continued to be viewed with some skepticism.[29]

As the security situation in Northeast Asia worsened, however, Tokyo policy makers became more convinced that the SDF needed to be ready and able to defend the country in wartime. This meant greater military cooperation with U.S. forces. The MSDF was a strong partner in the U.S. effort to build a regional maritime coalition and a core participant in the annual Rim of the Pacific exercise. As noted earlier, the MSDF was the first Japanese military service deployed abroad, and it participated in all of the major U.S.-led military coalitions in the wake of the Cold War. As the MSDF worked increasingly alongside other militaries far from home, ship commanders carefully followed the rules of engagement set out for them by Tokyo.

The antipiracy mission in the Gulf of Aden gave the MSDF greater experience operating in military coalitions, but there was little likelihood that Japanese ships would be seriously threatened. Antipiracy was largely a law enforcement mission, and the Japan Coast Guard officials on board the MSDF ships were tasked with making arrests. But what if another country's naval vessel was threatened? Should the MSDF just stand by? Diet members considered this as they deliberated the legislation for the mission. On June 19, 2009, the day the cabinet bill on counterpiracy finally passed, an LDP Diet member pointed out an incident in April 2008 in which a German naval vessel rescued a Japanese tanker attacked in the Gulf of Aden, arguing for Japan to do the same for others. Prime Minister Asō Tarō responded by saying that the main rationale for passing a new law for the antipiracy mission, rather than continuing to dispatch the SDF under a maritime security order, was to allow the MSDF to protect other countries' vessels against pirates. The Japanese navy was given permission to use force on behalf of other coalition participants.[30]

Real scenarios now presented the SDF with real command decisions—decisions that, without political authority, impinged on operational readiness. Missions critical to Japan's own defenses required close operational coordination with U.S. military forces. Ballistic missile defense (BMD), for example, raised even more intricate questions about collective self-defense. This new weapons system required ever more interoperability between the two militaries. The United States provided critical domain awareness for Japan's new BMD system, and as North Korea increased its testing of ballistic missiles, the question of when Japanese forces could shoot down a missile became less of a hypothetical conversation and more of an operational one. In the case of a missile directed at U.S. bases on Japanese soil, Japan's SDF could of course target it, but the government's interpretation of the constitution would prevent shooting down missiles aimed at the United States.[31] Without amending the government's interpretation of the right of collective self-defense, Japan's BMD system could not contribute to U.S.-Japan alliance operations in the case of a conflict.

Beyond Japanese territory, the SDF was far more cautious about its rules of engagement. The Japanese government's interpretation of the constitution meant that, despite the long-standing cooperation between U.S. and Japanese navies, MSDF commanders did not have authority to defend U.S. ships on the open seas. The U.S. Seventh Fleet depended heavily on not only U.S. bases in Japan and the home-ported aircraft carrier there but also on the support of Japan's MSDF, particularly valued for its antisubmarine warfare capabilities and for its patrols of regional sea lanes. Would Japanese destroyers be unable to defend U.S. ships if deployed together in the South China Sea? Or even further away in the Persian Gulf or

Indian Ocean? Japan's postwar navy had worked closely with the U.S. Seventh Fleet during peacetime, but should a conflict with China erupt on the high seas, a strict interpretation of the right of self-defense only permitted the MSDF to use force to defend its own ships. Again, without rethinking the government's interpretation on the right of collective self-defense, Japan's ship commanders would not have the legal authority to assist U.S. naval forces.

By 2007, Prime Minister Abe Shinzō decided to tackle the political challenge of rectifying this disconnect between existing laws and the SDF's growing operations with the U.S. military as well as with the UN's peacekeeping operations. Abe's commitment to a stronger military was well known, but there was no consensus on this within the LDP leadership. Abe, and others in the LDP, wanted Japan's military to be more self-reliant, a position argued forcefully much earlier in the Cold War by Nakasone Yasuhiro. Both conservatives spoke to their frustration at their country's willingness to rely solely on the United States to defend Japan, but these sentiments were also expressed at a time of growing concern over geopolitical changes in Asia. Nakasone's concept of autonomous defense (*jishu bōei*) came as U.S. forces were withdrawing from Asia after the Vietnam War; Abe argued for the spirit of self-reliance (*jijo seishin*) when it came to defending Japan against the growing military power of its neighbors.

The Abe cabinet sought to bolster the SDF's ability to operate seamlessly with U.S. forces and other partners in the region, especially on maritime operations. Like Nakasone, Abe wanted Japan's military to play a larger role in its own defense. Yet in the 1970s and 1980s, there seemed little need for a full integration of the two militaries in war planning. Two decades into the twenty-first century, however, Abe understood that integrating the SDF's war planning with U.S. operational plans would not only improve their readiness but pressures from foreign and potentially hostile forces now made it indispensable to Japan's security. The Asia that Abe faced posed far greater risk to Japan than the SDF faced decades earlier. Abe understood that he might need to order the use of force against North Korea's ballistic missiles and even perhaps against China's growing maritime forces.

Moreover, by the time Abe sat in the prime minister's office for the second time, the SDF was better able to offer military assets to the alliance as well as to others in the region concerned about Chinese maritime activities. Japan's military planners still thought that sustaining U.S. military dominance was the best hope for Japan's security, and thus Japan needed to develop its military to support and complement the use of U.S. military power in Asia.[32] Even some in the LDP's main opposition party, the DPJ, saw merit in this approach.[33]

Recognition of the right of collective self-defense did not bring full military reciprocity to the alliance, however. Even the Abe cabinet did not aspire to have Japan use military force to defend the territory of the United States, but he did want the Japanese military to use force to protect U.S. forces that were fighting for Japan's interests in Asia.[34]

## Designing an Alliance Deterrent

Alliance planners were hard-pressed to keep pace with the growing military capabilities of North Korea and China, and the U.S. and Japanese governments repeatedly adjusted their military priorities to the new dynamics of post–Cold War Asia. By 2005, the U.S.-Japan alliance identified common strategic objectives, including the peaceful resolution of disputes between Taipei and Beijing. This was the first strategic statement issued for the U.S.-Japan alliance since its inception, and it was followed shortly thereafter by a restructuring of U.S. and Japanese forces designed to consolidate and reposition forces to strengthen allied deterrence as Northeast Asia's military balance changed. The Japanese military was designed to include interoperable weapons systems so that its capabilities could be dedicated to military operations that both allies agreed were needed, such as BMD, maritime and in-air refueling, and an expanded investment in intelligence, surveillance, and reconnaissance capabilities. Building alliance capabilities, however, did not mean that Tokyo and Washington had a shared plan on how to use them should a conflict arise.[35]

The primary mechanism for upgrading military cooperation was the revision of the U.S.-Japan Defense Cooperation Guidelines. These were redefined as first Pyongyang and then Beijing demonstrated willingness to use new military capabilities to assert their interests in and around Japan. Moreover, the guidelines were coordinated with Japan's own national defense plans. Washington and Tokyo defined new "roles, missions, and capabilities" to deter aggression—and if necessary—to defend Japan. The guidelines were revised in 1997 in response to the regional implications of North Korea's proliferation, and in 2015, in response to Chinese maritime pressure on Japan's southern islands. Notable in the 1997 revision was Japan's acceptance of the primary role in its own defense and an expanded role in regional activities. In 2015, Japan traded emphasis on its role in regional security for a focus on its global military contributions, but the new SDF priorities incorporated in its previous National Defense Program Guidelines of BMD and island defenses were also included. This revision in U.S.-Japan military cooperation was aimed at ensuring a seamless alliance response to gray zone activities and to this end introduced the Alliance Coordination Mechanism. The 2015 guidelines also included cooperation in cybersecurity. In both revisions, the United States restated its commitment to maintaining an effective nuclear deterrent and to upgrading its forward-deployed forces.[36]

In the years after the Cold War, Tokyo also became more concerned about the U.S. nuclear umbrella. China's modernization of its nuclear arsenal in the mid-1990s raised the question of how the United States was prepared to ensure extended deterrence, and annual white papers from Japan's Ministry of Defense revealed a new focus on the nuclear balance in Asia. But Japanese public opinion was strongly against nuclear weapons. The atomic bombings of Hiroshima and Nagasaki at the end of World War II had revealed the terrible power of these weapons and wrought unspeakable devastation to civilians, and for over half a century, Japanese leaders avoided discussing the use of nuclear weapons on Japan's behalf. Politically, the nuclear umbrella so necessary to Japan's security could not be claimed as Tokyo's policy, but rather proffered by the United States as part of its military strategy.[37]

Sensitivity to "secret agreements" with the United States on the use of force, and on nuclear weapons use in particular, had long been part of a contentious public debate in Japan over military cooperation in the alliance. For decades, opposition parties had accused the ruling LDP of reaching "secret agreements" with Washington. In the renegotiation of the U.S.-Japan security treaty in the late 1950s, the Japanese government had requested prior consultation over the use of U.S. forces from Japanese bases. The treaty did not include this Japanese request, but Prime Minister Kishi Nobusuke and Secretary of State Christian Herter concluded a separate note that committed the U.S. government to consult with Japan on major military decisions regarding the use of the U.S. military stationed there. Japan wanted to be consulted on three types of decisions: first, significant change to U.S. troops deployed in Japan; second, the introduction of new weapons systems (specifically nuclear weapons); and, third, the use of forces and bases in Japan for combat in third countries.[38]

Within Japan, lawmakers clamored for a clear statement that Japan would not pursue the nuclear option nor would it allow the United States to bring nuclear weapons into Japan. Prime Minister Satō in 1967 announced his government's "three non-nuclear principles," in part to assuage international fears that Japan might acquire nuclear weapons but also to reassure domestic critics that Japan would not allow nuclear weapons to be "introduced" to Japanese territory by the United States. Fears that the Japanese government had come to some arrangement that effectively endorsed the use of these weapons had long stifled a policy debate on extended deterrence. Of particular note was the question of whether the Japanese government had allowed nuclear-armed ships to call at Japanese ports. When the DPJ assumed power in 2009, the new foreign minister, Okada Katsuya, ordered a search for these "secret agreements" and an assessment of the long-standing Japanese government position on the use of U.S. military force on Japan's behalf.[39]

This policy review of U.S.-Japan consultations on the U.S. military in Japan put to rest domestic concerns over an extralegal arrangement between Tokyo and Washington on the use of U.S. forces. But it did not answer the larger question of whether Japan should or should not allow the United States to use its nuclear arsenal on Japan's behalf. The DPJ's desire for transparency in the extended deterrence debate had cleared the air, but Foreign Minister Okada had to address this more pressing question in 2010. In the Diet, he put it as bluntly as any prior Japanese foreign minister: "My understanding is that the three non-nuclear principles were meant to keep Japan away from the threat of nuclear weapons. But in a crisis, can we rely on principles and norms to protect the security of the Japanese people or do we make an exception? That judgment ultimately has to be made by the government at that time. I think that to try to decide today over this possible future scenario would only tie the hands of those decision-makers." In the 2010 National Defense Program Guidelines, the Japanese Ministry of Defense noted for the first time that Japan and the United States would seek to improve the reliability of extended deterrence.[40]

The Japanese government's role in the UN Conference on Nuclear Disarmament and in the Nuclear Nonproliferation Treaty, as well as the strong civil society activism within Japan on nuclear disarmament, made greater advocacy for Washington's nuclear capabilities politically difficult. This became particularly apparent when the Obama administration began to consider a serious shift in thinking about the strategic role of U.S. nuclear forces. President Barack Obama's Prague speech in 2009, in which he called on the nuclear powers to move in the direction of ridding the world of nuclear weapons, resonated deeply in Japan. Particularly welcome in Japan was Obama's acknowledgment of the moral responsibility of the United States to lead this effort given that it was the only nation to have used nuclear weapons—and it had used them against Hiroshima and Nagasaki. But this worried some of Japan's security planners, for fear that Washington might compromise the nuclear balance in Asia at precisely the time when China seemed poised to assert its military power in the region and when North Korea seemed determined to complete its nuclear weapons ambitions.[41]

Asia's intermediate-range nuclear forces have been a serious concern for Japan. Although the United States and the former

Soviet Union had successfully negotiated a disarmament treaty on these forces in the 1980s, Japan took care to ensure that their negotiations did not adversely affect its own security. When Washington seemed willing to agree to allow Moscow to redeploy its SS-20s west of the Urals, Prime Minister Nakasone pointed out that this would increase their threat to Asia. Ultimately the Intermediate-Range Nuclear Forces Treaty eliminated these weapons and put in place safeguards against expanding the use of intermediate-range forces in ways that could threaten U.S. allies. China, however, was not subject to this U.S.-Russian agreement. Moreover, the United States had ended its own use of the Tomahawk cruise missile during the George W. Bush administration and thus did not have readily available a nuclear counter to Chinese forces deployed in the Asian theater. China's ability to marry nuclear warheads to intermediate-range ballistic missiles poses a formidable nuclear threat to Japan.[42]

The Japanese government was of two minds when it came to the Obama administration's nuclear policy. The Nuclear Posture Review in 2010 was the first statement of how the Obama administration would implement the president's Prague vision. In January 2010, Japan's foreign minister, Okada Katsuya, who had long been an advocate for a no first use policy, told the media that he had sent a letter to Secretary of State Hillary Clinton and Secretary of Defense Robert Gates suggesting a bilateral discussion on the possibility of no first use and what it would mean for U.S.-Japan cooperation. But the U.S. government was torn on moving forward with this declaratory policy, and the April 2010 Nuclear Posture Review did not present a shift to a no first use policy.[43] In the summer of 2016, this idea that the Obama administration might implement a no first use policy again reached the U.S. media. U.S. allies were said to have consulted on their misgivings in a *Washington Post* article. Abe denied that his government had concerns, but other politicians in Japan, including the president of the LDP's coalition partner, Yamaguchi Natsuo of the Kōmeitō, welcomed this shift in U.S. policy and urged Japan to support it.[44] The *New York Times* on September 5 described the divisions within Obama's cabinet over issuing an executive order to adopt a U.S. no first use policy, and two days later, the president's Deputy National Security Advisor Ben Rhodes said that there was no decision pending for the president. He went on to add that if U.S. declaratory policy were to be changed, the United States would consult with its allies, and that U.S. security guarantees to its allies are "rock solid and they will continue to be."[45]

A second debate over deterrence in Tokyo was also taking shape, and this focused on Japan's conventional forces and the possibility of developing offensive or strike capability. Japanese security experts and policy makers became increasingly worried that North Korea or even China might miscalculate unless Tokyo too maintained the ability to strike back. Japan's lack of even a conventional retaliatory capability had long been seen as a strategic weakness that could not be helped, given the strong antimilitary sentiment of the public. The U.S.-Japan alliance was deemed sufficient for nuclear deterrence, and it had long been assumed that forward deployed U.S. forces in Japan would also be sufficient to deter conventional attack.

Yet as Pyongyang increased the number of missiles that could strike Japan, Japan's own lack of conventional retaliatory capability stood out. Moreover, North Korea's arsenal of weapons of mass destruction, including its growing nuclear capabilities, raised questions about whether a conventional strike capability would be enough to deter use of these weapons against Japan. BMD provided only minimal protection. Equally worrisome was the potential for miscalculation in Pyongyang or—more dangerous still—a concerted effort by Beijing to convince Washington that the costs of using force on Tokyo's behalf would be too high. Without the ability to retaliate, Japan would have no recourse of its own. Few in Tokyo were ready to advocate for the nuclear option, but policy makers weighed their conventional options.

By the early 2000s, the merits of Japan's ability to launch a conventional strike were debated on the Diet floor. This echoed a debate half a century earlier on what kinds of forces Japan might need and how its constitution might affect military preparedness. In February 1956, Prime Minister Hatoyama Ichirō had refused to close the door on the option of Japan acquiring offensive weapons. If no other alternative, he argued, Japan should be able to defend itself by striking enemy bases in retaliation to a missile attack.[46] Almost fifty years later, the growing missile capabilities of Pyongyang made this scenario less theoretical for Japan's defense planners. Japan's political leaders not only began to argue for offensive weapons but also made clear these should not be seen as a last resort or as an alternative to U.S. defense assistance. Preemption might be necessary if Japan were about to be attacked. Interestingly, it was not only the conservative party that saw the logic in this option—some leading members of Japan's major opposition party, the DPJ, also supported it. Political leaders in both the LDP and the DPJ wanted to see their government conduct simulations of conflict with North Korea that included the ability to retaliate against North Korean bases in order to analyze Japan's defense needs. North Korea's testing of its intermediate-range missiles in July 2006 gave defense planners further cause for addressing Japan's missile gap.[47]

The successful launch in 2013 of a Taepodong missile, followed several years later by a sustained series of launches of shorter-range missiles from mobile launchers, including salvos of multiple simultaneous launches, exposed the potential limits of Japan's missile defenses. With North Korea possessing the ability to launch without warning and to launch enough missiles to make shooting them down difficult, the option of bolstering Japan's missile defenses with a retaliatory capability became far more appealing. Discussions within the Ministry of Defense on how Japan should respond to the growing regional missile threat had been ongoing.

When the LDP returned to government in late 2012, it took over planning for the next five-year defense plan, the National Defense Program Guidelines. In that plan, a "dynamic joint defense force" was envisioned for Japan's SDF. Both the soft and the hard capabilities of the SDF were to be upgraded, including readiness, sustainability, resiliency, and connectivity among all branches of Japan's military. Japan's C3I systems—command, control, communications, and intelligence—drew particular attention. Dynamic defense and a renewed emphasis on jointness would require constant attention. In December 2013, the parliamentary senior vice minister of defense, Takeda Ryota, convened a new committee (*Tōgō kidō bōeiryoku kōchiku iinkai*) to oversee this reorganization of Japan's military.

In March 2017, Imazu Hiroshi, head of the party's Research Commission on National Security, formally proposed the acquisition of conventional strike capability to Prime Minister Abe, and in May, former Defense Minister Onodera Itsunori, who had headed up the commission's ballistic missile team, traveled to Washington, DC, where he outlined Japan's need for a retaliatory strike capability. At a public symposium on the U.S.-Japan alliance, Onodera emphasized that Japan wanted to develop this capability *with* the United States to enhance the alliance deterrent. It was not an effort to acquire independent Japanese capability or to hedge against the failure of U.S. deterrence. Onodera also argued that Japan considered this capability to be used only in retaliation rather than in preemption.[48]

## Tokyo's Growing Fear of Abandonment

Deterrence against nuclear attack depends on the threat of nuclear retaliation, and Japan relies solely on U.S. strategic capabilities to accomplish this. Even with the ability to launch a conventional strike, Japan would be unable to deter its nuclear neighbors. Thus, as North Korea joined the ranks of nuclear-capable nations, Tokyo's strategic dependence on Washington deepened. China's growing military assertiveness also raised the specter of some sort of armed conflict, one in which Beijing's nuclear forces threatened to hold sway over a nonnuclear Tokyo. In the dynamics of the alliance, abandonment by the United States became far more concerning to Japan's decision makers.[49]

Yet Japan's security concerns grew not only from the rising capabilities of its neighbors. Political change in Washington had also brought home to Tokyo planners just how vulnerable Japan could be to a mercurial new president and to the possibility that the United States could sacrifice the interests of its allies as it pursued its own security priorities. Uncertainty deepened over the future of the U.S. role in Asia, and Japan's fear of abandonment has become ever more acute as leaders look at the accelerating dynamics of major-power competition in Asia.

These two sets of pressures—one from China's rising military power and the other from a far more unpredictable United States—have shaken Japanese perceptions of the alliance and raised the possibility that the U.S.-Japan alliance might not always be a reliable guarantor of Japan's security interests. Throughout the history of the alliance, Japan had played a supporting role in U.S. military strategy. Few imagined that Japan itself would be the target of a direct attack. For decades, an armed attack on Japan was considered to be likely only in the context of a broader regional conflict, most likely on the Korean peninsula, and even then, the Japanese military would be asked for rear-area support rather than become involved in combat operations abroad. But as the militaries of China and North Korea acquired the ability to directly threaten Japan and saw opportunity to test the U.S.-Japan alliance, military planners in Tokyo and Washington had to consider the possibility that Japan might become involved in armed conflict on its own.

Japan began to recognize China's growing military assertiveness in the 1990s, but the direct impact of Chinese military power on Japan's defenses was felt in 2012 when the two Asian powers clashed over the Senkaku Islands. After the fishing trawler incident in 2010, the sovereignty dispute came to a head, and despite efforts by Beijing and Tokyo to manage the crisis, within two years the maritime forces of both countries were mobilized to contest the other's claim of sovereignty over these small, uninhabited islands. Both countries deployed law enforcement vessels to Senkaku waters, but their navies were not far over the horizon.[50] This created a dilemma not only for Japan's defense authorities but also for the U.S.-Japan alliance.[51]

The rapid escalation of military tensions between Japan and China in the East China Sea took many in Washington by surprise and raised worries about the United States becoming involved in a war with China over these remote islands. Global media coverage of the dispute also propelled the crisis, as leaders in Tokyo and Beijing saw fit to emphasize their side of the dispute. China's decision to deploy its maritime law enforcement vessels to the Senkaku Islands was also informed by a Chinese challenge to Philippine sovereignty over the Scarborough Shoal in the South China Sea, and this created the distinct impression that Beijing's growing maritime forces were now to be used as an instrument of coercion in territorial disputes with its maritime neighbors across Asia's seas.

At the time, Tokyo and Beijing seemed unable to find an exit to the crisis. Political communication channels were shut, and public sentiment ran high in both nations. A Chinese naval vessel locked its fire control radar onto a Japanese ship in the early months of 2013, raising the level of tension even further. By November, China had declared an Air Defense Identification Zone (ADIZ) over an area of about two-thirds of the East China Sea, and the Chinese Ministry of Defense claimed it would take action against any aircraft entering that airspace. The United States immediately sent two B-52 bombers across the ADIZ, and the secretary of defense declared that the U.S. military would continue operate freely in international waters and airspace. The Abe cabinet refused to recognize the new ADIZ and sent civilian and military aircraft over the East China Sea without altering their normal flight paths. The United States, however, decided that commercial aircraft should follow the new ADIZ rules set by China.[52]

Washington sought to reassure Tokyo of its commitment to Japan's defense while also working to de-escalate the climbing tensions across the East China Sea. U.S. military forces were deployed to Japan to signal U.S. resolve, but the Obama administration was also pressed to make a clear declaration of its intention to defend Japan should the Chinese attempt to take the islands by force. U.S. policy had always been to apply Article Five of the bilateral security treaty to "territory under the administration of Japan," a legal reference that recognized Japan's administrative control over the islands. But U.S. policy since the reversion of Okinawa had also been to avoid taking a position on the sovereignty of the islands, leaving that to be resolved by Japan and China in accordance with international law. The Abe cabinet worried that the U.S. government was too ambiguous about its position on the Senkakus and that Beijing might try to force the issue by changing the status quo around the islands. Indeed, Beijing would then be able to make the case that the Senkakus were under its administrative control, weakening the long-held Japanese position that it was administering the islands since the turn of the twentieth century.

The Senkaku Islands crisis had raised the bar for U.S.-Japan military cooperation as it highlighted just how easily tensions could escalate between Tokyo and Beijing. Moreover, Tokyo planners worried about Chinese maritime activities in gray zone scenarios where Chinese ships might challenge Japan's sovereignty but do so with nonmilitary maritime forces. Maritime law enforcement, often referred to by experts as "white hulls," and maritime militia from China were far more numerous than similar Japanese ships, and China was rapidly expanding its fleet. Neither China nor Japan claimed to want a military conflict but preventing the creeping presence of Chinese vessels in Japan's waters brought the two Asian powers closer to the brink. Chinese forces made similar challenges to control of island territory against China's Southeast Asian neighbors. Japanese planners feared a Chinese landing on the Senkakus becoming a *fait accompli*. They had watched Beijing coerce Manila in the Scarborough Shoal, and wanted to avoid allowing Chinese forces to gain any advantage in the Senkakus. This would embarrass the Japanese government and force its hand on the defense of the islands. Deterring this kind of Chinese opportunism became a focal point of alliance consultations, and Tokyo asked for an update to the U.S.-Japan Defense Cooperation

Guidelines in 2015 to ensure seamless coordination in case of a gray zone conflict.[53]

The Obama administration increased its efforts to signal its support for Japan. After repeated assurances by Secretary of State Hillary Clinton and her successor, John Kerry, the president himself affirmed in Tokyo in 2014 that the United States considered the Senkaku Islands as being under the protection of Article Five of the U.S.-Japan security treaty. The revised guidelines also established the Alliance Coordination Mechanism, designed to offer full consultations in case of a crisis in order to prevent escalation to the use of force. Japan would not face another Senkakus crisis on its own. Not only would the alliance deter aggression and, if necessary, defend Japan, but Washington and Tokyo would work together to de-escalate a crisis should tensions flare.[54]

But a second—and far more serious—challenge to the alliance came from the United States. In the presidential campaign of 2016, candidate Donald J. Trump spoke openly of ending U.S. alliances, complaining of their strain on the U.S. economy. In an interview with the *New York Times* in March 2016, Trump went so far as to suggest that America's Asian allies would one day need to defend themselves against North Korea's nuclear weapons, saying, "If the United States keeps on its path, its current path of weakness, they're going to want to have [nuclear weapons] anyway with or without me discussing it, because I don't think they feel very secure in what's going on with our country."[55] Once elected, however, Trump and Abe met in a surprising pre-inauguration visit by the Japanese prime minister to Trump Tower, and Trump assured Abe privately that he would uphold the U.S. security commitment to Japan. Trade, rather than security, seemed to be the new president's largest concern. Trump had promised that within the first one hundred days of taking office, he would withdraw the United States from the

Trans-Pacific Partnership, a multilateral deal that Abe had advocated for and worked closely with the Obama administration on bringing to a successful close. When the Japanese prime minister visited the new U.S. president in February 2017, Trump had already implemented his promise. The United States had abandoned a regional economic vision it had created and championed with strong Japanese support.

But this would be only the first of many of Trump's abrupt diplomatic departures from a regional role that Tokyo had welcomed and supported. While Abe's overture to President-elect Trump had paid off, giving the Japanese leader a far smoother transition to this new administration than many other U.S. allies, Tokyo remained concerned about President Trump's rhetoric. The NATO meeting in the spring witnessed Trump's refusal to provide assurances of Article Five protections to European allies even as they worried about Russian's growing pressure on their eastern members. Australia's prime minister, Malcolm Turnbull, found himself on the receiving end of an angry outburst in the midst of his first call with President Trump, and when Moon Jae-in was elected president of South Korea in May, he faced a growing military crisis with North Korea as well as President Trump's insistence on renegotiating the U.S.-South Korea bilateral trade agreement. Abe managed to build a good working relationship with Trump, aided in part by the escalating crisis with Pyongyang, and regular consultations between Abe and Trump had firmed up their understanding of how best to manage Northeast Asia's biggest military threat (see figure 5.2).

Japan had long taken a tough line on sanctioning North Korean behavior. Ever since Prime Minister Koizumi had revealed that Japanese abducted by the Kim regime still lived in North Korea, Abe had been an ardent critic of the Japanese government's weak-

FIG. 5.2    President Donald J. Trump speaks to U.S. and Japanese armed forces at Yokota Air Base on November 5, 2017. © *Asahi Shimbun*

ness on Pyongyang. One of the most valued aspects of the Trump administration's response to North Korea's barrage of missile launches in 2017 was the harder line on sanctions. Abe used a host of multilateral meetings to advocate on behalf of international condemnation of North Korea's behavior, as well as making the North Korea problem the highlight of his bilateral meetings with world leaders. The passage on August 5 of UN Security Council Resolution 2371, which imposed sanctions on trade in four critical commodities (coal, iron ore, lead, and seafood products) was welcomed in Tokyo. At the UN General Assembly, Abe argued that past efforts to negotiate with North Korea had only been used by the Kim regime as a means of "deceiving us and buying time." Japan's prime minister made it clear that he believed that what was needed was "not dialogue, but pressure" on North Korea.[56]

Japan also took increasingly visible steps to respond to Pyongyang's missile launches. As noted earlier, the BMD alert status no longer was made public, and with the growing number of missiles heading in Japan's direction, the missile destruction order likely remained in place for much of the year. Trilateral exercises involving U.S. strategic forces accompanied by Japanese and South Korean fighter jets marked a deepening synchronization of the three allied militaries in Northeast Asia. Of course, Seoul was hesitant to allow Japanese forces on Korean soil, but when the North Koreans test-fired a long-range missile over Japanese territory, ROK forces along with United States Forces Korea demonstrated their lethality and alliance solidarity with Japan. A second test of the Hwasong-12 on August 29 came as exercises continued between U.S.-ROK forces. Synchronized with these exercises, the U.S. and Japanese militaries conducted missile defense exercises. The coordination of both U.S. alliances in response to the North Korean missiles was a notable step forward in alliance readiness (see figure 5.3).

But when President Trump shifted abruptly toward meeting the North Korean leader, Tokyo was caught off guard. President Moon's effort to use the Olympics as an opportunity for engagement had long been seen as a necessary effort at engagement, and so when Kim sent his sister, Kim Yo-jong, as well as the president of the Presidium of the Supreme People's Assembly, Kim Yong-nam, to the February games in Pyeongchang, Abe agreed to attend also. He greeted Kim's sister and met with the North Korean emissary. But the sudden shift in the U.S. position was alarming. Tokyo had not been consulted, nor was the aim of the Trump-Kim summit clear. In April, Prime Minister Abe traveled to the United States to share his thinking with President Trump. At the press conference held

FIG. 5.3   Japan's Air Self-Defense Force fighters fly with a U.S. B1-B bomber as part of a training exercise on August 15, 2017, near the Senkaku Islands. U.S. Department of Defense, photo courtesy Japan Air Self-Defense Force.

after their Mar-a-Lago meeting, Abe and Trump were in complete harmony on how to proceed with negotiations. Abe outlined Japan's three interests: the complete, verifiable, and irreversible denuclearization of North Korea, the reduction of ballistic missiles, and an accounting of the Japanese citizens who had been abducted by the North Korean regime. President Trump addressed all three of these interests, as he spoke warmly of his "good friend Shinzō." On trade, the two leaders had their differences, but overall the second Mar-a-Lago summit seemed a success for Abe. The United States and Japan remained on the same page on North Korea. They did, that is, until a week later when President Trump announced that he was calling off the meeting and Abe had to plan a return visit to Washington. The U.S.-North Korea summit was held in Singapore in June 2018, producing the first meeting between a U.S. president and a North Korean leader. What remains to be seen is how this overture will develop into a disarmament plan, and how close Washington and Tokyo will remain in the process. Should the United States choose to prioritize its own security over that of its allies, or worse yet, agree to an outcome that weakens U.S. military protection for Japan, the Abe cabinet will have to consider the consequences for its own military. Abandonment can come in many forms, and a U.S.-North Korea deal that leaves Japan more vulnerable to the North Korean threat would be viewed in Tokyo as a considerable setback.

. . .

The underpinnings of Northeast Asian stability were under challenge by the late 1990s, and Tokyo and Washington were forced to address the long-standing ambiguities that had characterized their military cooperation. The U.S. and Japanese governments also began to interpret threat differently. Even on the Korean Peninsula, where the United States and Japan had long discussed a possible crisis, the changing balance of military power was perceived differently. Nuclear proliferation by Pyongyang worried Washington more, especially the possibility that the North Korean regime could sell fissile material to terrorists, while Japanese planners focused on the growing number and range of its missiles. The launch of the Taepodong missile over Japan in 1998 brought a public outcry and raised questions about whether the United States was prepared to defend Japan against this new capability. Even as the United States sought to sanction North Korea's nuclear activities, Prime Minister Koizumi Jun'ichirō visited Pyongyang in 2002 to meet with North Korea's Kim Jong-il, and the two leaders announced a freeze in North Korean missile tests.

By the mid-2010s, the threat from North Korea had become far more lethal as Kim Jong-il's son, Kim Jong-un, grew confident in his regime's technological progress in building a significant nuclear and missile force. The younger Kim has wielded his growing arsenal of missiles and his more mature nuclear technology with skill, gaining considerable diplomatic advantage. By demonstrating that he was close to being able to threaten the United States, Kim could draw the United States into yet another round of talks about trading his nuclear weapons for economic investment. Japan had to face the fact not only that it was the only Northeast Asian state without the ability to retaliate against a missile strike but also that Pyongyang might present Washington with a difficult choice. While Japan had long been under nuclear and missile threat from other nations, such as Russia and China, the new Trump administration seemed particularly vexing as Japan's military planners worried that the United States could make decisions without regard for its non-nuclear Asian ally.

The United States and Japan also at times had difficulty in aligning their China policy as China's economic and military power upended Asia's balance of power. Tensions across the Taiwan Strait in 1996 had alerted Tokyo to Beijing's increasing willingness to use its military power to shape relations in the region, but Japanese security planners did not see a direct role for Japan's military in any effort to deter Chinese aggression. In the 1990s, Japan seemed to believe that only the United States could confront China's growing military challenge across the Taiwan Strait. But Japanese perceptions of the alliance with the United States changed fundamentally when China's military began to exert pressure directly on Japan. Tokyo saw Beijing's challenge to its administrative control over the Senkaku Islands as a grave risk to Japan's security. As tensions ratcheted up, from a Japan Coast Guard confrontation with a Chinese fishing trawler in 2010, to China's deployment of its own maritime patrols around the Senkaku waters, Tokyo could easily imagine a scenario that might bring the two Asian nations into direct military conflict. For the first time in the postwar era, Japan could be the object of aggression, and thus rather than worry about becoming entangled in a U.S. conflict, Japan's leaders had to confront the possibility that they could be abandoned by Washington if Beijing confronted Tokyo with military force.

While managing the alliance after the Cold War was difficult, many of the issues that were highlighted in U.S.-Japan consultations were familiar. Thinking on how to achieve reciprocity in an alliance relationship that was unique due to Japan's postwar restraint on the use of force evolved as Japan emerged as a dominant global economy. The tensions between citizens and the U.S. military eased somewhat, but their solution created the concentration of forces on the small island of Okinawa—exacerbating strains that already colored the relationship between the national and local governments. New capabilities were to be acquired, and new ways of imagining the division of labor between the two militaries were discussed.

The most consequential change was in Tokyo's perspective on its need for U.S. military force. The Cold War years were largely characterized by a fear of being dragged into Washington's wars, but the clash with Beijing in the East China Sea threw Japanese planners into deep anxiety over whether Washington would be willing to stand up militarily to China if Japan were attacked. While the Senkaku Islands seemed small and insignificant, they came to represent a far greater challenge for Japan's security planners: would the United States come to Japan's aid if its territory was challenged by China? Defense of the Senkakus became equated with the defense of Japan, and for the first time, Japan's leaders needed to ensure that their alliance with Washington would continue to be an effective strategic instrument.

The Japanese government had significant concerns about domestic criticism of the alliance and of the presence of U.S. forces in Japan in particular. But for planners, the value of the combination of U.S. and Japanese military power in Asia cannot be ignored. First and foremost, the bases that allow the United States a forward-deployed force posture gives it access across the Pacific and indeed across the Indo-Pacific. Second, Japan's own military capabilities—while constrained in imagining their role in a conflict—provide a net gain to the regional military balance. Despite the political constraints on the use of force, the SDF has a formidable arsenal and is well trained to use it if needed. Finally, embedded within a regional military strategy that serves the broader goal of stability in the Asia Pacific, Japan can claim its share of responsibility in the alliance and the public goods it provides beyond its shores. But convincing the United States to fight on Japan's behalf against a rising China creates a whole new dilemma for Tokyo's alliance management. The first step in this new challenge is to ensure the United States is firmly committed to avoiding an escalation to war.

But dealing with the heightened threats that Japan faces today will require more than assurances of the United States' commitment. It will necessitate contingency planning that involves both militaries, so as to anticipate when and how each military might initiate the use of force and to what end. If a conflict were to break out on the Korean Peninsula, U.S., Japanese, and South Korean forces would all be involved in a response. Yet there is no integrated command for all three allied militaries, nor is there a common understanding of how a conflict could be fought now that Japan is vulnerable to North Korea's missiles. The United States has largely been responsible for a strategic response against the North's growing nuclear capabilities. South Korea has also developed its own military response should North Korea attack, and since the 2010 sinking of the South Korean naval vessel, the *Cheonan,* and the shelling of Yeonpyeong Island, this has been organized independently from the UN Command's long-standing combined operational plans. Now if Japan decides to acquire conventional strike capability, when and how it will use that capability should be part of a U.S.-Japan alliance conversation. Sooner or later, the two militaries may have to fight together, and despite all the changes that have been made to the alliance over the years, Tokyo and Washington have yet to consider how they would organize for such a conflict.

The abandonment dilemma is not only about what might happen in a crisis or military conflict. It also affects expectations of continued cooperation in securing the interests of each ally in shaping the balance of power. Thus Japan's expectations of U.S. disarmament efforts are equally important when it comes to North Korea. Japan's leaders cannot be sanguine about the future of the alliance between the United States and Japan if a U.S. president begins to advocate for dismantling the global order that has sustained its security strategy. President Trump has cast doubt on the notion that the United States remains interested in a global leadership role similar to the one it undertook in the Cold War or even in the decades after the Cold War ended when U.S. power was the harnessed to a vision of global governance that reflected the norms and interests of the liberal democracies. Japan too embraced this vision of a global order and has been an active participant in the economic and political institutions designed to support it.

At the core of Japan's relationship with the United States, however, is a strategic bargain that trades American willingness to use military force on Japan's behalf for Japan's willingness to support American dominance in Asia. China is challenging the latter while the United States itself may be reconsidering its appetite for the former. Japanese leaders will be hard pressed to use the alliance as an instrument of their national strategy in the years ahead. Keeping China at bay while holding the United States close will be a difficult diplomatic strategy. But it will also require Tokyo to reexamine its own military power and decide whether it can—and should—play a greater role in shaping Japan's strategic options.

# Conclusion

For more than seven decades, generations of Japanese leaders have rejected the idea that the state can and should use force to resolve its international disputes. For much of that time, deploying its military abroad was anathema, and military cooperation with the United States, its ally, was limited. Japan rearmed, but as its name implies, the Self-Defense Force (SDF) continues to be dedicated to an exclusively defensive mission. Yet it boasts considerable capabilities. Japan's military today is a far cry from the "small but significant" military that its leaders once described. Rather, it is one of Asia's most potent. As world spending on arms grew in 2016, Japan ranked among the top ten highest in military spending, far below the spending of the United States and China, but roughly equivalent to U.S. allies in Europe.[1]

It was only in the fluid global politics after the end of the Cold War that the Japanese began to reconsider the value of their military. Many of the constraints on the SDF—imposed as a means of ensuring control over its use of force—have been lifted. For decades now, the SDF has been deployed abroad, serving in UN peacekeeping operations and other military coalitions around the globe. No longer limited to its own territory, Japan's military has been part of a global effort to assist conflict-ridden societies in rebuilding peace, as well as a coalition partner with the United States and other advanced industrial societies in countering terrorism and piracy to maintain open access to resources from the Persian Gulf.

At home, Japan's military is now a far more appreciated partner for civilian leaders who need its help in managing the nation's crises. Repeated natural disasters, and some conspicuous man-made challenges to public safety, have honed the cooperation between civilian and uniformed leaders. Outside of the national government, municipal and other local leaders have worked closely with the SDF in disaster relief. Nowhere was this more obvious than in the wake of the March 2011 Great East Japan Earthquake, when the Japanese military assumed the role of first responders in the devastated Tōhoku region. For many small communities whose local governments had been literally washed away by the accompanying tsunami, the SDF took on the role of directing their crisis response until help arrived weeks and even months later. Public opinion in Japan now ranks the SDF as one of the nation's most valued institutions.

## Tokyo's Growing Civil-Military Confidence

For much of the Cold War, Japanese decision makers defined domestic influences as the most important element in military policymaking. Indeed, it took decades for a national defense plan to emerge from the reconstituted bureaucratic processes that were designed to ensure an "exclusively defensive" military. Defeating the military's threat-based arguments over Japan's military aims, civilian planners instead sought to build a threat-neutral premise for military planning. The standard defense force concept (*kibanteki boeiryoku*) allowed for a minimal military organization that could power up should it need to, but which largely remained static in terms of its overall personnel and force posture. Instead of their own military power, Japanese decision makers looked to the bilateral framework of the U.S.-Japan alliance (*nichibei taisei*) to order their country's military priorities. The new dynamic defense posture reintroduced the notion that Japan's military readiness and capability must be premised on responding to the military capabilities of others.

While the alliance remained the frame for thinking about Japan's external defenses, Japanese thinking about their own military power was changing. Increasingly, Japan's conservative politicians and policy makers wanted to step up and rely less on U.S. military power. To be sure, some Japanese leaders had always wanted greater military self-reliance. As defense minister in 1970, Nakasone Yasuhiro put forward the concept of autonomous defense in response to the Nixon Doctrine. As prime minister, Nakasone argued for greater Japanese military responsibility in the alliance. Decades later, Prime Minister Abe Shinzō took up that mantle, adjusting to shifts in the regional military balance by arguing that Japan too must be more self-reliant when it comes to its defenses. But increasingly, Japan's military was also a valuable instrument its relations with other Asian maritime states as well as with other strategic partners, such as India and the EU. No longer solely operating with the bilateral alliance, Japan's SDF built ties with a variety of new national partners.

Along with a growing confidence in the military's utility abroad, Tokyo became more sensitive to external threat. Reforms to the way in which military policy was made accelerated, with long-standing sensitivities over the military's role in policy-making easing as the need for its expertise grew. New laws on how Japan might mobilize to defend itself should conflict erupt, the introduction of new technologies and new rules of engagement for their use, and the abandonment of the prohibition of defense technology competition all demonstrated how the pace of security policy reforms picked up as Japan entered the twenty-first century. What had long been seen as impossible had become routine. Japan was increasingly looking like other states when it came to government deliberations over military policy priorities.

Japan's military too deserves some credit for this growing comfort with military policy-making. The SDF accepted its growing missions abroad with little complaint, despite the lack of public consensus. From the vintage wooden minesweepers operating without modern technology in the Persian Gulf to the Maritime Self-Defense Force (MSDF) destroyers and Japan Coast Guard personnel sent to conduct antipiracy operations in the Gulf of Aden, the Japanese maritime forces led the way in demonstrating that their country could trust them to behave abroad. Japan's Air and Ground Self-Defense Force (ASDF and GSDF) also demonstrated their capabilities under the intense glare of domestic scrutiny in Kuwait and Iraq, respectively. Sent to these international coalitions with little support and training, the ASDF and GSDF acquitted themselves well in the midst of the far more well-equipped and politically supported dispatches of military units from a host of other U.S. allies and partners. And their role at home in disaster relief continued to build a reservoir of goodwill among the Japanese people. Once more, the Great East Japan Earthquake proved how much their country relied on them during a crisis. Yet while these internal shifts in the way Japanese relied on their military made many of the decisions possible, they were not the drivers of Japan's changing evaluation of military power.

Japan's leaders became acutely aware of the growing disadvantage their military was under as first North Korea and then China tested the readiness of the SDF. It was not the military's ability to contend with the growing threat, but rather the ambiguities surrounding how and when it could act, that was at the heart of Japan's military vulnerabilities. Hampered by an abundance of caution on the part of political leaders and by a deep-seated ambivalence built into the organizational processes for the application of military force, Japan's military commanders sought greater clarity in how to interpret their government's policy. As the missions assigned to the SDF increased, some of these questions had to be answered. The reinterpretation of the right of collective self-defense by the Abe cabinet in 2014 was controversial, but for a decade and a half, Japan had assigned its military abroad in coalition without giving it permission to use force in the performance of that mission. Until 2015, whether in UN peacekeeping operations, or in coalition deployments, the SDF was not permitted to use force on behalf of others.

Even at home, as the SDF was increasingly confronted with foreign militaries on Japan's doorstep, the use of force was to be limited. Yet as the SDF was called upon to defend Japanese waters and airspace, it became clear that civilian authorities would have to rely upon their judgment. Ballistic missile defenses necessitated a high degree of readiness and the judgment of Japan's military commander. Likewise, the experience and restraint of Japan's MSDF commanders were relied upon to implement a "maritime security order," whether against North Korean smugglers or Chinese submarines. The SDF became a crucial adviser as new military missions abroad were legislated and greater readiness at home was required.

As the readiness of the SDF increased in response to external pressures, Japanese political leaders showed little appetite for changing the core meaning of Article Nine of the Japanese constitution. Even Prime Minster Abe, who will likely be credited with implementing meaningful security policy reforms, never sought to transform the SDF's defensive orientation. His proposal to revise Article Nine, adding a sentence to note that the SDF is consistent with the spirit of the constitution, simply states what most Japanese already accept. Abe is looking to settle domestic controversy rather than move the needle on Japan's military. Some in his party want to tackle the ambiguous second paragraph and rewrite it to bolster their military's mission as well as their name. But no one challenges the first paragraph, and there seems little political gain to be had. Incremental changes reflecting ideas already widely accepted remain the preferred mode of policy reform even for those conservatives who want a more robust use of Japan's military power.

## The SDF as an Instrument of Foreign Policy

Japanese leaders today value their military as an instrument of national policy and are far more willing to use this instrument as a means of Japan's contribution to global security challenges than in the past. This integration of the military into Japan's foreign policy demonstrates how Tokyo has merged the self-restraint of the constitution with its growing sense of threat perception. Embedding its military within international coalitions not only demonstrates Japan's "proactive contribution to peace" but also ensures that the Japanese military will not be empowered to test the limits of civilian authority as it had been in the 1930s. Cooperative security— even in the defense of Japan—has been the preferred means of using military force. Going it alone militarily is no longer a Japanese preference.

The United States and other nations in Asia and Europe also see Japan's military as an asset in collective responses to global terrorism and piracy as well as in maritime challenges across the Indo-Pacific. This new post–Cold War effort to build military coalitions has created opportunity for the SDF to represent its nation's desire to assume greater responsibility for global security. Moreover, closer to Japan's own interests, the MSDF has been given far more latitude to assist in collective efforts to patrol sea lanes and ensure stable access to resources transiting through Asia's waters all the way to the Middle East.

Japan's leaders may increasingly use the military as an instrument of national policy, but they continue to shy away from difficult choices when it comes to planning for the use of force. Political elites champion civilian control but largely refuse to debate military policy in the Diet; they argue for international security cooperation but stop short of embracing the full responsibility of collective security; and they embed the SDF in coalitions abroad but micromanage from Tokyo its use of weapons in the face of danger. Adapting to the accelerating shifts in the military balance will require a firm political consensus on the use of force, and politicians will need to explain to the Japanese public the trade-offs ahead should their security environment worsen. To make the military a more effective instrument, Japan's politicians will need to embrace its role as a warfighting organization in addition to its role in keeping the peace.

While Japan's leaders have expanded their use of the military as an instrument of national power, the SDF has never fought a military conflict. Thus Japan's military policy choices are anticipatory; imagining how war might arrive on Japan's shores has largely been the task at hand for civilian leaders. Yet it seems increasingly likely that decision makers will need to order their military to use force. Asia's military balance is changing rapidly, and Japan is increasingly at a disadvantage. North Korea's growing arsenal of missiles and weapons of mass destruction as well as China's expanding maritime capabilities are changing Japan's defense requirements. As Japan's security and status have seemed jeopardized, its political leaders have gradually allowed their military to contribute to global security challenges and to improve their own defenses. Evidence of this can be found in the decision-making on sending the SDF abroad, crafting contingency laws to prepare for a military crisis, deliberating a revision of the Japanese constitution, and upgrading U.S.-Japan alliance coordination.

## Threat Perception and Military Readiness

The Japanese state has also prepared itself for the possible use of force in and around its territory. The rising military capabilities of its neighbors have heightened the sense of threat in Tokyo, leading to significant investment in new defensive weapons and in enhanced refinements to the defense coordination between the United States and Japan. Preparing for war has also meant considerable reforms within Japan, improving planning across government ministries but also building relationships and plans with local authorities and the SDF. Civil warning systems, long used only for natural disasters, have now been used for North Korean missile tests. Preparing both the Japanese military and the Japanese people is now part and parcel of Japanese defense planning.

Japanese military planning increasingly focuses on ensuring the U.S.-Japan alliance is ready to cope with any contingency in and around Japan. New scenarios are now driving alliance planning. North Korea's new missile capabilities have brought Japan within range of Pyongyang's direct attacks, a fact that Kim Jong-un has been eager to demonstrate since 2016. Moreover, these missiles now launch without much warning from difficult-to-detect mobile launchers, using solid instead of liquid fuel.[2] Just as challenging for Japan's defenses is the growing maritime presence of the Chinese military and paramilitary in and around Japanese waters. Beijing's challenge of Tokyo's administrative control over the Senkaku Islands adds greater urgency to the SDF's island defense mission. Both of these new threats have prompted a revision in the bilateral guidelines for military cooperation between Japanese and American militaries.

As others in Northeast Asia deploy greater military forces near Japan, crisis management is a high priority for the alliance. Notionally, the U.S. military has long been embedded in Japan's defense planning, especially for a possible conflict on the Korean Peninsula. But beyond this defining flashpoint in Northeast Asia, China's rise has increased tensions and complicated planning. After the island clash between Japan and China in 2012, the U.S. and Japanese governments created a new mechanism to facilitate crisis management.

Assigned to missions once thought to be beyond its responsibility, Japan's military has adapted and learned as it deployed abroad and as it confronted foreign armed forces in Japanese waters and airspace. As the SDF has learned from these missions, so too have Japan's civilian bureaucrats. More and more, the unique contributions that the SDF can make in cooperation with other national militaries abroad have become a valuable asset to Japanese diplomacy. Within Japan, the SDF's work with the national police, the Ministry of Foreign Affairs, the Japan Coast Guard, and the Japan International Cooperation Agency has led to partnerships among agencies that had long been suspicious of association with the military.

Similarly, the need for professional military expertise in handling Japan's rising regional security challenges has grown. For much of the Cold War, threat perception had been dismissed as a driver of military planning; few saw a direct military threat to Japan, and many across the Japanese government still saw the need to avoid an unbridled increase in military capabilities. Budgets were limited for precisely the same reason. The military voice in policy-making was limited to within the Defense Agency. But growing concern over the military buildup by countries surrounding Japan created more interest in the military perspective on policy choices. Within the Ministry of Defense, the balance of professional responsibility for the nation's defenses now rests more equally between civilian and uniformed policy makers. Across the Japanese government, other bureaucracies work regularly with their nation's military. The Ministry of Foreign Affairs sees in the SDF a welcome partner for global cooperation, especially in the UN; the Ministry of Economy, Trade and Industry now works closely with it on defense industrial cooperation; and the Ministry of Finance depends on the uniformed military's assessments as much as civilian planners when it decides on Japan's budgets.

## Reassessing the U.S.-Japan Alliance

Old habits in alliance policy-making also began to change. Washington had long demanded more in the way of defense spending and SDF capabilities. While this refrain was also heard in other alliances with South Korea and Europe, Japan's unique military restraints shaped that burden-sharing conversation through the end of the Cold War and into the decades that followed. Yet Tokyo faced an uncomfortable wake-up call in the first Gulf War. No longer would spending money in lieu of military action be sufficient. The George H. W. Bush administration began to argue that the time had come for Japanese "boots on the ground," a refrain also heard in other discussions with U.S. allies. Japan could no longer sit out of the military coalitions formed to cope with security threats globally, even as it increasingly upped its host nation support (HNS) for U.S. forces stationed in Japan. Japan's military support in a volatile Middle East became just one more metric for gauging reciprocity in the alliance, and by implication the ticket Tokyo needed to ensure continued U.S. support for Japan's own security.

Tokyo had never had to test the proposition that Washington would assist Japan if attacked. Article Five of the 1960 bilateral security treaty pledged U.S. defense assistance, and yet Japan seemed safe from direct threat or attack. The flashpoints of Asia were elsewhere—on the Korean Peninsula or across the Taiwan Strait. Relatedly, the U.S. nuclear umbrella was rarely discussed during the Cold War, especially in front of the Japanese public. But the reduction in U.S. nuclear forces after the Cold War worried Tokyo as it became clear that China remained committed to modernizing its nuclear arms and North Korea pursued its own nuclear arsenal. Ensuring that the nuclear umbrella was up to the task became more and more pressing for Tokyo, and so too was the need for the United States to declare its intentions to defend Japan in the face of increasing military assertiveness from both Pyongyang and Beijing.

The island dispute with China fundamentally changed Tokyo's perceptions of the alliance. Chinese pressure on the Senkaku Islands had escalated by 2012 as Beijing deployed maritime forces to the vicinity of the islands. For the first time, it was possible to imagine that Japan and China might find themselves at military loggerheads over these small, isolated islands. While no one wanted war, there was a risk that an incident or miscalculation by a local commander could set off a broader conflagration. In short, Japan could find itself at war with China. U.S. military support would be critical, and yet the two allies had never imagined this scenario, let alone practiced for it. Indeed, Japanese leaders had been loath to consider a direct Japanese military role in a conflict with China despite repeated crises across the Taiwan Strait. The Senkaku tensions offered a different scenario, one that involved an initial military response by Japan to be followed by a call for U.S. help. Military planners and politicians alike have shifted from worrying about being entrapped in U.S. wars elsewhere in the region to focusing more about ensuring the United States does not abandon Japan in a military confrontation with China. With U.S. forces forward deployed on Japanese bases, assistance could be easily provided. The critical question, however, was whether the United States would use force on Japan's behalf even if it meant going to war with China.

Tokyo has gone from being a hesitant military partner to being an advocate for military readiness. While polls reveal the Japanese regard with favor the U.S.-Japan alliance, Washington and Tokyo have not always agreed on strategic priorities. In the wake of the 9/11 terrorist attacks on the United States, Japanese governments had to advocate more strenuously for their interests, as the wars in Iraq and Afghanistan drew U.S. attention away from the Pacific.[3]

In Northeast Asia, Tokyo also saw its security priorities differently from Washington, causing some policy dissonance over how to cope with a changing region. On North Korea, for example, the George W. Bush administration's effort to pursue six-party talks left many in Tokyo concerned, especially about the prominent role China was assigned in the process. Perhaps the most challenging problem for Tokyo has been the deterioration of its relationship with Beijing and Beijing's assertive demonstration of its growing military interests in the East China Sea. China's rise has revealed differences over the geopolitical future of the region, and as Japan's relationship with a more assertive China has grown more difficult to manage, Tokyo has been forced to rely on Washington to advocate on its behalf with Beijing. Sensitivities to Washington's susceptibility to Beijing's plans in Asia have deepened.

On top of these strategic sensitivities in Asia, Tokyo—along with other U.S. allies—was startled by the tenor of the 2016 presidential election. Candidate Donald J. Trump suddenly raised fundamental questions about the future of U.S. policy toward Asia and about the U.S.-Japan alliance. For the first time since the 1960 security treaty was signed, a candidate for president openly questioned the value of the alliance to the United States. During the campaign, the Republican nominee raised alarm in Tokyo when he repeatedly mentioned Japan as an unfair trading partner, but his comments on the alliance were more worrisome. In a March 2016 interview with the *New York Times,* Trump argued that perhaps the time had come for Japan and South Korea to go it alone in defending themselves against North Korea. Trump also took aim at the Japanese contribution to U.S. forces there. Even after being told that Japan pays around 50 percent of the HNS costs, the highest amount of any ally, Trump responded by suggesting that Tokyo foot 100 percent of the bill.[4]

In Tokyo, senior officials responded promptly. Chief Cabinet Secretary Suga Yoshihide spoke first publicly, stating, "Whoever becomes president of the United States, the Japan-U.S. alliance, based on the bilateral security agreement, will remain the core of Japan's diplomacy," and Japan "will maintain its Three Non-Nuclear Principles"—not possessing, producing, nor permitting the introduction of nuclear weapons to Japan. Foreign Minister Kishida Fumio, a native of Hiroshima, echoed this rejection of nuclear weapons: "Japan abides by the Three Non-Nuclear Principles and the Atomic Energy Basic Act, and emphasizes the framework of the Nuclear Non-Proliferation Treaty. Therefore, I do not see any possibility of Japan possessing a nuclear arsenal." In the Diet, the Abe Shinzō cabinet was also confronted with questions about the Trump candidacy and what it meant for alliance policy. The prime minister was deeply committed to the Trans-Pacific Partnership, the twelve-nation trade agreement that the Obama administration had advocated, and he had initiated Diet ratification procedures in the hopes of providing momentum for a U.S. ratification process at the end of 2016. On the issue of the HNS and Trump's call for reciprocity, however, defense policy makers were clear that they had little appetite for increasing Japanese spending on U.S. forces even after Trump was elected. Instead, the incumbent defense minister and several former defense ministers argued for greater military self-reliance within the alliance. Defense Minister Inada Tomomi stated that this election result "provided the opportunity to think more seriously about what Japan could do on its own to defend itself." Former defense ministers Ishiba Shigeru and Onodera Itsunori made a similar case for how to manage any possible calls for Japan to increase its HNS; given the increasing military pressures on Japan, the SDF rather than U.S. forces would be more appropriate recipients of Japanese taxpayer money.[5]

Just as in previous transitions between U.S. presidents, the transition from Obama to Trump raised questions not only about the alliance but also about U.S. policy toward Asia. The Japanese government welcomed Obama's emphasis on a rebalance of U.S. foreign policy priorities to the Asia Pacific wholeheartedly, but as Tokyo's relations with Beijing soured, sensitivities in Tokyo about the Obama approach to China deepened and led them to question how this new U.S. Asia strategy was to be implemented.

Trump's campaign slogan "America First" raised far different concerns, however; would this mean a more isolationist approach to foreign policy or a more interventionist approach? Would trade conflict with China erupt at the cost of strategic cooperation among allies in Asia? Prime Minister Abe's quick move after the election to meet with then President-elect Trump, stopping off in New York on his way to the annual Asia Pacific Economic Community summit in Lima, Peru, suggested that the tenor of the campaign and especially Trump's focus on Japan had alarmed him.

While Abe's personal diplomacy seemed to reassure the Japanese government that President Trump would not be antagonistic toward the alliance, Trump's willingness to shake up U.S. relations with China as the president-elect introduced yet another variable into alliance management. Trump accepted a congratulatory phone call from Tsai Ing-wen, the president of Taiwan, on December 2, 2016, and became the first U.S. president-elect ever to have direct contact with a Taiwanese leader after 1979. Trump then went on to tweet his willingness to challenge the "one China" policy in the face of criticism. China responded quickly and harshly, and suddenly Tokyo began to wonder if a Trump administration might be too risky in its management of China.

As the Trump administration started out, however, it was the familiar challenge of North Korea that returned the alliance to steadier ground. During his visit to the United States, Abe met with Trump in Washington and issued a joint statement that reiterated U.S. support for the Senkaku Islands and for the broader security cooperation in the alliance. Moreover, the two leaders announced that they would initiate a separate dialogue on economic cooperation, led by Vice President Mike Pence and Deputy Prime Minister Asō Tarō. During the prime minister's visit to the president's estate in Florida, Pyongyang once again tested a missile aimed in Japan's direction, prompting the two leaders to call a press conference to protest this violation of the UN Security Council's most recent resolution. President Trump, standing with Prime Minister Abe, declared that the United States "stood behind Japan, 100 percent" in its efforts to defend itself against Kim Jong-un's provocations.[6]

North Korea's pressure on Japan's missile defenses prompted serious consideration of the ability to retaliate and has given Japanese planners even more reason to invest in their military capabilities. But the growing capabilities of Pyongyang have only exacerbated Tokyo's concern about the reliability of the U.S. extended deterrent. The Trump administration's initial tough stance on sanctioning North Korea was welcomed by the Abe cabinet. Indeed, Abe worked hard to support the UN Security Council's tough reckoning with North Korea on the costs of its threat to global security. Moreover, Tokyo was quite willing to up the military coordination with Seoul and to synchronize its military exercises with the United States to demonstrate just how lethal the combined forces of the United States and South Korea could be if threatened. But the abrupt diplomatic shift to diplomacy by President Trump caught Abe off guard, coming just weeks after the prime minister had traveled to the United States to confirm that the United States and Japan were on the same page when it came to the North. While publicly the Japanese government supported the idea of a negotiated denuclearization, the unpredictability of the U.S. president at the negotiating table was worrisome. Few in Japan felt that its interests would be adequately represented in the unfolding summitry with the North Korean leader, and Abe began to seek his own meeting with Kim Jong-un. With the increasing demonstrations of military force in Northeast Asia, Japan's strategic dependence on the United States deepened, and yet the Trump presidency had made the United States a far less reliable ally.[7]

# A Look Ahead

The growing military power of China and North Korea create pressures on Japan's defenses, and the unpredictability of decision-making in Washington raises new concerns about the future of the U.S.-Japan alliance. The Trump administration's call for greater allied burden sharing has led the Abe cabinet to consider how to up its spending on U.S. weaponry and to increase its military spending over the next five years. The midterm defense plan that will begin in 2019 is expected to increase military spending by at least 1 percent annually, a hefty increase by Japanese standards. But it is unlikely that this will significantly alter the way in which the SDF is armed, nor will it massively increase the size of Japan's military forces. For all of the recent changes in Japanese security planning, including the focus on military readiness, Japan's military continues to be organized for self-defense. Military capability—even the recent consideration of conventional strike forces—is still considered as a means to deter aggression. Developing a retaliatory capability is seen as the best means of ensuring neighboring countries will think twice before using force against Japan.

As tensions continue to rise in Northeast Asia, all eyes—in particular outside Japan—have been on Prime Minister Abe Shinzō and his security reforms. These reforms have been rolled out one after another under Abe, in a seeming cascade of security policy transformation. Yet many have been in the making for years. Moreover, despite Abe's efforts to fix the legal problems facing Japan's military, the political sensitivity over the use of force by the SDF—when and if it can use its weapons beyond Japanese territory—remains. No change has been made yet to the premise that the SDF will respond to violence only after Japan has been attacked. Early thinking on acquiring missiles, for example, considered preemptive strikes on missile launch pads, but with North Korea's move to mobile launchers, this no longer seems realistic. To date, Tokyo's discussion of acquiring potential retaliatory capability has been justified in terms of self-defense. But the use of this capability is liable to become just as conditioned by Diet concerns over the initiation of use of force.

Changes to Japan's policy on the use of force have largely been additive rather than innovative. Few in the Diet want to send the SDF to missions where it will need to use force, and an additional condition on its deployment, even within UN peacekeeping operations, is to keep the Japanese military far from situations where it may actually need to shoot. The South Sudan deployment, instead of facilitating SDF action on the ground, seemed just as hesitant regarding its role as in previous UN peacekeeping missions. The burden on others to provide the firepower needed to protect Japanese troops makes their utility in UN operations limited. In coalitions organized for collective security, the expectation is that all militaries will be able to use force if needed. Japan remains a reluctant partner still.

The Japanese public remains sensitive to the possibility of military action abroad. The SDF too have become accustomed to this low-risk conditioning of their overseas deployments. No member of the SDF has died abroad, while Japanese police, diplomats, and aid workers have lost their lives. Should Japan's military be found wanting in response to a dangerous situation abroad, or should the situation end up costing SDF lives, the Japanese will have to decide if they are ready to accept that. If the SDF is to be effective in international military coalitions, it will need to be able to confront risk.

Defense of the Japanese islands, however, will be expected. None of the legal changes made recently have fundamentally altered

Japan's desire to limit the use of military force to tasks that enhance its own security. Improvements in Japan's defense preparedness have been made, and the learning over time has proven invaluable to the discussions of how to improve and support the SDF as it prepares to confront North Korean and Chinese militaries. New capabilities—such as counterterror and amphibious units as well as Japan's new ballistic missile defense systems—are being developed, and additional capabilities are under consideration. Japan continues to upgrade its military technologies and to expand its cooperation with others in the Asia Pacific.

Little public attention has been given to whether the SDF is ready to fight, and win, a war, however. For the SDF, there is no comfort in the notion that the best defense might be a good offense. None of the new missions for the SDF involves coercion or punishment of other states. Preemption as a military tactic is still denied to the Japanese military. Even the call for an independent military strategy—a hedge against the possible decline in U.S. strategic protection—is absent in today's debate. If anything, Tokyo's security planners and the Japanese public seem to have doubled down on their investment in the alliance with the United States. Neither growing external pressures on Japan's defenses nor the worry about declining U.S. interest in alliances seems to have jolted the Japanese commitment to limiting their use of military force.

Japan's military today, however, is more thoroughly integrated into national strategy than ever before. Four generations of military leaders have now emerged at the top of the SDF, many who trained alongside U.S. forces or other national militaries in a variety of missions. The SDF's responsibility for—and responsiveness to—the Japanese people has been amply demonstrated in a series of natural disasters and other crises, and Japan's government today is much better prepared to deploy and support it. Hostile military action against Japan, of course, will present the ultimate test of the SDF and its growing capabilities. Japan's doctrine of military restraint works so long as there is no advantage to testing its military or its alliance with the United States; but it may not be effective if and when it becomes evident that others see the possibility—and the benefit—of coming out ahead by using force against Japan.

Worrisome signs are ahead. The U.S.-Japan alliance, while still embraced in Tokyo, seems less certain in Washington. Without a doubt, the cost of Japan's strategic bargain with the United States is rising, but the currency may also be changing. Burden-sharing debates are not new, but what is different today is this questioning of alliance equities that comes as Asia's balance of power is changing. China's military power is on the rise and increasingly felt in Asia—and cross the Indo-Pacific. The fate of U.S.-Chinese relations could unsettle Japanese calculations. A tougher U.S. line on China is welcome in Tokyo, but a downward spiral in relations between Washington and Beijing could easily produce a heated arms race, or worse yet, direct confrontation between the two major powers in Asia. Japan would be called upon to fight in that conflict, should it become a reality. Japan's vulnerability to missile strikes was laid bare in 2017 by North Korea—a fact that few in the region failed to notice. Only Tokyo has no ability to deal a serious military blow to a neighbor in a region of the world where the major powers intersect with often competing interests. Russia to the north, China to the east and south, and both nations on the Korean Peninsula are warily eyeing each other's militaries. Japan may not share a land border with any of these nations, but it has no real defenses against their ballistic missiles, and, without a robust U.S. defense of its interests, it is vulnerable to coercion by the nuclear weapons states. Deterrence may require another look at Japan's postwar doctrine if the United States no longer offers an unflinching willingness to strike on Japan's behalf.

Japan's preference for limiting its use of military power shaped more than seventy years of its strategy. In many ways, this reassured the Japanese as well as their neighbors. Three generations of civilian and uniformed policy makers gradually developed a more comfortable policy-making process on Japan's military aims and its capabilities, one responsive to elected leadership and one where those who wore the SDF uniform built strong ties with their communities and the citizens they serve. Yet as the United States becomes far less predictable and as Japan's neighbors reach far more readily for their military to demonstrate power, limiting Japan's military power may no longer make Japanese feel safe. Even Japan will find it necessary to assert its military power in this newly fraught Asia.

# · NOTES ·

## Introduction

1. President Obama's speech at Hiroshima can be found at: https:// obamawhitehouse.archives.gov/the-press-office/2016/05/27/remarks -president-obama-and-prime-minister-abe-japan-hiroshima-peace. According to a *Nikkei Shimbun* poll on May 26, 2016, 92 percent supported Obama's visit. An *Asahi Shimbun* survey from June 5 showed 90 percent support. For Japan's support of the Nonproliferation Treaty and how it fits into Japan's nonproliferation policy, see "Japan's Disarmament and Non-Proliferation Policy—Fourth Edition," Ministry of Foreign Affairs, Japan, https://www.mofa.go.jp/policy/un/disarmament/policy/pampho812 .html.

2. Prime Minister Abe's speech at Pearl Harbor can be found at: https:// obamawhitehouse.archives.gov/the-press-office/2016/12/28/remarks -president-obama-and-prime-minister-abe-japan-pearl-harbor.

3. The Air Self-Defense Force scrambled fighters 390 times against Russian aircraft in fiscal year 2017, which represented an increase of 89 times from the year prior and 43 percent of the total scrambles in FY2017, according to a Joint Staff press release: http://www.mod.go.jp/js /Press/press2018/press_pdf/p20180413_07.pdf.

4. Twenty-four percent of the Japanese have "confidence in Trump to do the right thing regarding world affairs." From Kristin Bialik, "Asian

countries on Trump's trip have largely positive views of U.S. but disagree on policy," Pew Research Center, November 3, 2017.

5. By the early 2000s, most scholars of Japanese security policy-making pointed to an incremental but significant process of "normalizing" defense planning in response to external changes. See Michael J. Green, *Japan's Reluctant Realism: Foreign Policy Challenges in an Era of Uncertain Power* (New York: Palgrave Macmillan, 2001). Andrew L. Oros examines the shifting normative constraints in the evolution of Japan's security policy. See *Normalizing Japan: Politics, Identity and the Evolution of Security Practice* (Stanford, CA: Stanford University Press, 2008). More recently, Oros has updated his analysis with *Japan's Security Renaissance: New Policies and Politics for the Twenty-First Century* (New York: Columbia University Press, 2017). Others point to Japan's growing sense of external threat. For example, see Christopher Hughes, *Japan's Foreign and Security Policy under the 'Abe Doctrine': New Dynamism or New Dead End?* (London: Palgrave MacMillan, 2015). Others argue that Tokyo is increasingly hedging as China's power rises relative to the United States. See Eric Heginbotham and Richard J. Samuels, "Japan's Dual Hedge: Not Another Britain," *Foreign Affairs* (September/ October 2002). For a decidedly different point of view, Amy Catalinac argues that this is less about threat perception and more about electoral redistricting in Japan: *Electoral Reform and National Security in Japan: From Pork to Foreign Policy* (New York: Cambridge University Press, 2016).

6. See, for example, the emphasis on normative dimensions of Japanese security decision-making in Peter J. Katzenstein, *Cultural Norms and National Security: Police and Military in Postwar Japan* (Ithaca: Cornell University Press, 1996) and Thomas Berger, *Cultures of Antimilitarism: National Security in Germany and Japan* (Baltimore: Johns Hopkins University Press, 2003).

7. MacArthur's notes on what he believed were the "must haves" for Japan's postwar constitution can be found through the National Diet Library: http://www.ndl.go.jp/constitution/e/shiryo/03/072/072_002l .html.

8. For years after the constitution was promulgated, the meaning of MacArthur's note would be scrutinized in Japan. In 1964, the Constitu-

tional Review Committee, established by the Japanese Diet, found that there was little evidence that U.S. occupation planners intended the full pacification of Japan. For example, there was no reference to an unarmed Japan in SWNCC-228, the planning document that set forth the aims of the Allied Occupation in Japan. Rather, the language used by MacArthur reflected his own personal thoughts at the time. See *Kenpō seitei no keika ni kansuru shō iinkai hōkokusho*, http://www.shugiin.go.jp /internet/itdb_kenpou.nsf/html/kenpou/chosa/shukenshi002.pdf/$File /shukenshi002.pdf, July 1964. For a full record of the Japanese deliberations over the drafting of the 1947 constitution, see the collection of documents at the National Diet Library of Japan, http://www.ndl.go.jp /constitution/e/outline/03outline.html.

9. For an analysis of these early Diet debates over how to limit Japanese military power, see Sheila A. Smith, "At the Intersection of the Cold War and the Postwar: The Japanese State and Security Planning" (PhD diss., Columbia University, 1996). One of the most persistent and effective Diet critics of successive LDP cabinets was Okada Haruo of the Japan Socialist Party. His memoirs present a vivid first-person narrative of the convictions that led him to challenge the Japanese government's rearmament plans. See *Kokkai bakudan otoko okapparu ichidaiki—Hansen heiwa ni kaketa giin seikatsu 40-nen* [A Biography of the Explosive Diet Member "Okapparu"—Forty Years as an Antiwar Advocate and Peace Legislator] (Tokyo: Gyōken, 1986).

10. On May 3, 2017, Abe released a video message to a meeting sponsored by the conservative Nippon Kaigi in which he stated his goals for constitutional revision. See *Asahi Shimbun*, May 3, 2017, http://www .asahi.com/ajw/articles/AJ201705030034.html.

11. Japan has upgraded its intelligence collection and analysis institutions in recent years. For a comprehensive historical analysis of Japanese intelligence capacity, see Richard J. Samuels, *Special Duty: A History of the Japanese Intelligence Community* (Ithaca, NY: Cornell University Press, 2019).

12. See Michael J. Green, *Arming Japan: Defense Production, Alliance Politics and the Postwar Search for Autonomy* (New York: Columbia University Press, 1998) for an in-depth look at early U.S. weapons sales to Japan. For a history of the Japan's own postwar defense industry, see Reinhard

Drifte, *Arms Production in Japan: The Military Applications of Civilian Technology* (London: Westview Press, 1986).

13. *Stockholm International Peace Research Institute (SIPRI) Yearbook 2011: Armaments, Disarmament and International Security* (Oxford: Oxford University Press, 2011), http://www.sipriyearbook.org/view /9780199695522/sipri-9780199695522-miscMatter-5.xml.

14. Prime Minister Abe outlined Japan's "proactive contribution to peace" at the United Nations in 2013: "Address by Prime Minister Shinzo Abe, at The Sixty-Eighth Session of The General Assembly of The United Nations," Cabinet Public Relations Office, September 26, 2013, https://japan.kantei.go.jp/96_abe/statement/201309/26generaldebate_e .html.

15. North Korea is consistently referred to as a "threat" in the Ministry of Defense White Papers, dating from the 1998 Taepodong missile launch over Japan. More recently in a piece for the *New York Times* entitled "Solidarity against the North Korean Threat," Prime Minister Abe described North Korea as a "grave and imminent threat." Abe's article can be found here: https://www.mofa.go.jp/p_pd/ip/page4e_000688 .html.

16. Ministry of Defense, Japan, *Japan Defense Focus* 19 (November 2010): 8, http://www.mod.go.jp/e/jdf/no19/interview.html.

17. Japan's defense spending rose in 2013, after eleven years of declining defense budgets. See Ministry of Defense, Japan, *Defense of Japan 2013*, 118, http://www.mod.go.jp/e/publ/w_paper/pdf/2013/28_Part2_Chapter2 _Sec4.pdf.

18. See Eric Heginbotham and Richard J. Samuels, "Japan's Dual Hedge," *Foreign Affairs* 81, no. 5 (September / October 2002): 110–121. See also Richard Samuels, *Securing Japan: Tokyo's Grand Strategy and the Future of East Asia* (Ithaca, NY: Cornell University Press, 2007) and Mike M. Mochizuki, "Japan: Between Alliance and Autonomy," *Strategic Asia 2004–2005*. For early discussions by Japanese security experts on why it may make sense to consider the nuclear option, see the project by the Society of Security and Diplomatic Policy Studies entitled "Facing the Inconvenient Truth: Re-examining Policy for Peace and Denuclearization of the Korean Peninsula," May 2017, and the op-ed by former Japanese Ambassador to the United States, Katō Ryōzō,

"核保有により得るもの、失うものは何か 日本の核問題を理性的に論ぜ
よ [Japan should rationally discuss the issue of what would be gained
and what would be lost if it possessed nuclear weapons]," *Sankei
Shimbun,* February 2, 2018.

## 1. Japan in the Cold War

1. The 1954 law that outlines the purpose and mandate of the SDF is the
   Self-Defense Forces Law. A separate law, the Defense Agency Establishment Law, created the bureaucracy tasked with defense planning.
   The full text of the Self-Defense Forces Law can be found in *Roppō
   zensho* [Full Text of Six Laws] (Tokyo: Yūikaku, 2017).
2. The Treaty of Peace with Japan can be found on the United Nations
   website: https://treaties.un.org/doc/publication/unts/volume%20136
   /volume-136-i-1832-english.pdf.
3. An account by Commander Nose Shōgo, who led Japan's minesweeping
   operation during the Korean War, *Chōsen sensō ni shutsudō shita nihon
   tokubetsu sōkaitei* [Japan's Special Minesweeping Force Dispatched
   During the Korean War] is available at http://www.mod.go.jp/msdf/mf
   /other/history/img/005.pdf.
4. Kishi Nobusuke's long-standing ambition for a more equal treaty is well
   documented in Hara Yoshihisa's definitive scholarship. See, for example,
   *Kishi nobusuke—Kensei no seijika* [Kishi Nobusuke—A Statesman of
   Power] (Tokyo: Iwanami Shinsho, 1995), *Nichibei kankei no kōzu—
   Anpo kaitei wo kenshō suru* [Composition of U.S.-Japan Relations—
   Examining Security Treaty Revision] (Tokyo: NHK Books, 1991), *Kishi
   nobusuke shōgenroku* [Testimony by Kishi Nobusuke] (Tokyo: Chūkō
   Bunko, 2014), and *Sengo nihon to kokusai seiji—Anpo kaitei no rikigaku*
   [Postwar Japan and International Politics—Power Dynamics of Security
   Treaty Revision] (Tokyo: Chūō Kōronsha, 1988). Public opinion in Japan
   was also trending against the United States. A high-profile case of a
   U.S. military guard shooting an elderly Japanese woman in the back
   drove the United States to reconsider prosecution of U.S. military
   personnel in Japan. The Girard case, as it came to be known, also
   reached U.S. courts as the guard's family accused the Department of

Defense of failing to protect their son. Moreover, bureaucratic wrangling over the security treaty negotiations leading up to negotiations with Washington is well documented in Yoshida Shingo's excellent analysis of the U.S.-Japan Alliance, *Nichibei dōmei no seidoka* [The Institutionalization of the U.S.-Japan Alliance] (Nagoya: Nagoya University Press, 2012), 33–78. Once the security treaty was renegotiated, mass demonstrations protesting the new treaty prevented President Dwight Eisenhower from visiting Tokyo. See the observations of George Packard, *Protest in Tokyo: The Security Treaty Crisis of 1960* (Princeton, NJ: Princeton Legacy Library, 1966).

5. The number of forces here is as of June 30, 1954, "Worldwide Manpower Distribution by Geographical Area," U.S. Department of Defense, Directorate for Information Operations and Reports, Statistical Information Analysis Division, https://www.dmdc.osd.mil/appj/dwp /dwp_reports.jsp. See also James Auer, *The Postwar Rearmament of Japanese Maritime Forces, 1945–1971* (New York: Praeger, 1973).

6. Sheila A. Smith, "At the Intersection of the Cold War and the Postwar" (PhD diss., Columbia University, 1996), 91.

7. Katō Yōzō, *Shiryoku—Jieitai shi: Keisatsu yobitai kara konnichi made* [A personal history of the history of the Self-Defense Force: From the National Police Reserve to Today] (Tokyo: Seiji Geppōsha, 1979).

8. Hatoyama and Yoshida had a difficult political history. U.S. authorities purged Hatoyama early in the occupation, largely for his prewar political role, choosing instead to elevate Yoshida as the Liberal Party leader and later prime minister. See Juha Saunavaara, "Occupation Authorities, the Hatoyama Purge and the Making of Japan's Postwar Political Order," *Asia-Pacific Journal*, vol. 7, issue 39, no. 2, September 2009. Hatoyama remained a vital voice in the Liberal Party and was less enthusiastic than Yoshida about the U.S. role in the deliberations over Japan's postwar military. In 1954, Hatoyama led a group of legislators out of the Liberal Party to create the Democratic Party. In a fury, Yoshida dissolved the Diet, famously yelling *baka yarō*—go to hell—at Hatoyama and his followers. Within a year, the Liberal and the Democratic Parties would come back together again to form the Liberal Democratic Party, the conservative party that governed Japan for much of the postwar era. For an excellent analysis of early party politics in Japan, see Masaru Kōno,

*Japan's Postwar Party Politics* (Princeton: Princeton University Press, 1997).

9. In the English language version of Article Nine, *senryoku* is translated as "war potential": "Aspiring sincerely to an international peace based on justice and order, the Japanese people forever renounce war as a sovereign right of the nation and the threat or use of force as means of settling international disputes. In order to accomplish the aim of the preceding paragraph, land, sea, and air forces, as well as other war potential, will never be maintained. The right of belligerency of the state will not be recognized."

10. Nishihiro Seiki, nicknamed Mr. Bōeichō ("Mr. Defense Agency"), was appointed director general of the Defense Policy Bureau, the post responsible for long-term defense policy planning, in 1985. Three years later, he became the first civilian policy maker raised within the agency to become administrative vice minister, the highest-ranking civil servant in any Japanese bureaucracy.

11. The Mitsuya Kenkyū, officially known as the 1963 Joint Staff Defense Study (Joint Staff Document 3, no. 30–38), was a major military study conducted between February and June 1963 and organized under the auspices of the Joint Staff. The Diet debate took place in the Lower House Budget Committee on February 10, March 3–4, March 10, March 19, and May 31, 1965. A special subcommittee on military planning was formed to investigate the Mitsuya case. For a more detailed discussion of this incident, see Smith, "At the Intersection of the Cold War and the Postwar," 62–113. See also Okada Haruo, *Kokkai bakudan otoko okapparu ichidaiki—Hansen heiwa ni kaketa giin seikatsu 40-nen* [A Biography of the Explosive Diet Member "Okapparu"—Forty Years as an Antiwar Advocate and Peace Legislator] (Tokyo: Gyōken, 1986).

12. The JSP had recognized that the SDF was created by constitutional means but maintained its existence contradicted the constitution. This position changed, however, in 1993 when the leader of the JSP, Murayama Tomiichi, joined with the LDP to form a coalition government. At that time, then Prime Minister Murayama stated that he recognized the existence of the SDF as an institution to use the minimal level of force for self-defense. See Social Democratic Party of Japan,

"Kyūjō ga arukara hairu jieitai [Joining the Self-Defense Force Thanks to Article Nine's Protection], Social Democratic Party Diet Members' Relay Column on Constitution," vol. 49, May 13, 2013, http://www5.sdp .or.jp/special/kenpo/49teruya.htm.

13. The Diet Law (Kokkaihō) was amended in October 1991 providing for the establishment of a standing committee on national security in the House of Representatives. The amendment passed in the Lower House on October 2 (Plenary Session, Lower House, Record no. 14, 121st Diet Session, October 2, 1991, http://kokkai.ndl.go.jp/SENTAKU/syugiin/121 /0001/12110020001014.pdf) and the amended Diet law came into force three days later on October 5 ("Kokkaihō [Diet Law]," Upper House, http://www.shugiin.go.jp/internet/itdb_annai.nsf/html/statics/shiryo/dl -dietlaw.htm). The official name of the Lower House committee is the National Security Committee (Anzen hoshō iinkai), and it began functioning in the 122nd Diet. In the House of Councilors, there is no standing national security committee. The Committee on Diplomacy and Defense (Gaikō bōei iinkai), established as a standing committee in 2000, discusses security issues. This new committee was included in the amendments to the Diet Law passed by the Lower House on November 31, 2000 (see Plenary Session, Lower House, 150th Diet Session, Record no. 19, November 31, 2000, http://kokkai.ndl.go.jp /SENTAKU/syugiin/150/0001/15011300001019.pdf) and entered into force on December 6, 2000. Accordingly, the committee started to function in the 151st Diet in 2001.

14. Early U.S. perspectives on the alliance can be found in the following volumes of the U.S. Department of State's *Foreign Relations of the United States: 1952–1954, China and Japan,* vol. 14, pt. 2, ed. David W. Mabon and Harriet D. Schwar, 1985; *1955–1957, Japan,* vol. 23, pt. 1, ed. David W. Mabon, 1991; *1958–1960, Indonesia; Japan; Korea,* microfiche supplement, vol. 17/18, ed. Madeline Chi, Louis H. Smith, Robert J. McMahon, and Glenn W. LaFantasie, 1994; and *1958–1960, Japan; Korea,* vol. 28, ed. Madeline Chi and Louis J. Smith, 1994. The joint statement after the discussions between Foreign Minister Shigemitsu and Secretary of State Dulles is available at "Nihon seiji kokusai kankei dētabēsu [Database of Japanese Politics and International Relations]" Institute of Advanced Studies on Asia, University of Tokyo, http://worldjpn.grips.ac.jp /documents/texts/JPUS/19550831.D1J.html.

15. See "Overview of Japan's Defense Policy," Ministry of Defense, http://www.mod.go.jp/e/d_act/d_policy/pdf/english.pdf.
16. See Richard M. Nixon, "Asia After Viet Nam," *Foreign Affairs* 46, no. 1, October 1967, 111–125. Nixon articulated how the Nixon Doctrine would translate into Asia policy through a press conference on Guam on July 25, 1969, a speech on November 3, 1969, and a Foreign Policy Report to Congress on February 18, 1970. For more information, see *Public Papers of the Presidents of the United States: Richard Nixon, 1969* (Washington, DC: Government Printing Office, 1971), 54–56.
17. On the fortieth anniversary of the publication of Japan's defense white paper, Nakasone shared his thoughts in the foreword of *Defense of Japan 2014*, http://www.mod.go.jp/e/publ/w_paper/pdf/2014/DOJ2014 _Foreword_web_1031.pdf. For a discussion of this period of defense policy-making, see Smith, "At the Intersection of the Cold War and the Postwar," as well as Ōtake Hideo, *Nihon no saigunbi to nashonarizumu— Hoshu, riberaru, shakai minshu shugisha no bōeikan* [Japan's Rearmament and Nationalism: The Defense Views of Conservatives, Liberals, and Social Democrats] (Tokyo: Chūkō Shinsho, 1988).
18. Nakasone's new plan presented a significant expansion of Japan's military capability over time. The obvious priority of the plan was on the development of the MSDF, and a major commitment of resources was made to building a larger naval force. The total cost of the plan was announced as 5,200 trillion yen. Smith, "At the Intersection of the Cold War and the Postwar," 189–191.
19. "Autonomous Defense and Defense Production," *Economisuto,* August 18, 1970, as cited in Smith, "At the Intersection of the Cold War and the Postwar," 174.
20. For an account of the debate over the "peacetime force posture," see Lower House Budget Committee deliberations, February 1973. See also *Bōeiryoku seibi keikaku wo chūshin to suru bōei seisaku no keii (Sono 2)* [Process of Defense Policy on Plan to Provide Security, Part 2], 25, for an outline of the Defense Agency's report entitled *Heiwaji no bōeiryoku* [A Force Posture for Peacetime]. See Sakata Michita's memoirs on his time as the head of the Defense Agency, wherein he talks about his desire to build greater public understanding of the SDF and its mission, *Chiisakutemo ōkina yakuwari* [The Self-Defense Force: Small but with a Significant Mission] (Tokyo: Asagumo Shimbunsha, 1977).

21. For a full discussion of Kubo's argument, and the military's strong reaction to it, see Smith, "At the Intersection of the Cold War and the Postwar," 161–222. This was a particularly rich era of debate within Japan's Defense Agency, and some of the leading civilian bureaucrats with considerable experience in military planning began to take their case to the public. A classic in Japanese defense thinking by the architect of the standard defense posture concept is Kubo Takuya, *Kokubōron* [On National Defense] (Tokyo: PHP Kenkyūjo, 1979). Some of the most interesting chronicles of the time are the writings of Kaihara Osamu, *Nihon bōei taisei no uchimaku* [Behind the Scenes Planning for Japan's Defense Posture] (Tokyo: Jiji Tsūshinsha, 1977) and *Watashi no bōei hakusho* [My Defense White Paper] (Tokyo: Jiji Tsūshinsha, 1975). Chronicles of this period include Chuma Kiyofuku, *Saigunbi no seijigaku* [The Politics of Rearmament] (Tokyo: Chishikisha, 1985), Hirose Katsuya, *Kanryō to gunjin* [Bureaucrats and the Military] (Tokyo: Iwanami Shoten, 1989), and Ōtake Hideo, *Bōei seisaku to kokunai seiji* [Defense Policy and Domestic Politics] (Tokyo: Sanichi Shobō, 1983).

22. "National Defense Program Outline," *Defense of Japan 1989*, 262–266. English translation can be found at http://www.ioc.u-tokyo.ac.jp /~worldjpn/documents/texts/docs/19761029.O1E.html.

23. For the Japanese position on the "residual sovereignty" of Okinawa, see the Ministry of Foreign Affairs website on Japanese territory, https://www.mofa.go.jp/region/asia-paci/senkaku/qa_1010.html.

24. Emblematic of this new Cold War competition was the Reagan administration's introduction of a technological race to develop a shield against nuclear weapons. For many, this quest seemed quixotic, and the idea of shooting down Soviet ballistic missiles was likened to something out of a Star Wars movie. But the push to develop ballistic missile defenses countered the basic framework of nuclear deterrence— mutually assured destruction. Building missile defenses would in fact destabilize that delicate balance by making it possible for the United States to gain first-strike capability. Japanese participation in this research and development project was a crucial signal that the techno- logical prowess of all advanced industrial economies would be harnessed to the Cold War competition. According to *Defense of Japan 1985*, Defense Agency, Japan, Japan received a letter in March 1985 from

Secretary of Defense Caspar Weinberger requesting allies' participation in Reagan's Strategic Defense Initiative (SDI). In September 1986, Chief Cabinet Secretary Gotōda announced Japan's decision to join the SDI research. See "SDI Kenkyū keikaku ni kansuru naikaku kanbō chōkan danwa" [Chief Cabinet Secretary's Statement Regarding SDI Research Plan], *Defense of Japan*, 1987, Ministry of Defense, Japan, http://www.clearing.mod.go.jp/hakusho_data/1987/w1987_9148.html.

25. The text of the Guidelines for Japan-U.S. Defense Cooperation, signed on November 27, 1978, can be found at http://www.mod.go.jp/e/d_act/anpo/19781127.html.

26. Japan's MSDF took responsibility for defending sea lanes one thousand nautical miles south of Japan. "Joint Communique Following Discussions with Prime Minister Zenkō Suzuki of Japan, May 8, 1981," Ronald Reagan Presidential Library, https://reaganlibrary.archives.gov/archives/speeches/1981/50881b.htm. Suzuki gave a specific number as one thousand nautical miles during the press conference at the National Press Club. "Japanese Premier Vows 'Even Greater Efforts' on Defense," *New York Times*, May 9, 1981. The ASDF, while focused largely on Japan's air defenses, operated at Japan's northern border, watching and challenging the Soviet Air Force. The MSDF's assumption of the sea lane defense mission, however, raised important questions for the ASDF about how it could provide air support. Studies at the time on *yōjō bōkū*, or "maritime air protection," sought to address this capability problem and bring the ASDF and MSDF in closer coordination. Finally, as U.S. strategy in the Western Pacific began to emphasize containing Russian submarines in the Sea of Okhotsk, the GSDF began to think of how its shore defenses in Hokkaido might also up the ante on Soviet forces in the Far East. See Nishimura Shigeki, "Thinking about Japan's Defense—A Global Approach to the Northern Forward Strategy," *Shin bōei ronshū* [Journal of National Defense] 12, no. 1 (July 1984): 8–17.

27. For Gotōda Masaharu's account of the cabinet debate and his opposition to sending the SDF to the Persian Gulf, see *Naikaku kanbō chōkan* [Chief cabinet secretary] (Tokyo: Kōdansha, 1989). Japan's media also watched this internal government debate closely. See, for example, "Perusha wan kōkensaku, junshisen haken ni shinchōron, gaimushō no omowaku hazureru [On efforts to contribute to the Persian Gulf,

caution against sending surveillance ships—Falling short of the Ministry of Foreign Affairs' expectation]," *Asahi Shimbun,* October 8, 1987.

28. Japan's GDP grew from 1.087 trillion USD in 1980 to 3.017 trillion USD in 1989. "World Bank Open Data," The World Bank Group, http://data .worldbank.org/indicator/NY.GDP.MKTP.CD?locations=JP; "U.S.-Japan Burden Sharing: Japan Has Increased Its Contributions but Could Do More," *Report to the Chairman,* Committee on Armed Services, House of Representatives, United States General Accounting Office, August 1989, http://www.gao.gov/assets/150/148034.pdf; Patricia Schroeder, "The Burden-Sharing Numbers Racket," *New York Times,* April 6, 1988.

29. "Zainichi beigun chūryū keihi futan no suii [Trends in the cost burden of stationing U.S. forces in Japan]," Ministry of Defense, Japan, http://www.mod.go.jp/j/approach/zaibeigun/us_keihi/suii_table_22-29 .html; Terri Moon Cronk, "U.S., Japan Agree to Host-Nation Support for U.S. Troops," Department of Defense, December 16, 2015, https://www.defense.gov/News/Article/Article/637009/us-japan-agree -to-host-nation-support-for-us-troops/. In the bilateral U.S.-Japan Host-Nation Support agreement of 2016, Japan agreed to an annual budget of 189.9 billion yen, or 1.6 billion dollars.

30. On the MiG pilot's defection, see "The Pilot Who Stole a Secret Soviet Fighter Jet," BBC, September 5, 2016, http://www.bbc.com/future/story /20160905-the-pilot-who-stole-a-secret-soviet-fighter-jet. Many accounts have since been published on the shooting of the KAL007 flight. For a journalistic account written soon after the incident, see Seymour M. Hersh, *"The Target Is Destroyed": What Really Happened to Flight 007 and What America Knew about It* (New York: Random House, 1986). For a more extensive academic analysis, see Kenneth C. Walker, "Incident off Sakhalin: The Destruction of KAL007," *Asian Affairs* 18, no. 3 (1987): 294–298.

31. "Text of Communiqué on Reagan-Suzuki Discussions," *New York Times,* May 9, 1981.

32. Japan's weekly tabloids were full of the story and there were many embellished accounts of his ambitions, but the mainstream Japanese media focused their attention on the one sentence delivered by General

Kurisu that cost him his job: "現行の自衛隊法には不備な面が多く、奇襲
攻撃を受けても法的に即応できない場合がある。その際は第一線指揮官
が独断で超法規的な行動をとるだろう. [There are many aspects of the
current SDF law that are insufficient, and if Japan were to suffer an
armed attack, legally the SDF are not in a position to respond. At such a
time, local SDF commanders will likely have to make their own decision
to act in ways that go beyond existing law.]" "Kurisu Hiroomi shi (moto
bōeichō tōgō bakuryō kaigi gichō) shikyo [Mr. Kurisu Hiroomi, former
chairman of the Joint Staff Council, dies]," *Yomiuri Shimbun*, July 21,
2004.

33. Even relying solely on its economic influence, Tokyo faced considerable
resentment in Asia. Economic power was not without its tensions, and
relations with Southeast Asia grew tense as Japanese influence began to
dominate the region. Prime Minister Fukuda Takeo in 1977, on the cusp
of his tour of the region, spoke to the need to temper Japanese commer-
cialism and yet again reemphasized his country's commitment to peace
and prosperity. This too emerged as a new diplomatic doctrine for Japan,
the Fukuda Doctrine, that identified good relations with Japan's
Southeast Asian neighbors as critical to its national strategy. "Waga
gaikō no kinkyō [Current status of our diplomacy]," Ministry of Foreign
Affairs, Japan, 1978, http://www.mofa.go.jp/mofaj/gaiko/bluebook/1978
/s53-shiryou-002.htm.

34. This coalition of militaries was organized into the multinational North
Atlantic Treaty Organization (NATO) in Europe, but in Asia, the U.S.
military became a hub around which other national militaries would
organize. For a history of U.S. alliances in Asia, see Victor Cha,
*Powerplay: The Origins of the American Alliance System in Asia* (Princeton,
NJ: Princeton University Press, 2016). Major General Henry C.
Stackpole III, commander of Marine Corps bases in Japan, called U.S.
forces "a cap in the bottle" to prevent a rearmed, resurgent Japan. Fred
Hiatt, "Marine General Says U.S. Troops Must Stay in Japan," *Washington Post*, March 27, 1990.

35. A number of Japanese terms have been used to describe greater military
self-reliance. Defense Agency Director General Nakasone used the term
*jishu bōei* [autonomous defense] in 1970, which at the time was translated
as "autonomous defense." Today, defense policy makers refer to greater *jijo*

[self-help]. Both are employed with largely the same meaning—Japan needs to rely on its own military capability more. From 1963 to 1965, the U.S. Fifth Air Force studied Japanese air defenses, and this led to a full transfer of responsibility to Japan's ASDF. What was called Operation Clearwater resulted in a withdrawal of all U.S. Air Force units from Japan other than those dedicated to offensive operations elsewhere in Asia.

## 2. The Self-Defense Force Abroad

1. Michael H. Armacost, *Friends or Rivals? The Insider's Account of U.S.-Japan Relations* (New York: Columbia University Press, 1996), 98–127. "Tai iraku 'nishigawa bundan' ni keikai wo—Bei taishi, shushō ni daitōryō shinsho" [A warning on the "West's division of labor" in Iraq—U.S. ambassador hands president's letter to prime minister], *Nikkei Shimbun*, December 4, 1990; "Zoku bei taishi jimin jitsuryokusha tsūji eikyōryoku nerau" [U.S. ambassador seeks to influence Liberal Democratic Party's power brokers], *Asahi Shimbun*, October 26, 1990.

2. "What Japan's 'Checkbook Diplomacy' Isn't Buying," *Business Week*, December 10, 1990. The advertisement sponsored by the Kuwait government thanking the coalition ran in the *Washington Post*, March 11, 1991. The phrase "too little, too late" is often used to describe the shortcomings of Japan's response to the Gulf War. See, for example, Teshima Ryūichi, *Gaikō haisen—130 oku doru wa suna ni kieta* [A diplomatic defeat—13 billion dollars disappear in the sand] (Tokyo: Shinchōsha, 2006) and Tanaka Hitoshi, "Nihon yo shutaisei wo hakki seyo" [Japan, it's time to take the initiative], *Nikkei Bijinesu*, November 14, 2011, https://www.jri.co.jp/page.jsp?id=20478.

3. For an analysis of the impact of the Gulf War on Japanese policy on national security, see Michael J. Green and Igata Akira, "The Gulf War and Japan's National Security Identity," in Funabashi Yoichi and Barak Kushner, *Examining Japan's Lost Decades* (New York: Routledge, 2015), 158–175; "War in the Gulf: Germany; Germans Are Told of Gulf War Role," *New York Times*, January 31, 1991; "Doitsu ga jindō-teki shien wo riyū ni wangan e sōkai butai haken bei yōsei uke hatsu no NATO ikigai"

[Germany dispatches its minesweepers outside of NATO for the first time at U.S. request, claiming they are for humanitarian assistance], *Yomiuri Shimbun,* March 7, 1991.

4. At a U.S.-Japan Honolulu symposium, organized by the *Yomiuri Shimbun* and the East West Center, Auer stated, "[Japan] can make a significant contribution by sending Japan's high-tech minesweeping vessels along with its financial support." See "Nichibei honoruru shinpo kaimaku sōkaitei haken ni sekkyokuron mo nihon no wangan kōken sakude" [U.S.-Japan Honolulu symposium opens: Positive voice for Japan's dispatch of minesweepers as contribution to the Gulf], *Yomiuri Shimbun,* August 25, 1990. Auer also advocated for the SDF's contribution in refugee rescue operations in a *Nikkei Shimbun* interview, "Nanmin kyūshutsu e jieitai haken wo awā moto bei kokubōsōshō nihon buchō ni kiku genkōhō wakunai de kanō" [The dispatch of the Self-Defense Force to rescue refugees would be possible under current Japanese law], says Auer, former Japan Desk officer at the U.S. Department of Defense] *Nikkei Shimbun,* September 12, 1990. See also James E. Auer, The *Postwar Rearmament of Japanese Maritime Forces, 1945–71* (New York: Irvington, 1973). For the account by Commander Nose Shōgo, who led Japan's minesweeping operation during the Korean War, see *Chōsen sensō ni shutsudō shita nihon tokubetsu sōkaitei* [Japan's special minesweeping force dispatched during the Korean War], http://www.mod.go.jp/msdf/mf /history/img/005.pdf; Agawa Naoyuki, *Umino yūjō—Beikoku kaigun to kaijō jieitai* [Maritime Friendship: The U.S. Navy and Japan's Maritime Self-Defense Force] (Tokyo: Chūkō Shinsho, 2001); "Bei e no shisha senkyo ya fukkōsaku de kanshoku saguru—Wangan sensō to nihon 20" [A Japanese emissary sent to U.S. for update on the election and reconstruction—Gulf War and Japan, 20], *Asahi Shimbun,* February 14, 1991.

5. See "After the War Gulf Is Swept for Mines," *New York Times,* March 19, 1991. For Captain Ochiai's account, see Ochiai Taosa, *Operation Gulf Dawn,* 2001, http://www.mod.go.jp/msdf/mf/other /history/img/001.pdf.

6. This account was included in Sakurabayashi Misa, *Umi wo hiraku— shirarezaru sōkai butai* [Paving the way across the seas—The must read story of Japan's minesweeping forces] (Tokyo: Namiki Shoboō, 2008).

Her account includes extensive interviews with those who commanded the mission both in the Persian Gulf and from Tokyo, and those in the MSDF with direct knowledge of the mission verified the account. Analysis based on interviews with those who were on the mission include Ikari Yoshirō, *Perushyawan no gunkanki: Kaijō jieitai sōkai butai no kiryoku* [Flying the military flag in the Persian Gulf: A chronicle of the Maritime Self-Defense Force minesweeping force] (Tokyo: Kōjinsha, 2015). See also Agawa, *Umino yūjō* [Maritime Friendship].

7. Japan's role in peace negotiations in Cambodia (or Kampuchea) dated back to 1980 when Vietnam invaded Cambodia, according to L. William Heinrich Jr. Also, Heinrich points out that MOFA wanted to be a part of UN peacekeeping since the United Nations showed interest in 1988. Thus it was this longtime involvement in restoring peace in Cambodia, rather than U.S. pressures during the Gulf War, that led to the first dispatch of the SDF in UN peacekeeping there. See Heinrich, "Seeking an Honored Place: The Japanese Self-Defense Force and the Use of Armed Force Abroad" (PhD diss., Columbia University, 1997), 194–251. For an overview of the scope of the UN mission in Cambodia, see "Cambodia—UNTAC: Facts and Figures," United Nations, http://www.un.org/en/peacekeeping/missions/past/untacfacts.html.

8. Heinrich, "Seeking an Honored Place," 231–235.

9. The original bill was passed in the Lower House on December 3, 1991, with 311 for and 167 against (478 MPs present), http://kokkai.ndl.go.jp/SENTAKU/syugiin/122/0001/1221203000107.pdf). It was amended in the Upper House on June 9 and approved by a vote of 137 for and 102 against, Plenary Session, Lower House, 123rd Diet Session, June 9, 1992, http://kokkai.ndl.go.jp/SENTAKU/sangiin/123/0010/12306090010023.pdf. The amended bill was returned to the Lower House and passed on June 15 with 329 for and 17 against, Plenary Session, Lower House, 123rd Diet Session, June 15, 1992, http://kokkai.ndl.go.jp/SENTAKU/syugiin/123/0001/12306150001033.pdf.

10. See "Outline of Japan's International Peace Cooperation," Ministry of Foreign Affairs, Japan, May 14, 2015, http://www.mofa.go.jp/fp/ipc/page22e_000683.html.

11. Other personnel included sixteen SDF personnel assigned to monitor the cease-fire and forty-one others (including national and local

government officials as well as nongovernment personnel). See "International Peace Cooperation Assignment in Cambodia," Cabinet Office, Government of Japan, Secretariat of the International Peace Cooperation Headquarters, http://www.pko.go.jp/pko_e/result/cambo/cambo02 .html. The Japanese page includes official documents related to this assignment, http://www.pko.go.jp/pko_j/result/cambo/cambo02.html.

12. The report concluded with this assessment of next steps: "We are thinking primarily of how Japan can utilize its valuable experience in Cambodia to contribute to improving the implementation of our peacekeeping cooperation law as well as our capacity to fulfill the peacekeeping mission. We would like to continue to encourage international cooperation based on the international peacekeeping law while increasing our public's understanding of and support for these activities." See the government's final report on Japan's participation in the United Nations Transitional Authority in Cambodia, "Kanbojia kokusai heiwa kyōryoku gyōmu no jisshi no kekka" [Results of implementation of Japan's international peace cooperation operations in Cambodia], November 1993, Secretariat of International Peace Cooperation Headquarters, Cabinet Office, Government of Japan, http://www.pko.go.jp/pko_j/data/pdf/04/data04_02.pdf. There were many outside of government who saw this new role for Japan in peacekeeping as a significant contribution to global peace. See, for example, Daisuke Akimoto, "The shift from negative pacifism to positive pacifism: Japan's contribution to peacekeeping in Cambodia," *Ritsumeikan Journal of Asia Pacific Studies*, Volume 31, 2012.

13. The Local Autonomy Minister's visit was covered by *Nikkei Shimbun* on May 11, 1993. International criticism of Japan's growing discomfort with the UNTAC mission intensified from the spring to summer of 1993. See for example, "Japan Grows Wary of Cambodia Role," *New York Times*, April 29, 1993; "Japan Presses U.N. on Cambodia Peril," *New York Times*, May 10, 1993; "U.N. Eases Risk for Japanese in Cambodia," *Washington Post*, May 11, 1993; "Cambodia gambit may backfire: Global role put in jeopardy," *Japan Times*, May 24, 1993; "Japanese in Cambodia: Far from Samurai," *The Wall Street Journal*, June 1, 1993; and, "Actions of Japan Peacekeepers in Cambodia Raise Questions and Criticism," *New York Times*, October 24, 1993.

14. The PKO Law was revised in 1998, 2001, and 2015.

15. "Speech by Minister for Foreign Affairs of Japan Mr. Masahiko Kōmura—Japan: A Builder of Peace," Ministry of Foreign Affairs, Japan, January 24, 2008, http://www.mofa.go.jp/policy/un/pko /speech0801.html.

16. The United Nations began to use the term postconflict *peacebuilding* to refer to a series of operations necessary for postconflict reconstruction. See the report, *An Agenda for Peace,* presented to the General Assembly by the UN Secretary General, Boutros Boutros-Ghali in January 1992, available at: http://www.un.org/ga/search/view_doc.asp?symbol=A/47 /277.

17. "Matsubara Ken'ichi, Rikujō jieitai tōbu hōmentai dai 12 shidanchō" [Matsubara Ken'ichi, commander of Twelfth Division, Ground Self-Defense Force Eastern Army], *Asahi Shimbun,* May 24, 1993.

18. "PKO hō minaoshi e junbi, seifu yotō mazu mondaiten seiri—Gyōmu han'i ya shikiken shōten" [Preparing to revise PKO Law, government and ruling party lay out issues with focus on range of mission and command], *Nikkei Shimbun,* September 19, 1993.

19. "Nihon wa anzen ka daiichi bu kiki ha sokoni (6) PKO kōken ni ashikase" [Is Japan safe? (I.) A looming crisis (6) The shackles on our PKO contribution], *Yomiuri Shimbun,* April 12, 1998. The revised law in 1998 can be found at "Kokusai rengō heiwaiji katsudō-nado ni taisuru kyōryoku ni taisuru hōritsu no ichibu wo kaisei suru hōritsu" [Law to amend the Act on Cooperation for United Nations Peacekeeping Operations] (Law no. 102), House of Representatives, Japan, http://www.shugiin.go.jp/internet/itdb_housei.nsf/html/housei /h142102.htm.

20. A sixteen-member expert panel was established to advise Japan's prime minister on how to improve and strengthen Japan's capacity for international peace cooperation. Their conclusions are available at http://www.kantei.go.jp/jp/singi/kokusai/kettei/021218houkoku .html.

21. Prime Minister Koizumi referred to the preamble in his policy speech to the 153rd Diet (*shoshin hyōmei enzetsu*) as follows:

卑劣極まりないテロに対して、全世界が、これに屈することなく、敢然と闘おうとしています。我が国は、日本国憲法前文に

おいて、「われらは、いづれの国家も、自国のことのみに専念して他国を無視してはならないのであつて、政治道徳の法則は、普遍的なものであり、この法則に従ふことは、自国の主権を維持し、他国と対等関係に立たうとする各国の責務であると信ずる。日本国民は、国家の名誉にかけ、全力をあげてこの崇高な理想と目的を達成することを誓ふ」との決意を世界に向かって明らかにしています。世界人類の平和と自由を守るため、国際協調の精神の下、我が国としても、全力を挙げて、この難局に立ち向かおうではありませんか。国民並びに議員各位のご理解とご協力を心からお願い申し上げます。

[The entire global community stands undaunted and ready to fight resolutely the unprecedented cowardly acts of terrorism. In the preamble of the Constitution of Japan, we have declared to the world our firm resolve: "We believe that no nation is responsible to itself alone, but that laws of political morality are universal; and that obedience to such laws is incumbent upon all nations who would sustain their own sovereignty and justify their sovereign relationship with other nations. We, the Japanese people, pledge our national honor to accomplish these high ideals and purposes with all our resources." Now is the time for our nation to confront the present difficulties with its full power in a spirit of international cooperation in order to defend peace and freedom for all humankind. Here I sincerely ask for the understanding and cooperation of the people of Japan and the members of the Diet.]

"Dai 153 kai kokkai ni okeru koizumi naikaku sōri daijin shoshin hyōmei enzetsu," Prime Minister of Japan and His Cabinet, September 27, 2001, http://www.kantei.go.jp/jp/koizumispeech/2001/0927syosin.html. English translation of the speech is available at "Policy Speech by Prime Minister Koizumi Junichirō to the 153rd Session of the Diet," Prime Minister of Japan and His Cabinet, September 27, 2001, http://japan .kantei.go.jp/koizumispeech/2001/0927syosin_e.html.

22. See the sophisticated analysis of Japan's decision-making in the aftermath of 9/11 by Jeffrey Wayne Hornung, "Learning How to Sweat: Explaining the Dispatch of Japan's Self-Defense Forces in the Gulf War and Iraq War" (PhD diss., George Washington University, 2009).

23. Japanese ships supplied fuel for coalition ships, fuel for onboard helicopters, as well as water to other nations' militaries. A destroyer accompanied each supply ship for protection. The MSDF was also responsible for protecting the ships being refueled, which took one to two hours. See "Tero taisaku kaijō sōshi katsudō ni taisuru hokyū shien katsudō no jisshi ni kansuru tokubetsu sochihō ni motozuku hokyū shien katsudō no kekka "[The results of refueling operations based on the Special Measures Law for Preventing Terrorism at Sea], Ministry of Defense, Japan, April 2010, http://www.mod.go.jp/j/approach/kokusai _heiwa/hokyushien/pdf/kekka.pdf.

24. United Nations Security Council Resolution 1368 (2001).

25. Koizumi spoke again of Japan's promise to the world, embedded in the preface of its constitution, that it would not stand by and ignore the plight of others in a January 19, 2004, speech before the 159th Session of the Diet, http://www.eda-jp.com/pol/koizumi/159.html. See http://www.mofa.go.jp/region/n-america/us/pmv0305/overview.html.

26. United Nations Security Council Resolution 1483 (2003), adopted by the Security Council at its 4761st meeting, on May 22, 2003, https:// documents-dds-ny.un.org/doc/UNDOC/GEN/N03/368/53/PDF /N0336853.pdf?OpenElement.

27. "Press Conference 2 December 2003," Ministry of Foreign Affairs, Japan, http://www.mofa.go.jp/announce/press/2003/12/1202.html; "Prime Minister Attends the Funeral of the Officials of the Ministry of Foreign Affairs of Japan Who Died in Iraq," Prime Minister of Japan and His Cabinet, December 6, 2003, http://japan.kantei.go.jp /koizumiphoto/2003/12/06sougi_e.html. Later, MOFA published a report on this incident, http://www.mofa.go.jp/mofaj/area/iraq/pdfs /jiken_js.pdf.

28. Satō's account of his experiences in Iraq was a bestseller, Satō Masahisa, *Iraku jieitai 'sentōki'* ["A battle diary" of the SDF in Iraq] (Tokyo: Kōdansha, 2007). Satō was later elected to the Upper House, where he took a strong interest in Japan's military policy and was still happy to be referred to as "Satō with the mustache." His website can be accessed here: http://hige-sato.jp/.

29. The GSDF prepared an extensive internal history of the Iraq deployment. The details and analysis that follow are drawn from this report: *Iraku fukkō shien katsudō kōdōshi* [The history of Iraq reconstruction

support operation activity], May 2008, Ground Staff Office, available per request based on Japan's Information Disclosure Act (the official name of the act is Act on Access to Information Held by Administrative Organs). This report was first made available upon the request of a journalist, Fuse Yūjin. Tsujimoto Kiyomi, a member of the Democratic Party of Japan, made the entire report available on her website on July 16, 2015, http://www.kiyomi.gr.jp/blog/5969/. The Diet debate on this report began on July 10, 2015, during the Lower House Special Committee on Security Legislation. See page 27 for a description of the unrest that interrupted the GSDF's operations in Samawah.

30. For details, see "Japan's Official Development Assistance White Paper 2006," Ministry of Foreign Affairs, Japan, http://www.mofa.go.jp/policy /oda/white/2006/ODA2006/html/honpen/hp202020401.htm.

31. Al Jazeera television broadcast the three abducted Japanese nationals, reportedly held by the group identifying itself as the Mujahadeen Squadron. The hostages were identified as Imai Noriaki, Kōriyama Sōichirō, and Takatō Nahoko. "Hostages put Tokyo in bind," Al Jazeera, April 8, 2004, http://www.aljazeera.com/archive/2004/04 /2008410926569161144.html. "Iraqi Group to Free Japanese Hostages," Al Jazeera, April 10, 2004, http://www.aljazeera.com/archive/2004/04 /200849162520336183.html. Then Minister of Foreign Affairs Kawaguchi Yoriko noted on April 15, 2004, "I strongly warn you—please avoid visiting Iraq for any reason." In Japanese, 今後とも、イラクへの渡航はどのような目的であっても絶対に控えて頂きたいということを強く勧告申し上げます。"Gaimu daijin kaiken kiroku" [Press briefing record by foreign minister], Ministry of Foreign Affairs, Japan, April 15, 2004, http://www.mofa.go.jp/mofaj/press/kaiken/gaisho/g_0404.html#7-B.

32. *Japan's Official Development Assistance White Paper 2006.*

33. See the discussion of lessons learned during the Iraq mission in the concluding section of *Iraku fukkō shien katsudō kōdōshi*, 185–187.

34. The Ministry of Defense White Paper notes as follows:

> In February this year, Dutch military troops started withdrawing from the Province of Muthanna after winding up their mission of ensuring the security of the province. The GSDF has received support from the Dutch military on various fronts, including cooperation extended to the GSDF's advance team

which was sent to Samawah for the research mission before the dispatch of core GSDF units, the GSDF units in their actual deployment, and the GSDF units after they started undertaking humanitarian and reconstruction operations in Samawah. On March 7 this year, British troops replaced the Dutch troops to help ensure security in the province. In May, Australian troops began deployment to Samawah. At present, British and Australian troops are operating for ensuring security in the province. It is important for the dispatched GSDF units to keep in close cooperation with troops of the British and Australian forces when conducting their assigned missions. In order to promote such cooperation, the GSDF units and those of the British and Australian forces sent liaison officers to each other's camps, and sponsored regular meetings to exchange views, or put on various cultural events.

*Defense of Japan 2005,* Ministry of Defense, Japan, p. 57, http://www.mod .go.jp/e/publ/w_paper/pdf/2005/4.pdf.

35. The official name of the antiterror law is Special Measures Law Concerning Measures Taken by Japan in Support of the Activities of Foreign Countries Aiming to Achieve the Purposes of the Charter of the United Nations in Response to the Terrorist Attacks Which Took Place on 11 September 2001 in the United States of America as well as Concerning Humanitarian Measures Based on Relevant Resolutions of the United Nations (Law no. 113, 2001).

36. A GSDF officer later analyzed the mission challenges of the Japanese in Samawah and suggested that by June 2005, the positive attitude toward the GSDF seemed to diminish. Sakaemura Yoshiyuki [Lt. Col, GSDF], "A New Role for Armed Forces in a Nonpermissive Environment: On the Coordination between the Japan Self-Defense Forces' International Peace Cooperation Operations and the Official Development Assistance in Iraq," Japan Peacekeeping Training and Research Center, Working Paper no. 201301, July 15, 2013, http://www.mod.go.jp/js/jsc/jpc/research /image/eng04.pdf. See the MOFA update on Samawah projects at http://www.mofa.go.jp/policy/oda/region/middle_e/future_iraq_e.pdf. Sakaemura uses the *Asahi Shimbun* polls, but the polls are hardly definitive as no other polling data can be compared for other locales

around Iraq and to Iraqi responses to other militaries. Japan was very concerned about how the local population perceived the GSDF, however. In 2004, for example, the *Asahi* reported that 85 percent of those who were aware of the SDF's work viewed it favorably, but many in Samawah were unaware of the SDF personnel and what they were doing. "Jieitai chūryū, samawa shimin ra no 85 pāsento sansei asahi shimbunsha kyōdō yoron chōsa" [85 percent of Samawah citizens support SDF's presence, finds *Asahi Shimbun*'s co-survey], *Asahi Shimbun*, June 29, 2004; "Iraku musanna shu, asahi shimbunsha kyōdō yoron chōsa" [*Asahi Shimbun*'s co-survey in Iraq's Muthanna Province], *Asahi Shimbun*, November 26, 2004.

37. See *Iraku fukkō shien katsudō kōdōshi*. This GSDF report became fodder for Diet debate in 2015 when Diet member Tsujimoto Kiyomi of the DPJ reminded Prime Minster Abe of now General Banshō's claim that the Iraqi mission was in fact a "purely military operation." Opposition critics accused the LDP of trying to claim that Japan's UN peacekeeping and its humanitarian support in Iraq was in fact a noncombat mission and thus in keeping with the spirit of Article Nine of the Japanese constitution. See Tsujimoto's exchange with Defense Minister Nakatani Gen: Special Committee on Security Legislation for the Peace and Security of Japan and the International Community, Lower House, 189th Diet Session, July 10, 2015, vol.19, http://kokkai.ndl.go.jp/SENTAKU/syugiin/189/0298/18907100298019.pdf.

38. Sakaemura, "A New Role for Armed Forces in a Nonpermissive Environment," 16–17.

39. *Yomiuri*'s December 14, 2004, poll revealed 27.8 percent supported the extension while 49.5 percent opposed it; *Asahi*'s poll revealed on December 21 that 31 percent supported it, and 58 percent opposed the extension; and *Nikkei* on December 29 showed 32 percent supported it, and 54 percent opposed it.

40. UN Resolution 1816 condemned acts of piracy and armed robbery off Somalia's coast, and UN Resolution 1838 authorized "all necessary means" to repress such acts. Japan cosponsored both resolutions. Additional UN Security Council resolutions would be passed, ultimately tasking a multinational naval effort at monitoring and deterring piracy and enforcing international law should pirates be detained. See United Nations Security Council Resolutions 1846, 1851, and 1897. The Combined

Maritime Forces are an all-voluntary multinational naval force with rotating participation by member states of the United Nations. In 2016, thirty-one navies participated in the Combined Maritime Forces. For information on the mission, see https://combinedmaritimeforces.com.

41. The exchange can be found in the deliberations of the Special Committee on International Terrorism and Japan's Cooperation and Support Activities As Well As Iraq Reconstruction Efforts [in Japanese], Lower House, 170th Diet Session, October 17, 2008, http://kokkai.ndl.go.jp /SENTAKU/syugiin/170/0133/17010170133003.pdf.

42. *Defense Focus,* Ministry of Defense, Japan, no. 13 (March 2009), http://www.mod.go.jp/e/jdf/no13/policy.html.

43. The website of the Regional Cooperation Agreement on Combating Piracy and Armed Robbery against Ships in Asia (ReCAAP) is located at http://www.recaap.org/Home.aspx.

44. The mission of the Combined Task Force 151 (CTF 151), one of three task forces operated by the Combined Maritime Forces, is described as follows: "In accordance with United Nations Security Council Resolutions, and in cooperation with non-member forces, CTF 151's mission is to disrupt piracy and armed robbery at sea and to engage with regional and other partners to build capacity and improve relevant capabilities in order to protect global maritime commerce and secure freedom of navigation." For further details on the Combined Maritime Forces, see https://combinedmaritimeforces.com. For an update on Japanese contributions to the antipiracy effort in the Gulf of Aden, see "Japan's Actions against Piracy off the Coast of Somalia," Ministry of Foreign Affairs, Japan, February 15, 2016, http://www.mofa.go.jp/policy/piracy/ja _somalia_1210.html.

45. A report on the Ministry of Foreign Affairs observers' mission to Sudan in January 2011 is available at *Sūdan jūmin tōhyō kanshi kokusai heiwa kyōryoku tai (nanbu sūdan jūmin tōhyō kanshidan) katsudo hokokusho* [Sudanese Referendum Monitoring International Peace Cooperation Team (South Sudan's Referendum Monitoring Commission) Activities Report] [Available in Japanese with only limited English translation] March 24, 2011, Cabinet Office, Government of Japan, Secretariat of the International Peace Cooperation Headquarters, http://www.pko.go.jp /pko_j/archive_jp/jisseki/sudan/sudan2011.pdf.

46. Reports on the annual Australia-Japan-United States Trilateral Strategic Dialogue can be found at http://www.mofa.go.jp/mofaj/area/jau/.

47. The details of the loan agreement between the Republic of Philippines and Japan can be found at "Signing of Japanese ODA Loan Agreement with the Republic of the Philippines," Japan International Cooperation Agency, December 16, 2013, https://www.jica.go.jp/english/news/press /2013/131216_01.html, and Japan-Philippines Summit Meeting, Ministry of Foreign Affairs, Japan, September 6, 2016, http://www.mofa.go.jp/s _sa/sea2/ph/page3e_000568.html. Abe sent a personal message before the first Malabar exercise: "Message by Prime Minister Abe," Ministry of Defense, Japan, http://www.mod.go.jp/j/photo/pdf/20140725b.pdf.

The description of Acquisition, Technology, and Logistics Agency (ATLA) in the *Defense White Paper 2016* is as follows:

> On October 1, 2015, ATLA was established as an extra-ministerial organization, by bringing together and consolidating equipment procurement related departments regarding procurement, research, and development in the Ministry of Defense (MOD). This has been implemented as a part of MOD reform along with the integration of duties related to actual unit operations into the Joint Staff. ATLA has been established to aim at: 1) implementation of unified project management throughout the life cycle from an integrative perspective; 2) smooth and prompt reflection of the operational needs of units to the equipment to be procured; 3) active engagement in new areas (such as further internationalization of defense equipment and investment in cutting edge technology research); and 4) simultaneous achievement of acquisition reform and maintaining and strengthening defense production and technological bases.

48. On Japan's "three principles on defense exports," see "Japan's Policies on the Control of Arms Exports," Ministry of Foreign Affairs, Japan, http://www.mofa.go.jp/policy/un/disarmament/policy/.

49. See *Defense of Japan 2018* reporting on SDF participation in international peace cooperation activities, available at: http://www.mod.go.jp/j /publication/wp/wp2018/html/ns057000.html. An English language

account can be found on pp. 507–509 of the *Defense of Japan 2017*, available at: http://www.mod.go.go.jp/e/publ/w_paper/pdf/2017 /DOJ2017_reference_web.pdf.

## 3. Mobilizing the Military

1. While plans to draw down U.S. forces in NATO proceeded, by 1995 U.S. planners had frozen the number of U.S. forces in the Asia Pacific at one hundred thousand to contend with the emerging security concerns in the region. U.S. Department of Defense, *United States Security Strategy for the East Asia-Pacific Region* (February 1995). For the logic of this approach to Asia, see Joseph S. Nye Jr., "East Asia Security: The Case for Deep Engagement," *Foreign Affairs* 74, no. 4 (July/August 1995): 4, 90–102.

2. In 1996, the two governments revisited their bilateral Defense Cooperation Guidelines with an eye to laying out the ways in which the two militaries might work in "situations in areas surrounding Japan." Afterward, the SDF and the U.S. forces in the Pacific began exercising together to perform what became known as SIAS-J missions. On the interaction between President Bill Clinton and Prime Minister Hosokawa Morihiro, see the *Mainichi Shimbun* series "A Triangle for the New Century," especially part two of the series: "Shin seiki e no toraianguru dai ni bu: Nichibeidōmei no kyojitsu beigun to ittaika no osore" [A triangle for the new century, part 2: The real risk of integrating military forces in the U.S.-Japan alliance], *Mainichi Shimbun,* May 16, 1997. A more recent series in the *Yomiuri Shimbun* on the 2015 new security legislation also analyzes why Japan earned a reputation for being "unable" to change in the immediate aftermath of the Cold War. See "Kenpō kō tankan anpo hōsei 1 'dekinai nihon' no henka" [Shift in thinking on constitution: Part 1, Security legislation—From a Japan that couldn't to a Japan that could], *Yomiuri Shimbun,* July 2, 2014.

3. See, for example, Ozawa Ichirō, *Blueprint for a New Japan: The Rethinking of a Nation* (Tokyo: Kōdansha International, 1994).

4. In 2005, Tokyo and Washington eventually announced shared strategic goals for the U.S.-Japan alliance. While this was largely a list of policies already in place in Tokyo and Washington, it was the first statement of

U.S.-Japanese intentions in Northeast Asia. A year later, the United States and Japan announced a new force posture to back this up, calling it a U.S.-Japan deterrent force posture. A decade or more into the post–Cold War era, Tokyo was far more ready to embrace a shared strategic agenda and to act in concert with the United States in ensuring regional deterrence. http://www.mofa.go.jp/region/n-america/us /security/scc/joint0502.html.

5. See *Japan Times*, August 6, 2008. https://www.japantimes.co.jp/news /2008/08/06/national/woman-left-in-coma-by-aum-94-gas-attack-dies /#.W6pcUFVKi70).

6. In late April, the *Asahi Shimbun* reported that several SDF officers had collaborated with the Aum after the incident, telling them of their alert status, and one member of the SDF was suspected of attempting to build a bomb. It is documented in this Lower House memorandum of questions: Itō Masayoshi, "Genshoku Jiēkan ni yoru ōmu shinrikyō ni taisuru bunai shiryō teikyō ni kansuru shitsumon shuijo" [Memorandum on questions about the serving Japanese Self-Defense Forces official's provision of internal documents to Aum Shinrikyō], 132nd Session of the Diet, Upper House, May 31, 1995, http://www.sangiin.go.jp/japanese /joho1/kousei/syuisyo/132/syup/s132021.pdf.

7. Major media coverage of the Kōbe earthquake was exhaustive, particularly on the government debate over the causes for delay in the dispatch of the SDF. See, for example, *Asahi Shimbun*, January 19 and 24, 1995, *Yomiuri Shimbun*, January 22 and 27, 1995, and the *Nikkei Shimbun*, January 23, 24, and 27, 1995. On the December 1995 deliberations on revising the Disaster Countermeasures Basic Law, see *Asahi Shimbun*, December 1, 1995. For a full account of Japan's response to the Kōbe disaster and subsequent natural disasters by a senior advisor to the Japanese government, see Iokibe Makoto, *Daisaigai no jidai—Mirai no kokunan no sonaete* [In the Era of Major Disasters: Preparing for the Japanese Nation's Difficulties Ahead] (Tokyo: Mainichi Newspaper Publishing, 2016), especially chapter two.

8. The JSP had been an ardent critic of the SDF throughout the postwar years, only grudgingly acknowledging in 1984 that the SDF had been created "constitutionally." This legal issue is discussed in *Defense of Japan 1988*, Defense Agency, Tokyo. The JSP did not formally accept the SDF as constitutional until 1994, when the leader of the party joined the LDP

to form a coalition government. For a critique of Japanese defense policy by a JSP member, see Ueda Tetsu, *Sensōron* [Theory of War] (Tokyo: Marujyusha, 1989).

9. For a discussion of the political factors that shape Japan's debate over the nuclear option, see Sheila A. Smith, "Realists, Not Rightists, Shape Japan's (Non) Nuclear Choice" (working paper for the Nonproliferation Policy Education Center), Arlington, VA, 2017.

10. Some Japanese politicians did not think so. The Diet deliberations in the immediate aftermath of the Taepodong launch produced a flurry of interest in developing a Japanese satellite capability independent of the United States. The MOFA's *Diplomatic Bluebook of 1999*, https://www .mofa.go.jp/policy/other/bluebook/1999/I-b.html#2, incorporates the cabinet decision to acquire information-gathering satellites by 2002.

11. "Japan-DPRK Pyongyang Declaration," Ministry of Foreign Affairs, Japan, September 17, 2002, http://www.mofa.go.jp/region/asia-paci/n _korea/pmv0209/pyongyang.html.

12. Japan participated in the Six Party Talks begun in 2003 that included China, the United States, Russia, South Korea, and North Korea. The Japanese government has sought repeatedly to persuade Pyongyang to account for those Japanese citizens abducted by the DPRK. See the Ministry of Foreign Affairs website dedicated to the abductees, http://www.mofa.go.jp/region/asia-paci/n_korea/abduction/. See also Robert S. Boynton, *The Invitation-Only Zone: The True Story of North Korea's Abduction Project* (New York: Farrar, Straus and Giroux, 2016). In 2014, Kim Jong-un attempted to rekindle diplomacy with Japan by promising to reopen an investigation on those Japanese citizens Tokyo believed to still be in North Korea. The effort made little progress. See Sheila A. Smith, "Pyongyang's New Overtures and Abe's Diplomacy," May 31, 2014, http://38north.org/2014/05/ssmith053114/and "Reading Pyongyang's Intentions with Japan," November 25, 2014, http://38north .org/2014/11/ssmith112514/.

13. The Japanese government explained in the Diet in April 2008 that the total cost of BMD would be somewhere between 800 billion yen and 1 trillion yen. "Misairu bōeihi 1.5 bai chō seifu sōtei goe ruikei 1 chō 5800 en" [Missile defense cost 1.5 times more than the original government estimate—totaling 1.58 trillion yen], *Mainichi Shimbun*, February 23,

2016. But in 2017, the Ministry of Defense stated that Japan had spent far more, estimating that since 2004, it had spent a total of 1.85 trillion yen on BMD systems, including four Aegis BMD-capable destroyers, seventeen batteries of PAC-3, and eleven radars. This was more than double the initial cost estimates, and moreover, did not include the operational or personnel costs associated with BMD. [Interview by author with Ministry of Defense officials, June 27, 2017.]

14. Diet deliberations over this new legal framework for mobilizing in case of an attack began in May 2002, and the laws were passed in the Lower House on May 15 and the Upper House on June 6, 2003. A full description of the package of laws included in this contingency legislation is included in *Defense of Japan 2005*, Ministry of Defense, Japan, 199–214.

15. "第3章　国民保護への対応," Fire and Disaster Management Agency, 2012, http://www.fdma.go.jp/html/hakusho/h27/h27/html/3-2-1.html.

16. See *Defense of Japan 2006* for details on the rationale for the creation of a Joint Staff Office, http://www.mod.go.jp/e/publ/w_paper/pdf/2006/3-1-1.pdf. In Japanese, the Joint Staff Council was referred to as the *tōgō bakuryō kaigi* (統合幕僚会議), and the Joint Staff Office is called the *tōgō bakuryō kanbu* (統合幕僚監部). For an outline of the JSO's responsibilities, see Ministry of Defense, Japan: http://www.mod.go.jp/js/Joint-Staff/js_jurisdiction.htm. See also Yuki Tatsumi, *Japan's New Defense Establishment: Institutions, Capabilities and Implications* (Washington, DC: Stimson Center, 2007) for an in-depth look at the institutional changes under way within the bureaucracy responsible for defense planning.

17. "National Defense Program Guidelines for FY2014 and Beyond," Ministry of Defense, Japan, http://www.mod.go.jp/j/approach/agenda/guideline/2014/pdf/20131217_e2.pdf.

18. For the JCG's account of the interdiction, see "Kaijō hoan repōto 2003" [Japan Coast Guard Report 2003], Ministry of Land, Infrastructure, Transport, and Tourism, Japan, http://www.kaiho.mlit.go.jp/info/books/report2003/special01/01_01.html. For more on the Proliferation Security Initiative, see "The Proliferation Security Initiative (PSI)," Ministry of Foreign Affairs, Japan, http://www.mofa.go.jp/policy/un/disarmament/arms/psi/psi.html.

19. "Response to Submarines Submerging in Territorial Waters," *Defense of Japan 2005,* Ministry of Defense, Japan, 43–44, http://www.mod.go.jp/e /publ/w_paper/pdf/2005/3.pdf. Whether it was a deliberate attempt to challenge Japanese defenses, or a commander's mistake, is unclear. See Peter A. Dutton, *Scouting, Signaling, and Gatekeeping: Chinese Naval Operations in Japanese Waters and the International Law Implications,* U.S. Naval War College China Maritime Studies, no. 2 (Newport, RI: Naval War College Press, 2009) and Minemura Yoshito, "Han kyu sensuikan no ryokai shinpan jian—CMSI Scouting, Signaling, and Gatekeeping wo yonde" [A Han-class submarine's invasion of Japanese territorial waters: Reading CMSI *Scouting, signaling, and gatekeeping*], *Japan Maritime Self-Defense Force Command and Staff College Review* 1, no. 1 (May 2011): 90–100.
20. For a Ministry of Defense description of the submarine incursion, see http://www.mod.go.jp/j/press/news/2018/01/11a.html. Minister of Defense Onodera Itsunori criticized the incursion in a press conference on January 16, 2018, http://www.mod.go.jp/j/press/kisha/2018/01/16.html.
21. For details on Japan's missile defense enhancements, see *Defense of Japan 2016,* Ministry of Defense, Japan, 290–293.
22. The United States and Japan have cooperated in developing this new missile defense capability, working closely on the SM-3 interceptors. Japanese MSDF combat units have deployed to Kauai, Hawaii, to exercise and test new technological improvements to this ship-based system.
23. "Waga kuni no BMD seibi e no torikumi no henkan [History of efforts for BMD development in Japan]," *Defense of Japan 2016,* Ministry of Defense, Japan, http://www.clearing.mod.go.jp/hakusho_data/2016 /html/ns044000.html.
24. Under Article 76 of the SDF Law, the minister of defense can mobilize the SDF if there is clear intent to launch a missile that could pose a danger to Japan. When the intention of the launch is unclear, a cabinet decision must be made before the minister can issue a destruction order under Article 82, and this is to be issued without public notification. *Defense of Japan 2009,* Ministry of Defense, Japan, 183–193.
25. "Mr. Chikao Kawai, Vice-Minister for Foreign Affairs, Lodges a Protest against Dr. Han Zhiqiang, Acting Ambassador of the People's Republic

of China to Japan," Ministry of Foreign Affairs, Japan, December 13, 2012, http://www.mofa.go.jp/announce/announce/2012/12/1213_03.html; Sheila A. Smith, "Beijing's Test of Tokyo," *Asia Unbound,* Council on Foreign Relations, December 13, 2012, http://blogs.cfr.org/asia/2012/12/13/beijings-test-of-tokyo/.

26. The Minster of Defense discussed the intrusion of a Chinese drone into Japanese airspace and response measures at a press conference on September 10, 2013. A transcript of the press conference is available at "Press Conference by the Defense Minister (04:55–05:13 P.M. September 10, 2013)," Ministry of Defense, Japan, http://www.mod.go.jp/e/press/conference/2013/09/10.html. The next month, Prime Minister Abe approved new rules of engagement that would authorize the SDF to shoot down unmanned aircraft that enter Japanese airspace. "Japan to Shoot Down Foreign Drones That Invade Its Airspace," *Japan Times,* October 20, 2013.

27. The 2004 NDPG notes the following: "Since in our judgment, the likelihood of full-scale invasion of Japan has declined and is expected to remain modest in the foreseeable future, we will modify our current defense force building concept that emphasized Cold War–type anti-tank warfare, anti-submarine warfare and anti-air warfare, and will significantly reduce the personnel and equipment earmarked for a full-scale invasion." See "National Defense Program Guidelines, FY2005-," Ministry of Defense, Japan, http://www.mod.go.jp/e/d_act/d_policy/pdf/national_guidelines.pdf. Additionally, the 2010 Mid-Term Defense Program states the following: "The GSDF will establish a new coastal surveillance unit and will begin to form a first-response unit to station in the island areas of southwestern Japan." "Mid-Term Defense Program (FY2011–FY2015)," Ministry of Defense, Japan, http://www.mod.go.jp/e/d_act/d_policy/pdf/mid_termFY2011-15.pdf. These joint exercises, dubbed *Chinsei* [Tranquility in the West], were held annually from 2013 [interview by the author with General Banshō Koichirō, July 2014].

28. For a fuller analysis of the domestic politics on the Senkaku Islands dispute, see Sheila A. Smith, *Intimate Rivals: Japanese Domestic Politics and a Rising China* (New York: Columbia University Press, 2015). In Japanese, *Nitchū Shin'ainaru Shukuteki: Henyōsuru Nihon Seiji to Taichū*

*Seisaku*, trans. Fushimi Taketo, Sato Yuko, and Tamaki Nobuhiro (Tokyo: Tokyo University Press, 2018).

29. For more on the relocation, see "Japan Defense Focus No. 74", Ministry of Defense, Japan, March 2016, http://www.mod.go.jp/e/jdf/pdf/jdf _n074.pdf. For more on China's Air Defense Identification Zone, see Sheila A. Smith, "China Ups the Ante in East China Sea Dispute," *Asia Unbound*, Council on Foreign Relations, November 25, 2013, https://www.cfr.org/blog-post/china-ups-ante-east-china-sea-dispute.

30. The 2015 revision of the Guidelines for U.S.-Japan Defense Cooperation lays out a plan for the Alliance Coordination Mechanism with the aim of improving operational coordination between the SDF and the U.S. military through new communications infrastructure and joint training. For the joint statement from the Ministry of Defense and the U.S. Department of Defense, see "Guidelines for Japan-U.S. Defense Cooperation," April 27, 2015, p. 3, http://www.mofa.go.jp/files/000078188.pdf.

31. On the discussion between Diet members Ishiba Shigeru and Maehara Seiji, see Sugio Takahashi, "Dealing with the Ballistic Missile Threat: Whether Japan Should Have a Strike Capability Under its Exclusively Defense-Oriented Policy," originally published in Japanese, *Bōei kenkyūjo kiyō* (NIDS Security Studies), vol. 8, no. 1, (October 2005): 105–121, http://www.nids.mod.go.jp/english/publication/kiyo/pdf /bulletin_e2006_4_takahashi.pdf. This discussion of the "so-called capability to attack enemy bases" (*Teki kichi kōgeki nōryoku*) was explained in *Defense of Japan 2013*, Ministry of Defense, Japan, http://www.clearing.mod.go.jp/hakusho_data/2013/2013/html/nc004000 .html.

32. See, for example, the *Defense of Japan 2013* discussion of possible future defense capabilities. "Shin 'bōei keikaku no taikō' sakutei ni kakaru teigen ('bōei o torimodosu')" [Recommendations for the new National Defense Program Guidelines (Restoring Defense)], National Defense Subcommittee of the Liberal Democratic Party, June 6, 2013. The subtitle, "Restoring Defense," echoes the LDP's campaign slogan of "Restoring Japan."

33. Full statement by Prime Minister Abe from the Upper House is as follows:

> The LDP has long debated on the issue of whether it will continue to be acceptable for Japan to ask U.S. forces to strike

missiles that are aimed at Japan . . . I believe we need to fully consider what constitutes an effective deterrent, in other words we have to have those who would attack Japan hesitate because they believe that attacking Japan would harm their own national interest or the lives of their own citizens. (Prime Minister Abe Shinzō, May 8, 2013, Upper House Budget Committee).

この点に関し、安倍内閣総理大臣は、「今まさに日本を攻撃しようとしているミサイルに対して、米軍がこれは攻撃してくださいよと（中略）日本が頼むという状況でずっといいのかどうかという問題点、課題はずっと自民党においても議論をしてきたところでございます。（中略）相手に、これはやはり日本に対してそういう攻撃をすることは自分たちの国益あるいは自分たちの国民の命にも大きな影響力があると思って思いとどまらせるようにするという、抑止力を効かせる上においてどうすべきかという議論はしっかりとしていく必要があるんだろうと、このように思っております。」（13（平成25）年5月8日　参議院予算委員会　安倍内閣総理大臣答弁）

From *Defense of Japan 2013*, Ministry of Defense, Japan.

## 4. The Constitution Revisited

1. The full text of Article Nine is as follows: "Aspiring sincerely to an international peace based on justice and order, the Japanese people forever renounce war as a sovereign right of the nation and the threat or use of force as means of settling international disputes. In order to accomplish the aim of the preceding paragraph, land, sea, and air forces, as well as other war potential, will never be maintained. The right of belligerency of the state will not be recognized."
2. For a critical analysis of the role of the Cabinet Legislation Bureau, see Richard J. Samuels, "Politics, Security Policy and Japan's Cabinet Legislation Bureau: Who Elected These Guys, Anyway?" (Japan Policy Research Institute Working Paper no. 99, March 2004), http://www.jpri .org/publications/workingpapers/wp99.html.
3. Ozawa Ichirō, the secretary general of the LDP at the time of the Gulf War, was one such lawmaker. He went on to argue for a new approach

to Japan's international responsibility, one where the SDF could play a role in the UN efforts to ensure peace, in his book *Nihon kaizō keikaku* [Blueprint for a new Japan] (Tokyo: Kōdansha, 1993). In English: Ozawa Ichirō, *Blueprint for a New Japan: The Rethinking of a Nation* (Tokyo: Kōdansha International, 1994).

4. Koizumi also ensured that the SDF deployed to Iraq would not use force abroad: "In personnel terms, given that the situation in Iraq is one that cannot always be described as being safe, I have decided to dispatch the SDF which have had a daily training regimen, and capable of operating efficiently and avoiding danger in hostile environments. They will not use force. They will operate in regions free from military action and in a case when such action occurs near the site of their operations, the SDF will temporarily suspend their operations or take shelter and seek the directive of the Minister of State for Defense. We will take every possible measure to ensure their safety." "General Policy Speech by Prime Minister Koizumi Junichirō to the 159th Session of the Diet," Ministry of Foreign Affairs, Japan, January 19, 2004, http://www.mofa.go.jp/announce/pm/koizumi/speech040119.html.

5. The official name of the Antiterrorism Special Measures Law is the "Special Measures Law Concerning Measures Taken by Japan in Support of the Activities of Foreign Countries Aiming to Achieve the Purposes of the Charter of the United Nations in Response to the Terrorist Attacks Which Took Place on 11 September 2001 in the United States of America as well as Concerning Humanitarian Measures Based on Relevant Resolutions of the United Nations." For details of operations included in this law, see "The Antiterrorism Special Measures Law" [tentative English summary], Prime Minister of Japan and His Cabinet, October 2001, http://japan.kantei.go.jp/policy/2001/anti-terrorism/1029terohougaiyou_e.html. This information is also presented in detail in the 2003 Ministry of Defense White Paper, http://www.clearing.mod.go.jp/hakusho_data/2003/2003/pdf/15420000.pdf. The Antiterror Law was submitted to the Diet on October 5, 2011, and passed about three weeks later, on the 29th. "Heiwa gaikō, shikin-seki ni tero tokusohō seiritsu, 'chūritsu' sokonau osore mo" [Antiterror Law Passes with Peaceful Diplomacy as Milestones—The Risk of Damaging 'Neutrality'], *Asahi Shimbun*, October 30, 2001.

6. For the final vote tally, see http://www.sangiin.go.jp/japanese/joho1 /kousei/vote/153/153-1029-v003.htm.

7. The official name of this law is "Law Concerning the Special Measures on Humanitarian and Reconstruction Assistance in Iraq."

8. See Jeffrey Wayne Hornung, "Learning How to Sweat: Explaining the Dispatch of Japan's Self-Defense Forces in the Gulf War and Iraq War" (PhD diss., George Washington University, 2009), 201–265.

9. Morimoto Satoshi, *Iraku sensō to jieitai haken* [Iraq War and Self-Defense Force Dispatch] (Tokyo: Tōyōkeizai Shinpōsha, 2004). Hornung explores the thinking of a secret team directed by the prime minister's office to consider Japan's options. Assistant Chief Cabinet Secretary for Security Affairs Ōmori Keiji and Assistant Chief Cabinet Secretary for Foreign Affairs Yachi Shōtarō in the prime minister's office were the link with the Defense Agency and the Ministry of Foreign Affairs, respectively. Ōmori put together a team to develop an action plan that included ideas of what the SDF might be able to accomplish depending on how the war unfolded. The cabinet approved the ideas in the plan by the end of March. See Hornung, "Learning How to Sweat," 201–265.

10. Once drafted, the legislation was based on UN Security Council Resolutions 678, 687, 1441, and 1483. The *yūji hōsei,* or contingency legislation, is discussed in Chapter 3.

11. The bill was headline news on June 14, 2003, on the *Asahi Shimbun, Yomiuri Shimbun,* and *Nikkei Shimbun.* The *Japan Times* reported the bill in English. See Hornung, "Learning How to Sweat" for a detailed description of the discussions among legislators and in the Diet.

12. The DPJ-sponsored bill consisted of three mandates: (1) to delete from the government-proposed bill reference to UN Security Council Resolutions 678, 687, and 1441 as justification for the attack against Iraq by the United States and the United Kingdom; (2) to delete from the bill all aspects associated with the dispatch of the SDF; and (3) to shorten the term of the bill from four years to two years. "Iraku tokuso hōan de jieitai haken sakujo no shūseian teishutsu wo kettei" [Decision to Submit a Proposal to Delete the Dispatch of Self-Defense Force in Iraq Special Measures Law], Democratic Party of Japan, July 1, 2003, http://www1.dpj.or.jp/news/?num=3822. This DPJ proposal was voted

down two days later, when the original bill passed the Diet's Special Committee on Iraq.

13. See "Table 3.8 (Asahi): Support-Opposition to SDF Dispatch to Iraq," in Hornung, "Learning How to Sweat: Explaining the Dispatch of Japan's Self-Defense Forces in the Gulf War and Iraq War," 112. Data from the *Yomiuri Shimbun* on various dates (July 15, 2003; December 16, 2003; January 27, 2004; and February 27, 2004) show that in July 2003, only 30.5 percent supported the SDF dispatch to Iraq and 43.2 percent opposed. By December, 17.8 percent of respondents called for the SDF to be dispatched as soon as possible; 48.2 percent supported the dispatch after the situation in Iraq became stable; and 29.8 percent opposed the dispatch. In January 2004, a total of 53 percent supported the decision made to dispatch the SDF to various degrees while 44 percent opposed it. The support increased by 5.4 percentage points in the following month after the SDF was dispatched. Data from the *Nikkei Shimbun* from various dates (June 23, 2003; August 4, 2003; December 22, 2003; and February 16, 2004, show that the Iraq Special Measures Law bill initially garnered 43 percent approval and 41 percent disapproval in June 2003. Yet, asked more specifically about the SDF dispatch in August, shortly after the bill passed the Diet, 52 percent opposed the dispatch while only 28 percent supported it. The support for the dispatch gradually grew—from 28 percent in August, to 33 percent in December, and finally to 43 percent in February 2004— while the opposition remained constant with 52 percent in August and December polls and slightly declined to 42 percent in February. According to the cabinet secretariat's polling, in 2000, 82 percent saw the SDF favorably; in 2003, it fell slightly to 80 percent, and then rose to 85 percent in 2006. See surveys conducted by the Cabinet Office in 2000, 2003, and 2006 (or under the years Heisei 12, Heisei 15, and Heisei 18 using the Japanese imperial calendar) on "Jieitai ni taisuru inshō" [Impressions of the Self-Defense Force], Cabinet Office, Government of Japan, http://survey.gov-online.go.jp/h26/h26-bouei/zh/z07.html.

14. For the details of the operation in the Indian Ocean, see "Tero taisaku kaijō soshi katsudō ni taisuru hokyū katsudō no jisshi ni kansuru tokubetsu sochihō ni motozuku hokyū shien katsudō no kekka" [Results

of Replenishment Support Activities Based on Act on Special Measures Concerning Implementation of Replenishment Support Activities Toward the Antiterrorism Maritime Interdiction Operation], Ministry of Defense, Japan, April 2010, http://www.mod.go.jp/j/approach/kokusai_heiwa/hokyushien/pdf/kekka.pdf; "First ASDF relief flights land in Islamabad," *Japan Times*, October 10, 2001.

15. Article Sixty-Six states, "The Cabinet shall consist of the Prime Minister, who shall be its head, and other Ministers of State, as provided for by law. The Prime Minister and other Ministers of State must be civilians. The Cabinet, in the exercise of executive power, shall be collectively responsible to the Diet." From *The Constitution of Japan*, https://japan.kantei.go.jp/constitution_and_government_of_japan/constitution_e.html.

16. In 2001, the Ministry of International Trade and Industry was replaced by the Ministry of Economy, Trade and Industry.

17. These three conditions for ordering the use of force for self-defense were once again put forward in Diet debate by the director of the Cabinet Legislation Bureau, Takatsuji Masami, on March 10, 1969, in the Budget Committee of the Upper House. They were further refined by the testimony of the government on September 27, 1985, in the Lower House. The government's three conditions on the use of force necessary for self-defense recognized under Article Nine are as follows: (1) an unlawful attack on Japan, (2) there are no alternative means of repelling this, and (3) only the minimal necessary level of force should be used.

The government will determine whether these three conditions are fitting at that time. *Bōei Handobukku 2011* [Defense Handbook 2011] (Tokyo: Asagumo Shimbunsha, 2011), 643. The English version of the 2013 Ministry of Defense's White Paper presents a wordier version: (1) when there is an imminent and illegitimate act of aggression against Japan, (2) when there is no appropriate means to deal with such aggression other than by resorting to the right of self-defense, and (3) when the use of armed force is confined to the minimum necessary level. *Defense of Japan 2013*, 101, http://www.mod.go.jp/e/publ/w_paper/pdf/2013/22_Part2_Chapter1_Sec2.pdf.

18. Initially, these three principles for the exercise of Japan's right of self-defense were put forward by the director of the Cabinet Legislative Bureau in the deliberations over the 1954 Self-Defense Law. See Dai 19-kai Shugiin Naikaku iinkai dai 21 [Cabinet Committee of the Lower House, 19th Session of the Diet], April 7, 1954, cited in Umeda Sayuri, *Japan: Article Nine of the Constitution,* Library of Congress, https://www .loc.gov/law/help/japan-constitution/article9.php#_ftn104.

19. Here the language is very specific to Japan's defenses. The SDF by law can use force to "defend our country" [*waga kuni wo bōei suru tame*]. The contingency laws passed in 2003–2004 had outlined a response to an armed attack against Japan. What would be required in the event of an armed attack, as well as how to ensure cooperation with Japanese citizens and other government agencies, was outlined therein. A new law, entitled the Law to Ensure the Peace and Independence of our Nation as well as the Security of Our People and Our Country in the Case of an Armed Attack ['Buryoku' Kōgeki Jittai nado ni okeru Wagakuni no Heiwa to Dokuritsu narabini Kuni oyobi Kokumin no anzen no kokubō ni kansuru hōritsu], was passed. Included in that bundle of laws were Measures to Support U.S. Military Operations, the Law Regulating Maritime Transport, the Law Governing the Treatment of POWs, Regulations on Violations of International Humanitarian Protections, Law on the Exceptional Use of Public Facilities, and the Law on the Protection of the Japanese Citizens. For a full treatment of the evolution of Japan's defense laws, see the text assigned to Japan's SDF officers on the legal basis for their activities: Tamura Shigenobu, Takahashi Kenichi, and Shimada Kazuhisa (eds.), *Nihon no Bōei Hōsei,* 2nd ed. (Tokyo: Naigai Shuppan, 2012), particularly chapter 9.

20. Ishiba Shigeru, an LDP defense expert and former minister of defense, felt strongly that Japan's legal system needed to be revamped. Ishiba spoke and wrote about national defense and on what reforms were needed. After serving in the cabinet, Ishiba wrote *Kokubō—Subete wo shirubeki tokiga kita* [The time has come to know everything about Japan's defenses] (Tokyo: Shinko Bunko, 2011). As secretary general of the LDP from 2012, Ishiba lobbied hard for changing the government's interpretation of the right of collective self-defense. See *Nihonjin no tame no 'shūdanteki jieiken' nyu mon* [Allowing the right of collective

self-defense for the Japanese people] (Tokyo: Shinkosha, 2014). Ishiba also advocated for constitutional revision in *Nihon wo Torimodosu. Kenpō wo torimodosu* [Restore Japan. Restore our constitution] (Tokyo: PHP Kenkyūsha, 2013).

21. For an examination of how civilian control was defined after World War II, see Hikotani Takako, "The Paradox of Antimilitarism: Civil-Military Relations in Post World War II Japan" (PhD diss., Columbia University, 2014).

22. Most of the controversies of the past were eventually resolved as civilian leaders took steps to improve Japanese security planning, but they took time and were politically sensitive. During the Cold War, the political controversy over the Mitsuya Study, a contingency planning exercise leaked in the mid-1960s, eventually led to the initiation of bilateral talks with the United States and produced the U.S.-Japan Defense Cooperation Guidelines. Chairman of the Joint Staff Council, General Kurisu Hiroomi's statement that local commanders might have to defend their country with or without the proper laws led to his firing, but Prime Minister Fukuda Takeo then initiated discussions on how to develop the legal measures necessary to ensure the defense of Japan. It took almost three decades before the contingency legislation (*yūji hōsei*) was created and passed into law, but the controversy Kurisu stirred up revealed a critical weakness in Japan's military planning. See Sheila A. Smith, "At the Intersection of the Cold War and the Postwar" (PhD diss., Columbia University, 1996).

23. For an analysis of the institutional responsibilities and reforms of the relationships among civilian and uniformed policy makers, see Yuki Tatsumi, *Japan's National Security Policy Infrastructure: Can Tokyo Meet Washington's Expectations?* (Washington, DC: Stimson Center, 2008).

24. See *Defense of Japan 2014* for a discussion of MOD reform, Ministry of Defense, Japan, http://www.mod.go.jp/e/publ/w_paper/pdf/2014 /DOJ2014_4-2-3_web_1031.pdf.

25. Tamogami was the only officer punished because only his essay was published. The APA group is a real estate and development group, and according to its website, the annual essay competition is part of the APA's broader effort to "contribute to society." The essay contest is entitled *A Genuine Historical Perspective on the Modern Era,* and it is part

of a broader set of activities designed to achieve "The Revival of Japan."
The Japanese title of the contest is *Shin no kin gendai shikan* (真の近現代
史観). The website states: "This effort to honor these essays is to
encourage research on Japan's modern history, international relations,
politics, and policy that contribute to the growth and development of
our proud homeland, Japan. In addition, we would like to widely
disseminate the results of this excellence in research. From books and
essays published over the past five years that have received nomination,
our selection panel selects the most distinguished for the grand prize."
[本表彰制度は、誇りある祖国である日本の成長発展に資する近現代史、
国際関係、政治・政策等の分野における研究を促すとともに、優れた研
究成果を広く周知していきたいと考えています。過去5年以内に発刊され
た書籍や発表された論文のうち、推薦人による推薦を受けた作品の中か
ら、審査委員によって本大賞の趣旨に照らして最も優れた作品を選定致
します。] See the current essay contest link on the APA website [in
Japanese], http://ronbun.apa.co.jp/.

"Tamogami kūbakuchō kōtetsu: Kenshō ronbun, fukusū jieikan ga
ōbo, bōeishō, naiki ihan no chōsa kentō" [ASDF Staff Chief Tamogami
Gets Fired: Multiple SDF Officers Apply for Essay Contest, Ministry
of Defense May Investigate Violation of International Rules], *Mainichi
Shimbun,* November 2, 2008.

"Tamogami kūbakuchō kōtetsu: Shin'nen de ronbun kaita kako
'sonnano kankei ne'" [ASDF Staff Chief Tamogami Gets Fired: "I
Wrote the Article with Conviction," "It Doesn't Matter" He Says in
Past], *Mainichi Shimbun* (west), November 1, 2008.

"Tamogami shi, ronbun jushō wo egao de hōkoku kichi tomono kai
kessei yōsei kai jimu kyokuchō akasu" [Mr. Tamogami Happily Reports
Essay Award and Requests Establishment of Association of Friends of
Bases—Association's Secretary General Reveals], *Asahi Shimbun,*
November 12, 2008. According to the *Asahi Shimbun,* Tamogami
supported the Japanese Society for History Textbook Reform, a group
known for its revisionist views of Japan's prewar history.

26. Minister Mabuchi Sumio of the Ministry of Land, Infrastructure,
Transport, and Tourism was eventually sanctioned in the Upper House
proceedings, with a censure motion passed on November 27, 2010;
Plenary Sessions, Upper House, November 26–27, 2010. See full Diet
debate here: http://kokkai.ndl.go.jp/SENTAKU/sangiin/176/0001

/17611260001010.pdf and http://kokkai.ndl.go.jp/SENTAKU/sangiin
/176/0001/17611270001011.pdf. LDP Diet members also reacted critically
to the language used by the DPJ's chief cabinet secretary during a
budget committee hearing when he referred to the SDF as an "instrument of violence" [*bōryoku sōchi*]. Chief Cabinet Secretary Sengoku
Yoshito stated in the Upper House's budget committee that "the SDF,
which is an instrument of violence . . . well, a type of military institution . . . need be kept under civilian control." The Diet record records
Sengoku as changing his statement somewhat in response to the
reaction: "You have just mentioned *De l'esprit des lois*. In the world of
civil servants, similarly, I believe that political neutrality is essential.
Because JSDF, an instrument of violence [some people speak up],
can be recognized as a military organization [some people speak up], the
civilian control of the military has to be enforced. Additionally, from
the experience before World War II, we should never . . . [some people
speak up] . . . ok, I take your opinion and take my word back to redefine
JSDF as organization that uses force."

In Japanese, "今、法の精神と言われました。公務員という世界で
は、同じように政治的な中立性が求められると思います。そしてさら
に、この暴力装置でもある自衛隊⋯⋯⋯（発言する者あり）まああある種
の、ある種の軍事組織でありますから⋯⋯⋯（発言する者あり）⋯軍
事組織でもありますから、これはシビリアンコントロールが利かなけれ
ばならないと。それから、まあ戦前の、戦前の経験からしまして、決し
て⋯⋯⋯（発言する者あり）じゃ、実力組織というふうに訂正させても
らいます。" Remarks by Sengoku Yoshito, Upper House Budget
Committee, November 18, 2010, http://kokkai.ndl.go.jp.

27. The report from the MOD's special investigation on the South Sudan
logs is available here: http://www.mod.go.jp/igo/inspection/pdf
/special04_report.pdf. On the day the report was released, July 27, 2017,
Vice-Minister of Defense Kuroe and the Ground Staff Office chief of
staff, General Okabe Toshiya, resigned. Defense Minister Inada
resigned on July 28. In February 2017, Lower House member Gotō
Yūichi from the Democratic Party asked about the existence of logs
from the GSDF's Iraq deployment, but Inada replied she was not
aware of any; Lower House Budget Committee, February 20, 2017,
http://kokkai.ndl.go.jp/SENTAKU/syugiin/193/0018/19302200018013
.pdf.

After an internal search effort, the existence of logs from the GSDF deployment in Iraq was reported to Defense Minister Onodera in March 2018, and he made this information public in April. *Asahi Shimbun,* April 3, 2017, http://www.asahi.com/ajw/articles /AJ201804030044.html.

28. One hundred seventy belong to the Zenkoku Take no Kai (or Zenkoku Bu no Kai), according to a blog written by an Upper House member, Satō Masahisa, http://ameblo.jp/satomasahisa/entry-12053091434.html ?frm_src=favoritemail. For profiles of the former SDF officers in the Diet, see their websites: Nakatani Gen (http://www.nakatanigen.com /profile/); Nakatani Shin'ichi (https://nakatani.tv/profile/); Uto Takashi (http://www.utotakashi.jp/profile/), and Satō Masahisa (http://hige-sato .jp/profile.html). Morimoto Satoshi, former defense minister, also has a website: http://www.office-morimoto.net/about. At the time of his appointment, there was also criticism of Morimoto's appointment to the cabinet because he was not an elected official. "Shin bōeishō hatsu no minkanjin kanbō chōkan bunmin tōsei no kanten kara mo mondai nashi" [First Private Citizen Appointed as New Defense Minister, Chief Cabinet Secretary Says No Problems With Civilian Control], NHK News, June 4, 2012.

29. Other laws have also been changed. The new security laws of 2015 included changes not only to the SDF law but also to the UN Peace-keeping law, Act on Measures to Ensure the Peace and Security of Japan in Perilous Situations in Areas Surrounding Japan, and Act on Measures Conducted by the Government in Line with U.S. Military Actions in Armed Attack Situations. See the full list here: http://www.cas.go.jp/jp /gaiyou/jimu/pdf/sinkyuu-heiwaanzenhouseiseibihou.pdf. The list of revisions of SDF law can be found here: http://hourei.ndl.go.jp /SearchSys/viewEnkaku.do?i=nH9Wu%2Ffb7Goek6%2BGNPCncQ%3 D%3D.

30. This constraint on the SDF differentiated the U.S.-Japan alliance from other Cold War alliances. By the end of the decade, however, the Defense Agency head, Sakata Michita, recognized that it could end up impairing Japan's own defense preparedness, and he opened talks with the United States on what the military division of labor could be between U.S. and Japanese forces. The U.S.-Japan Defense Cooperation Guidelines were thus first established in 1978, yet they were focused only

on exercises and studies for a contingency that threatened Japan. By the mid-1990s, as the United States grew more concerned about North Korea's nuclear ambitions, the United States and Japan revised these guidelines to expand their scope to regional contingencies, and once again, after the Chinese began to put pressure on Japan around the Senkaku Islands, these guidelines would be revised to focus on "gray zone" contingencies. Yet all three of these revisions in how the U.S. and Japanese militaries would work together stopped short of allowing the SDF to use force beyond the mission of Japan's defense. "The Guidelines for Japan-U.S. Defense Cooperation," Ministry of Defense, Japan, November 27, 1978, http://www.mod.go.jp/e/d_act/anpo/19781127.html; "The Guidelines for Japan-U.S. Defense Cooperation," Ministry of Defense, Japan, September 23, 1997, http://www.mod.go.jp/e/d_act/anpo /19970923.html; and, "The Guidelines for Japan-U.S. Defense Cooperation," Ministry of Defense, Japan, April 27, 2015, http://www.mod.go.jp/e /d_act/anpo/shishin_20150427e.html.

31. "Report of the Advisory Panel on Reconstruction of the Legal Basis for Security," Prime Minister of Japan and His Cabinet, June 24, 2008, http://www.kantei.go.jp/jp/singi/anzenhosyou/report.pdf. By the time this report came out, Abe had already stepped down as prime minister.

32. "Report of the Advisory Panel on Reconstruction of the Legal Basis for Security," Prime Minister of Japan and His Cabinet, May 15, 2014, http://www.kantei.go.jp/jp/singi/anzenhosyou2/dai7/houkoku_en.pdf.

33. Advocates of constitutional reinterpretation were supportive of this new expanded view of Japan's defense needs, but many thought Abe did not go far enough. Akiyama Masahiro, president of a prominent conservative think tank, the Tokyo Foundation, dubbed Abe's effort a "crusade" and yet felt it did not go far enough in addressing Japan's defense needs during peacetime. See http://www.tokyofoundation.org/en/articles/2014 /redefining-self-defense. Others, including Kitaoka Shin'ichi, the lead scholar in the prime minister's advisory group, had hoped that the prime minister would embrace collective security—the core principle of the United Nations—as the most appropriate means of ensuring Japan's security, a position that would have allowed Japan to come to the aid of others under attack. "The U.S.-Japan Alliance: Next Steps and Future Vision, Dialogue with Dr. Shin'ichi Kitaoka," Center for Strategic and

International Studies, June 16, 2014, https://www.youtube.com/watch?v =8uBum83FlaM.

34. The report argued, "Tensions have been rising especially in the Asia-Pacific region. Territorial and other destabilizing elements exist. The rise of China's influence is evident. . . . Against the background of the increase in military budget, China has installed and quantitatively expanded its arsenal of latest weapons such as modern combat aircraft and new types of ballistic missiles in a dramatic manner. . . . In addition, there have been attempts to unilaterally change the status quo by force based on their own territorial assertions. This makes it imperative that Japan fulfills an even greater role for ensuring peace and stability in the region, as the risks have been increasing." The Advisory Panel on Reconstruction of the Legal Basis for Security, "Report of the Advisory Panel on Reconstruction of the Legal Basis for Security," May 15, 2014, https://www.kantei.go.jp/jp/singi/anzenhosyou2/dai7/houkoku_en.pdf.

35. "Three New Conditions for the 'Use of Force' as Measures for Self-Defense Permitted Under Article Nine of the Constitution," *Defense of Japan 2016*, Ministry of Defense, Japan, 165–166. According to media reporting by the *Nikkei* and the *Asahi*, for example, the Kōmeitō pressured the government to change a few words to further narrow the conditionality, such as from "おそれがある" [poses a danger] to "明白な 危険がある" [poses a clear danger] and from "他国" [a foreign country] to "密接な関係にある他国" [a foreign country that is in a close relationship with Japan], while the LDP changed from "国民の権利を守 るために他に適当な手段がない" [When there is no other appropriate means available to repel the attack and protect the right of its people] to "我が国の存立を全うし、国民を守るために他に適当な手段がない" [When there is no other appropriate means available to repel the attack and ensure Japan's survival and protect its people].

"Shūdanteki jieiken de ōsuji gōi LDP-Kōmeitō kōshi yōken shūsei icchi" [Major agreement on right of collective self-defense: LDP and Kōmeitō agree to correct on condition for use of force], *Nikkei Shimbun*, June 25, 2014. For more detailed account of each meeting, see https://www.Kōmei.or.jp/news/detail/20140521_14024.

"Kōmei iron wo kakaeta mama 'yōnin' shūdanteki jieiken de ichinin toritsuke" [Kōmeitō defers on the right of collective self-defense, acceptance with disagreement], *Nikkei Shimbun,* July 1, 2014. LDP Vice President Kōmura echoed Yamaguchi's statement by saying, "憲法9条が ある限り、これ以上のことはできない。ほぼ限界点だ." "Shūdanteki jieiken: Jikō gōi konseki ni kakugi kettei buryoku kōshi hadome naku" [Right of collective self-defense: LDP-Kōmeitō agrees, cabinet decision this evening, no breaks on the use of force], *Mainichi Shimbun,* July 1, 2014.

36. Media polling revealed a mixed picture. The *Yomiuri Shimbun,* for example, showed a sharper decline in support for the Abe cabinet after its decision in July 2014 (9 percent) than during the Diet deliberations over the new security legislation in September 2015 (4 percent). The *Nikkei Shimbun* reported a 5 percent drop in approval in July 2014 but a 6 percent drop in September 2015. The liberal *Asahi Shimbun,* however, showed a 1 percent increase in approval in July 2014 while registering a 1 percent drop in approval in September 2015. *Yomiuri Shimbun,* July 4, 2014, and September 21, 2015; *Nikkei Shimbun,* July 28, 2014, and September 21, 2015; and *Asahi Shimbun,* July 6, 2014, and September 21, 2015.

37. In September 2015, a *Nikkei Shimbun* survey showed that 78 percent of the public thought the government had insufficiently explained the security bills. Polls conducted by the *Yomiuri Shimbun* and *Mainichi Shimbun* put that number at 82 percent and 78 percent, respectively.

38. Quoted in Sheila A. Smith, "Reinterpreting Japan's Constitution," *Asia Unbound,* Council on Foreign Relations, July 2, 2014, http://blogs.cfr.org /asia/2014/07/02/reinterpreting-japans-constitution/.

39. "(Kenpō kō) tenkan anpo hōsei (4) guē zōn kiki hinpatsu (rensai)" [(Constitution examined) shift with security legislation (4) repeated crises in the gray zone (series)], *Yomiuri Shimbun,* July 8, 2014. In Japanese, Kōmura stated, "これは、軍と警察の100年戦争だ。今回の 整理で50年ぐらいに縮まったが、これ以上突っ込んだら大変なことに なる。"

40. Sheila A. Smith, "Japan's Future Strategic Options and the U.S.-Japan Alliance," in *Japan's Nuclear Option: Security, Politics, and Policy in the 21st Century,* ed. Benjamin L. Self and Jeffrey W. Thompson (Washington, DC: Stimson Center, 2003).

41. Speaking to Japan's National Press Club (日本記者クラブ) on May 17, 2017, Onodera Itsunori called for the government to consider acquiring

the ability to strike enemy bases, arguing that "neutralizing a missile before it is launched is the surest way of defending against a missile attack." In Japanese, "撃つ前のミサイルを無力化するのが一番確実なミサイル防衛だ。" *Mainichi Shimbun,* May 18, 2017.

42. For the report by the ballistic missile subcommittee of the Policy Research Council, see https://jimin.ncss.nifty.com/pdf/news/policy/134586_1.pdf. On the subject of a conventional strike, it says, "政府は、わが国に対して誘導弾等による攻撃が行われた場合、そのような攻撃を防ぐのにやむをえない必要最小限度の措置として、他に手段がない場合に発射基地を叩くことについては、従来から憲法が認める自衛の範囲に含まれ可能と言明しているが、敵基地の位置情報の把握それを守るレーダーサイトの無力化、精密誘導ミサイル等による攻撃といったの要な装備体系については「現在は保有せず、計画もない」との立場をとっている。"

43. The Abe cabinet passed a resolution for revising the Implementation Plans for the International Peace Cooperation Assignment for the United Nations Mission in South Sudan on November 15, 2016. The revised plan included the following: "With regard to the duration of international peace cooperation mission, even if the five basic principles on our nations' participation in the United Nations Peace Keeping Forces are met, the National Security Council will order the South Sudan International Peace Cooperation Unit to withdraw if it sees that Japanese forces cannot operate in safety and perform their mission." In Japanese, "国際平和協力業務が行われる期間中において、我が国として国際連合平和維持隊に参加するに際しての基本的な五つの原則が満たされている場合であっても、安全を確保しつつ有意義な活動を実施することが困難と認められる場合には、国家安全保障会議における審議の上、南スーダン国際平和協力隊を撤収する。" See "Minami sūdan kokusai heiwa kyōryoku gyōmu jisshi keikaku" [Implementation Plans for the International Peace Cooperation Assignment for the United Nations Mission in South Sudan], Prime Minister's Office and His Cabinet, November 15, 2011, http://www.pko.go.jp/pko_j/data/pdf/02/data02_27.pdf. "Shin ninmu ni kansuru kihonteki na kangaekata" [Basic Understanding of Assigning New Missions], Prime Minister's Office and His Cabinet, Cabinet Secretariat, Ministry of Foreign Affairs, Ministry of Defense, November 15, 2016, http://www.kantei.go.jp/jp/tyoukanpress/201611/__icsFiles/afieldfile/2016/11/15/20161115shiryou.pdf.

44. In the Diet, opposition legislators challenged the government's management of the South Sudan deployment after internal memos written by the GSDF in July were revealed. The Abe cabinet announced that the SDF would return to Japan by the end of May 2017. Chief Cabinet Secretary Suga Yoshihide denied on March 11 that the withdrawal decision was due to the deteriorating security situation in South Sudan. Abe echoed this in the Upper House Budget Committee by saying that this withdrawal was not due to deterioration of public order [in South Sudan], and it was simply a policy decision to put a break. "Minami sūdan tesshūan 16 nen 9 gatsu fujō kanbōchōkan 'chian to mukankei'" [The Proposal to Withdraw Forces from South Sudan Surfaced in September 2016—Chief Cabinet Secretary Suga Says "Nothing to Do with its Public Order"], *Nikkei Shimbun*, March 11, 2017. "'Chian akka gen'in de nai shushō, minami sūdan tesshū de san'in yosan'" ['Deteriorating Public Order Was Not the Reason,' Says Prime Minister on Withdrawal of Forces from South Sudan at the Upper House Budget Committee], *Yomiuri Shimbun*, March 14, 2017.

45. On polls on the right of collective self-defense, see "Kenpō kaishaku henkō 'hantai' 51 percent, shūdanteki jieiken kōshi de honsha yoron chōsa" [Reinterpreting constitution 'oppose' 51 percent—Our survey on exercise of collective self-defense], *Nikkei Shimbun*, May 25, 2014. The *Asahi Shimbun* surveyed the divergent methodologies and particular characteristics of Japanese media polling on the reinterpretation of the constitution. See "(Ikegami Akira no shimbun naname yomi) Shūdanteki jieiken to yoron chōsa kokumin no mayoi ga tsutawaru ka" [Ikegami Akira's diagonal reading: Collective self-defense and polls, would people's hesitancy be heard?], *Asahi Shimbun*, May 30, 2014. Also see *Asahi Shimbun*, May 26, 2014. Two months later, another *Asahi* poll found opinion was divided over the policy change, but a majority (63 percent) felt that the way Abe had approached reinterpretation was inappropriate, and even more (72 percent) felt that there was insufficient debate over the reinterpretation of the constitution. "Shūdanteki jieiken yōnin 'yoku nakatta' 50 percent and naikaku shijiritsu 44 percent—Asahi Shimbunsha yoron chōsa" [Collective self-defense 'not a good idea' 50 percent, cabinet approval rating 44 percent—Asahi Shimbun Public Survey], *Asahi Shimbun*, July 6, 2014. On Prime Minister Abe's views on

the current constitution, see *Sankei Shimbun,* April 27, 2013, in which he stated, "It is simply an illusion to argue that we, the Japanese, can take credit for opening a new, postwar era when we drafted it. In 1946, our constitution was made up by amateurs in the General Headquarters (GHQ) with no background in constitutional or international law in only eight days." "New Year's Reflection by Prime Minister Shinzō Abe," Prime Minister of Japan and His Cabinet, January 1, 2014, http://japan.kantei.go.jp/96_abe/statement/201401/newyear_e.html.

46. According to the *2012 White Paper* of the Ministry of Land, Infrastructure, Transport and Tourism, a height of over 9.3 meters (the prior maximum height recorded by the Japan Meteorological Agency's domestic tsunami observatory locations) was recorded at Soma in Fukushima sixty-five minutes after the earthquake. Various academics and research institutions have looked into tsunami damage, one of which affirmed that the tsunami inundated the Japanese coastline at the point of a 30m altitude. Judging from that research, it is thought that the tsunami was higher than recorded at some areas, resulting in extraordinary damages: http://www.mlit.go.jp/english/white-paper/2010.pdf. Six days after the earthquake, CNN reported that 450,000 were displaced by the earthquake and tsunami: "Six Days Later, Japanese Still Confronting Magnitude of Quake Crisis," CNN, March 17, 2011. As of September 28, 2018, the Reconstruction Agency reported that 56, 842 people are still unable to return to their homes: http://www.reconstruction.go.jp/topics/main-cat2/sub-cat2-1/20180928_hinansha.pdf. The most recent survey by the Cabinet Secretariat was conducted in 2015. See http://survey.gov-online.go.jp/h26/h26-bouei/zh/z07.html.

47. The tables are compiled from the *Yomiuri Shimbun's* surveys on Japan's constitution, found here: "2002–2016 What Should We Do with Article Nine? (Yomiuri)," http://i.cfr.org/content/newsletter/files/Yomiuri%20Article%20Nine%202002-2016.pdf; and "1995–2016 Reasons for Supporting Constitutional Revision (Yomiuri)," http://i.cfr.org/content/newsletter/files/Yomiuri%20Article%20Nine%201995-2016.pdf. Sheila A. Smith and Ayumi Teraoka, "Early Postwar Attitudes on Constitutional Revision," *Asia Unbound,* Council on Foreign Relations, July 28, 2016, https://www.cfr.org/blog-post/early-postwar-attitudes-constitutional-revision. Masatoshi Asaoka and Ayumi Teraoka,

"Japanese Public Opinion on Constitutional Revision in 2016," *Asia Unbound,* Council on Foreign Relations, August 1, 2016, https://www.cfr.org/blog-post/japanese-public-opinion-constitutional-revision-2016.

48. The *Yomiuri Shimbun* proposed draft revisions of Japan's constitution three times—in 1994, 2000, and 2004. The text of all three versions can be found here: https://info.yomiuri.co.jp/media/yomiuri/feature/kaiseishian.html. The *Sankei Shimbun*'s proposal in 2013, entitled "Kokumin no kenpō" [The People's Constitution], can be found here: http://www.sankei.com/politics/news/141030/plt1410300023-n1.html.

49. In January 2000, the Diet Committee on Constitutional Revision (*Kenpō chōsa kai*) was formed and included the majority of political parties in the parliament. A range of issues were discussed in considering what might be included in a revised constitution. In the Lower House committee, the initial topics for discussion were local governmental autonomy, fundamental human rights, and subsidies for private schools. The Upper House discussed Japan's contribution to international security and the bicameral structure of the Diet. See *Yomiuri Shimbun,* January 3, 2000. The committee released an interim report of more than nine hundred pages on November 1, 2002, revealing the difficulties of devising a consensus on what a revised constitution might look like. A final report was released three years later, on April 15, 2005. These findings can be found at http://www.shugiin.go.jp/internet/itdb_kenpou.nsf/html/kenpou/chosa/index.htm.

50. The purpose of this cross-party commission was to draft a bill supported by various parties, but this was not possible. The ruling coalition of the LDP and Kōmeitō submitted their bill, and the largest opposition party, the DPJ, submitted its bill on May 26, 2006. A detailed history of the Diet committees on the constitution can be found here: http://www.shugiin.go.jp/internet/itdb_kenpou.nsf/html/kenpou/keii.htm.

51. The full Japanese term is 日本国憲法の改正手続に関する法律 (*Nihonkoku kenpō no kaisei tetsuzuki ni kansuru hōritsu*). A few revisions were introduced into the law in May and June 2014. The Lower House Diet record says that the bill was passed by a majority vote on April 16, 2007. A copy of the law is available at http://kokkai.ndl.go.jp/SENTAKU/syugiin/166/0001/16604130001022.pdf). The vote in the Upper House was 122 for and 99 against (221 MPs present), and the bill was passed on

May 14: http://kokkai.ndl.go.jp/SENTAKU/sangiin/166/0001
/16605140001024.pdf.

52. Sheila A. Smith, "Voters Give Abe an Opening for Constitutional Debate," *Asia Unbound,* Council on Foreign Relations, July 11, 2016, https://www.cfr.org/blog-post/voters-give-abe-opening-constitutional -debate.

53. "Shushō kaikenan Kōmei ga rikai 'Jieitai meiki' Ishin kangei, minshin hanpatsu" [Kōmeito expresses sympathy for prime minister's constitution revision proposal; Japan Innovation Party welcomes mentioning the Self-Defense Force; and the Democratic Party opposes it], *Yomiuri Shimbun,* May 4, 2017.

"Ji kō i kaiken giron e jietiai meiki shushōan ni dōi" [LDP, Kōmeitō, and JIP move forward with constitutional revision, agreeing with prime minister's proposal to mention the Self-Defense Force], *Yomiuri Shimbun,* May 4, 2017.

54. Abe's political future seemed in jeopardy as his cabinet faced repeated revelations of an influence scandal. Two examples of favorable government ment decisions, one discounting the sale of government land to a school that claimed Abe's wife as a board member and another giving preferential tial treatment to a friend of the prime minister's, threatened to unravel the cabinet. Public approval ratings plummeted twice—once in the summer of 2017 when the scandals were discovered, and again in early 2018 when it was revealed that bureaucrats had doctored documents presented to the Diet during an inquiry. Nonetheless, in a snap election for the Lower House, Abe led his party to victory again, and continued to push for revising Article Nine. See *Japan Decides 2017: The Japanese General Election,* ed. Robert J. Pekkanen, Steven R. Reed, Ethan Scheiner, and Daniel M. Smith (London: Palgrave Macmillan, 2018), particularly chapter 16, "Constitutional Revision in the 2017 Election," 297–312, by Kenneth Mori McElwain.

55. Abe Shinzō, *Utsukushii kuni e* [Toward a beautiful country] (Tokyo: Bungei Shunjū, 2006), later revised as *Atarashii kuni e* [Toward a new country] (Tokyo: Bungei Shunjū, 2013). On the seventieth anniversary of the end of World War II, Abe drafted a new prime ministerial statement that included reference to Japan's erroneous decision and postwar recovery in which he noted his generation's responsibility to future generations of Japanese to apologize for the past. See Sheila A. Smith, "Japan-China

Relations in the Post-Reconciliation Era," *Journal of Asian Studies* 74, no. 4, November 2015, 803–809, for a comparison of the Japanese and Chinese commemorations of the end of World War II in 2015.

## 5. Relying on Borrowed Power

1. The sense in Japan that the U.S.-Japan alliance was in peril in the wake of the Cold War is captured in Funabashi Yoichi's seminal work, *Alliance Adrift* (New York: Council on Foreign Relations Press, 1999). Funabashi, at the time the chief diplomatic correspondent for the *Asahi Shimbun*, chronicles the disconnect between Washington and Tokyo as they sought to respond to North Korean proliferation, the base crisis in Okinawa, and the effort to revamp the guidelines for military cooperation.

2. Two articles in the 1960 Treaty of Mutual Defense and Cooperation between the United States and Japan reflected this strategic bargain: Article Five provided that the United States and Japan "would act to meet the common danger" in case of "an armed attack against either Party in the territories under the administration of Japan." Article Six obligated Japan to provide bases and facilities for U.S. forces "for the purpose of contributing to the security of Japan and the maintenance of international peace and security in the Far East." See Chapter 1.

3. Sakamoto Kazuya, *Nichibei dōmei no kizuna—Anpo jōyaku to sōgosei no mosaku* [The bonds of U.S.-Japan alliance—The security treaty and search for reciprocity] (Tokyo: Yūikaku, 2000).

4. This memorandum on "prior consultation," referred to as the Kishi-Herter Note, reflected the growing concern within Japan that U.S. forces could be used for purposes that were not in the interest of Japan. The note can be accessed from the National Graduate Institute for Policy Studies' The World and Japan database project: "Exchanged Notes, Regarding the Implementation of Article VI of Treaty of Mutual Cooperation and Security between Japan and the United States of America," http://worldjpn.grips.ac.jp/documents/texts/docs/19600119 .T2E.html.

5. "Joint Statement by President Nixon and Prime Minister Eisaku Satō," November 21, 1969, http://ryukyu-okinawa.net/pages/archive/sato69

.html. For analysis of the impact of the Vietnam War on Japan, see Thomas R. H. Havens, *Fire across the Sea: The Vietnam War and Japan, 1965–1975* (Princeton: Princeton University Press, 2014).

6. U.S. discontent with its European allies over burden sharing reached a peak in 1971, with Senator Mike Mansfield's proposal of an amendment to the Selective Service Bill that would have halved the number of U.S. troops stationed in Europe; Phil Williams, "The Mansfield Amendment of 1971," in *The Senate and US Troops in Europe* (London: Palgrave Macmillan, 1985). In 2014, at a summit in Wales, NATO leaders agreed to meet defense spending levels of 2 percent of GDP by 2024; "Wales Summit Declaration," September 5, 2014, https://www.nato.int/cps/ic /natohq/official_texts_112964.htm.

7. The SOFA accompanied the 1960 treaty and set the terms for managing the presence of U.S. forces on Japanese soil. It covered a range of issues, from taxes, to the status of criminal jurisdiction, to imports of personal goods, and it largely provided extraterritorial protections to U.S. military personnel and in some cases to their dependents. As defense minister in 1978, Kanemaru argued in the Lower House that Japanese should have some compassion (*omoiyari*) for the United States as it struggled to fulfill its military commitments. Japan provided 6.2 billion yen in support of U.S. forces that year. For more information, see *Bōei shisetsu chō kankeishi* [History of Defense Facilities Administration Agency], Defense Facilities Administration Agency, 2007, 160–162, http://www .mod.go.jp/j/profile/choushi/choushi.html.

8. For a detailed account of U.S. involvement in protecting tankers during the Iran-Iraq War, see George K. Walker, "The Tanker War 1980–88: Law and Policy," *International Policy Studies* 74, 2000: 33–105. For a discussion of the late Cold War negotiations between Tokyo and Washington on increasing Japan's fiscal support for the U.S. military, see Sheila A. Smith, "At the Intersection of the Cold War and the Postwar" (PhD diss., Columbia University, 1996), 266–331.

9. U.S. Congress, Senate, Committee on the Budget, *Defense Burden-Sharing*, 101st Congress, 1st sess., 1988, 52.

10. Foreign Minister Maehara's opening remarks in a press conference with U.S. Ambassador to Japan John Roos included this statement: "In the viewpoint that this is a special agreement with strategic importance to

Japan's security and diplomacy, I regard the word 'omoriyari yosan' [compassion support] no longer appropriate. I would like to use the term 'host nation support' going forward." In Japanese, "日本の安全保障、外交における戦略的な特別協定であるという観点から、もはや「思いやり予算」という言葉は適当ではないというのが、私（大臣）の思いでございまして、「ホスト・ネーション・サポート」という言い方を今後はさせていただきたいと考えております" When a journalist asked Maehara to clarify what he meant, he said, "The U.S. forward presence is not only critical for Japan's security but also as a public asset to this region's stability, and the core of this treaty is Article Six. . . . I feel that the nuance of this word 'omoiyari' is not right. In other words, it is in both U.S. and Japan's national interests for U.S. forces to station and for Japan to cover its necessary cost to a certain extent, and it is our strategic decision [to cover the cost]. Thus, the word 'omoiyari' misses the mark, and I would like to use the term 'host national support' from now on." In Japanese,

> この米国のプレゼンスというものについては、日本の安全保障のみならず、この地域の安定の公共財として極めて有用であるという観点から、根本になっているのは日米安保条約の第6条です。...私（大臣）の気持ちとして、思いやりという言葉とはニュアンスが違うということです。つまりは米軍が駐留し、ある程度の必要な経費を日本が負担するということは、日本の国益に資するのだと、両国の国益に資する戦略的な判断なのだという点から、思いやりという言葉はずれているということを申し上げて、ホスト・ネーション・サポートという言葉をそのまま使わせていただきたいということを申し上げているわけでございます

The full text is available at "Gaimu daijin kaiken kiroku" [Record of press briefing by foreign minister], Ministry of Foreign Affairs, Japan, January 21, 2010, http://www.mofa.go.jp/mofaj/press/kaiken/gaisho/g _1101.html#5-A.

11. Emma Chanlett-Avery and Ian E. Rinehart, *The U.S.-Japan Alliance* (Congressional Research Service, February 9, 2016). For the Ministry of Foreign Affairs text of the 2016 Special Measures Agreement, see https://www.mofa.go.jp/mofaj/press/release/press4_003168.html.

12. "The Basic Plan Regarding the Measures Based on the Law Concerning the Special Measures on Humanitarian and Reconstruction Assistance in Iraq," press conference by Prime Minister Koizumi Junichirō, December 9, 2003, http://japan.kantei.go.jp/koizumispeech/2003/12/09press_e.html.

13. "Historical Reports—Military Only—1950, 1953–1999—Worldwide Manpower Distribution by Geographical Area (M05)," Defense Manpower Data Center, Department of Defense, https://www.dmdc.osd.mil/appj/dwp/dwp_reports.jsp.

14. Much of the land in Okinawa used by the U.S. military was private land that had been forcibly taken during World War II, and landowners had long sought redress for the continued use of the land for military purposes. Okinawa's governors had always stepped in when individual landowners refused to sign the leases, but in the midst of the 1995 crisis, Ōta became the first to render these leases unconstitutional. Sheila A. Smith, "Challenging National Authority: Okinawa Prefecture and the U.S. Military Bases," in *Local Voices, National Issues: The Impact of Local Initiative in Japanese Policy-Making,* ed. Sheila A. Smith (Ann Arbor: University of Michigan Press, 2000), 75–114; Masamichi S. Inoue, *Okinawa and the U.S. Military: Identity Making in the Age of Globalization* (New York: Columbia University Press, 2007).

15. See Chapter 1.

16. Both an interim report and a final report by the Special Action Committee on Okinawa can be found here: http://www.mofa.go.jp/region/n-america/us/security/seco.html and http://www.mofa.go.jp/region/n-america/us/security/96saco1.html. Over the years it took to plan the relocation of Futenma, the Japanese and U.S. governments spent vast sums of taxpayer dollars. The Japanese government expenses included relocation of U.S. Marine training exercises, subsidies for local communities, and the continued rent of Futenma base land. The U.S. government also assessed basing needs and force posture reorganization, as well as the establishment of cultural and educational training and outreach necessary for improving relations with the local community in Okinawa. Perhaps most costly was developing a workable proposal for a new runway that would be acceptable to Tokyo, Okinawa officials, and the U.S. military.

17. Inoue, *Okinawa and the U.S. Military.*

18. Tokyo policy makers and security experts bemoaned Okinawan efforts to gain economic benefit from the base issue. One leading negotiator, former Ministry of Defense Vice Minister Moriya Takemasa, wrote a scathing critique of Governor Inamine when he retired from the Ministry. Moriya was later convicted of bribery and remains in jail. Morimoto Satoshi, a professor of international security at Takushoku University, also wrote of this period in the base negotiations, chronicling the role of U.S., Japanese, and Okinawan negotiators in the complex effort to address the mid-1990s protest movement. See 普天間の謎―基地返還問題迷走15年の総て [The enigma of Futenma—An overview of a 15-year odyssey of Okinawa base consolidation] (Tokyo: Kairyusha, 2010). Morimoto went on to become the minister of defense from June 2012 through December 2012 in the Noda cabinet, the third and final DPJ government.

19. "Denny Tamaki, critic of U.S. bases on Okinawa, wins election," *AP News*, October 1, 2018.

20. *Defense of Japan 2016,* Ministry of Defense, Japan, 257, http://www.mod.go.jp/e/publ/w_paper/pdf/2016/DOJ2016_2-4-4_web.pdf.

21. The Japan Coast Guard tracks the number of Chinese vessels that enter the territorial waters of the Senkaku Islands and the contiguous sea: http://www.kaiho.mlit.go.jp/mission/senkaku/senkaku.html.

22. "F-15s Transferred to Okinawa Base to Strengthen Defense against China," *Mainichi Shimbun,* February 1, 2016, http://mainichi.jp/english/articles/20160201/p2a/00m/ona/007000c.

23. Policy makers and analysts in Washington continue to urge Tokyo to consider deeper integration of military planning in order to improve the alliance's ability to respond to the growing military pressures on Japan. See, for example, the 2018 report, "More Important Than Ever: Renewing the U.S.-Japan Alliance for the 21st Century," led by former Deputy Secretary of State Richard L. Armitage and former dean of Harvard University's Kennedy School of Government, Joseph S. Nye Jr. The report was published by the Center for Strategic and International Studies and is available here: https://www.csis.org/events/us-japan-alliance-more-important-ever.

24. Article Five of the treaty for NATO provides for reciprocity in the defense of its signatories. Not only did the United States commit itself

to the defense of its NATO allies, but NATO allies were also committed to assist the United States should it be attacked. This provision has only been used once since NATO was concluded, and that was by the United Kingdom after the terrorist attacks on the United States on September 11, 2001. The United Kingdom Royal Air Force took to the skies off of North America to provide assistance in the defense of the U.S. mainland. See more on Article Five on NATO's website, http://www.nato.int/cps/en/natohq/topics_110496.htm. Also see "After the Attacks: The Alliance; For First Time, NATO Invokes Joint Defense Pact with U.S.," *New York Times,* September 13, 2001.

25. See Patrick M. Cronin and Michael J. Green, *Redefining the U.S.-Japan Alliance: Tokyo's National Defense Program* (Washington, DC: Institute for National Strategic Studies, 1994). Also see the report chaired by Richard L. Armitage, *The United States and Japan: Advancing Toward a Mature Partnership* (Washington, DC: Institute for National Strategic Studies, 2000); and Richard L. Armitage, and Joseph S. Nye Jr., *The U.S.-Japan Alliance: Getting Asia Right through 2020* (Washington, DC: Center for Strategic and International Studies, 2007).

26. The 1997 guidelines begins by stating its aim: "The aim of these Guidelines is to create a solid basis for more effective and credible U.S.-Japan cooperation under normal circumstances, in case of an armed attack against Japan, and in situations in areas surrounding Japan." It went on to explain the term "areas surrounding Japan":

> Recognizing that a situation in areas surrounding Japan may develop into an armed attack against Japan, the two Governments will be mindful of the close interrelationship of the two requirements: preparations for the defense of Japan and responses to or preparations for situations in areas surrounding Japan.
>
> . . . Situations in areas surrounding Japan will have an important influence on Japan's peace and security. The concept, situations in areas surrounding Japan, is not geographic but situational. The two Governments will make every effort, including diplomatic efforts, to prevent such situations from occurring. When the two Governments reach a common assessment of the state of each situation, they will effectively

coordinate their activities. In responding to such situations, measures taken may differ depending on circumstances.

"The Guidelines for Japan-U.S. Defense Cooperation," Ministry of Defense, Japan, September 23, 1997, http://www.mod.go.jp/e/d_act/anpo /19970923.html.
27. In a 1985 debate in the Upper House of the Diet over U.S.-Japan defense cooperation, Prime Minister Nakasone clarified the Japanese government's position on military command in the U.S.-Japan alliance as follows:

> We resolutely guarantee that the U.S.-Japan security treaty, and the various agreements that are based on it, are premised on the decision-making authority of the Japanese people. Even in considering under the U.S.-Japan Defense Cooperation Guidelines how to respond with U.S. forces in the case of an emergency (conflict), we have been resolute in our separation of command for Japanese forces. I would like you to be aware that this is how our forces are structured.
>
> In Japanese: 日米の安全保障条約、それに基づくもろもろの協定、取り決め等におきましては、毅然として日本の民族自決権というものは確保されておるのでありまして、有時のときの共同対処に対しても、ガイドライン等におきまして指揮系統は毅然として分かれておる、そういう形になっておるということを御認識願いたいと思うのであります。

Remarks by Nakasone Yasuhiro, Upper House, Plenary Session, 103rd Diet Session, October 18, 1985, http://kokkai.ndl.go.jp/SENTAKU /sangiin/103/0010/10310180010003.pdf.
28. Kusunoki Ayako, "Yoshida Shigeru to nichibei dōmei no keisei" [Yoshida Shigeru and formation of U.S.-Japan Alliance] (conference paper, National Institute for Defense Studies, 39–47), http://www.nids .mod.go.jp/event/other/just/pdf/05.pdf. Kusunoki refers to the declassified memorandum from the U.S. Joint Chiefs of Staff: Joint Chiefs of Staff, Decision on JCS 2180/71, a memorandum by the Chief of Staff, U.S. Army, "Proposed Agreement between the U.S. and Japan to Establish Combined Defense Measures for Japan," June 2, 1952, Geographic File, 1951–1953, 092 Japan (12-12-50), Sec. 12, RG 218,

National Archives and Records Administration, College Park, Maryland.

29. Not all U.S. strategic planners welcomed Japan's growing military power, however. Over the years, U.S. military leaders made no secret of their belief that the alliance was the primary mechanism for keeping Japanese military power in check. Major General Henry C. Stackpole, commander of Marine Corps bases in Japan, in an interview with the *Washington Post* in March 1990, argued against the withdrawal of U.S. forces from Asia after the Cold War. Noting that Japan already had a "very, very potent military," Stackpole stated publicly what many only said in private: "No one wants a rearmed, resurgent Japan.... So we are a cap in the bottle, if you will." See Fred Hiatt, "Marine General: U.S. Troops Must Stay in Japan," *Washington Post,* March 27, 1990.

30. Tsuchiya Shinako, Plenary Session, Lower House, 171th Diet Session, June 19, 2009, http://kokkai.ndl.go.jp/SENTAKU/syugiin/171/0001 /1710619000104I.pdf. Asō's full comment is as follows:

サーチライトとか音響マイクとか、ああいったものだけで十分対応はこれまでのところはできておりますが、今後そうならないケースのことも考えておくというのが大事なところでありまして、そういったことを考えていったら、これはいずれも強盗というか海賊相手の話なので、基本的には海上警備行動というもので対応できるというように考えております。基本はそう思っております。

ただ、今問題になってきているのは、隣の日本国籍に所属していない艦船に対してということで、向こうから救助を求められたというようなときが、だんだんその範囲が、同じ地域にいれば、そっちの方は助けるけれども、こっちは助けないというようなことができるかなという現実問題を考えたときに、今回の法案を出させていただいたという経緯を考えた場合、今回の考え方としては、基本的には間違っていないと思っております。

Asō Tarō, Special Committee on Counterpiracy and Counterterrorism and Japan's Cooperation and Support Activities, Lower House, 171th Diet Session, April 23, 2009, http://kokkai.ndl.go.jp/SENTAKU/syugiin/171 /0202/17104230202007.pdf. The DPJ's majority in the Upper House slowed passage of the bill, and it went through the Lower House twice as a result. The DPJ also proposed an alternative bill that strengthened Diet oversight of the dispatch of the SDF and the Japan Coast Guard.

31. The command structure for BMD was set forth in July 2005 in a partial revision of the Defense Agency Establishment Law of 1954. In cases where the defense ministry recognized the need to defend against the harm to the lives or the property within Japan's sovereign territory, the minister could, with the approval of the prime minister, order the SDF to destroy incoming missiles. The text in Japanese is as follows:

> 第八十二条の二　長官は、弾道ミサイル等（弾道ミサイルその他その落下により人命又は財産に対する重大な被害が生じると認められる物体であつて航空機以外のものをいう。以下同じ。）が我が国に飛来するおそれがあり、その落下による我が国領域における人命又は財産に対する被害を防止するため必要があると認めるときは、内閣総理大臣の承認を得て、自衛隊の部隊に対し、我が国に向けて現に飛来する弾道ミサイル等を我が国領域又は公海（海洋法に関する国際連合条約に規定する排他的経済水域を含む。）の上空において破壊する措置をとるべき旨を命ずることができる。
>
> 　　2　長官は、前項に規定するおそれがなくなつたと認めるときは、内閣総理大臣の承認を得て、速やかに、同項の命令を解除しなければならない。
>
> 　　3　長官は、第一項の場合のほか、事態が急変し同項の内閣総理大臣の承認を得るいとまがなく我が国に向けて弾道ミサイル等が飛来する緊急の場合における我が国領域における人命又は財産に対する被害を防止するため、長官が作成し、内閣総理大臣の承認を受けた緊急対処要領に従い、あらかじめ、自衛隊の部隊に対し、同項の命令をすることができる。この場合において、長官は、その命令に係る措置をとるべき期間を定めるものとする。
>
> 　　4　前項の緊急対処要領の作成及び内閣総理大臣の承認に関し必要な事項は、政令で定める。
>
> 　　5　内閣総理大臣は、第一項又は第三項の規定による措置がとられたときは、その結果を、速やかに、国会に報告しなければならない。

See http://www.shugiin.go.jp/internet/itdb_housei.nsf/html/housei
/16220050729088.htm.

32. Abe's thinking was expressed in his personal writings, as well as in his
comments in the Diet. In his book *Atarashii kuni e* [Toward a new
country] (Tokyo: Bungei Shunju, 2013), Abe expresses his deep
frustration about his nation's lack of willingness to defend itself and its
reliance on others to defend the peace. Later, when he returned to the
prime minister's office, Abe followed through on his idea of reinterpreting the right of collective self-defense. When the Abe cabinet
announced its decision to change the government's interpretation, Abe
noted, "Our peace is not given to us by others. There is no other path
than to build it ourselves," http://www.kantei.go.jp/jp/96_abe/statement
/2014/0701kaiken.html.

33. Before taking office in 2009, some members of the DPJ expressed
interest in possibly allowing the right of collective self-defense. For
example, Okada Katsuya, then secretary general of the party, stated the
following in a roundtable discussion held by the *Yomiuri Shimbun* in
2003:

> 集団的自衛権は非常に幅広い概念だ。第三国が米国と戦争にな
> った時、日本が出かけて行って武力行使をするのは憲法を逸脱
> している。米国本土が攻撃された場合も憲法上は問題だ。た
> だ、日本を防衛するために活動している米軍が攻撃された場
> 合、日本に対する行為と見なし、日本が反撃する余地を残すの
> は十分合理性がある。今の憲法は、すべての集団的自衛権の行
> 使を認めていないとは言い切っておらず、集団的自衛権の中身
> を具体的に考えることで十分整合性を持って説明できる。た
> だ、日本を守るため公海上に展開している米軍艦艇が攻撃され
> た場合という限られたケースなので、むしろ個別的自衛権の範
> 囲を拡張したと考えた方がいい。集団的自衛権という言葉を使
> わない方がいい。

"Yoyatō kanjichō kenpō zadankai seiji no kasseika kokusai kōken wo
genjitsuteki shiten de—tokushū" [A roundtable discussion on constitution among secretary generals of ruling and opposition parties: In a
realistic viewpoint of international cooperation and revitalization of
politics—Special edition], *Yomiuri Shimbun,* May 3, 2003.

34. The advisory panel that Abe appointed to consider constitutional reinterpretation discussed the idea of collective security. "Report of the Advisory Panel on Reconstruction of the Legal Basis for Security," The Advisory Panel on Reconstruction of the Legal Basis for Security, Prime Minister of Japan, June 24, 2008, http://www.kantei.go.jp/jp/singi /anzenhosyou/report.pdf.

35. Secretary of State Condoleezza Rice, Secretary of Defense Donald Rumsfeld, Minister of Foreign Affairs Asō Tarō, and Minister of State for Defense Nukaga Fukushirō, "United States-Japan Roadmap for Realignment Implementation," United States-Japan Security Consultative Committee Document, May 1, 2006, http://www.mofa.go.jp/region /n-america/us/security/scc/doc0605.html.

36. Each of the three texts of the U.S.-Japan Defense Cooperation Guidelines can be found on the Ministry of Defense website: 1978 (http://www.mod.go.jp/e/d_act/anpo/pdf/19781127.pdf), 1997 (http://www.mod.go.jp/e/d_act/anpo/pdf/19970923.pdf), and 2015 (https://www.mofa.go.jp/files/000078188.pdf).

37. This passivity with regard to Japan's reliance on the U.S. nuclear umbrella is the premise of a new book by one of Japan's leading security thinkers and practitioners. Satō Yukio, in the prologue to *Sashikakerareta kasa—Beikoku no kaku yokushiryoku to nihon no anzen hosho* [Under an extended umbrella: U.S. nuclear deterrence and Japan's security] (Tokyo: Jiji Tsushinsha, 2017), notes an early statement to Japan's press by then Foreign Minister Shīna Etsusaburo. In 1966, when Shīna was asked by a reporter if Japan was under U.S. nuclear protection, the foreign minister responded, "Yes, there are times when umbrellas are proffered." Satō noted that this passive voice could no longer be used today, and yet it reflects the way in which Japanese leaders have approached extended deterrence.

38. The defining academic account of the Japanese negotiations for a revised U.S.-Japan security treaty led by Prime Minister Kishi can be found in Hara Yoshihisa, *Kishi Nobusuke—Kensei no Seijika* (Tokyo: Iwanami Shinsho, 1995). A second opportunity for defining Japanese interests with regard to U.S. military forces in Japan came when the Ryūkyū and Bonin Islands were returned to Japan. Here again U.S. and Japanese interests in the U.S. military stationed in Japan diverged. The Nixon

administration, in wanting to decrease its ground forces in Asia, nonetheless wanted to ensure its ability to use strategic forces should a conflict erupt on the Korean Peninsula. Gaining Japanese acquiescence to this was essential for the Joint Chiefs, who were uncomfortable with the Japanese government's imposing control over what had been the free use of U.S. forces from occupied Okinawa. Prime Minister Satō Eisaku, however, had promised to put Okinawa's U.S. bases on the same footing as the main islands (*hondo nami*). This meant a more restricted use of the bases under the provisions of the "prior consultation notes" of the 1960 treaty. Significant negotiations between the White House and the prime minister's office produced a compromise that allowed the United States to introduce nuclear weapons should they be needed in a crisis. According to the report of the Ministry of Foreign Affairs on the "so-called secret agreements," a memo prepared in 1968 by then director general of the North American Affairs Bureau, Togo Fumihiko, became the basis of briefings for subsequent prime ministers and foreign ministers with regard to the use of U.S. military forces in Japan. The Ministry of Foreign Affairs, Japan, describes it thus (https://www.mofa.go.jp/mofaj/gaiko/mitsuyaku/pdfs /hokoku_naibu.pdf):

　（ハ）歴代総理、外務大臣への説明
　　　＊上記の昭和 43 年東郷北米局長メモ(文書 1-5)は、同年 1 月 30 日に三木外務大臣、 同 2 月 5 日に佐藤総理大臣、同 12 月 11 日愛知外務大臣に回覧された模様であり、 欄外にそれぞれ「御閲読済」と記述がある。
　　　＊この東郷北米局長のメモは、その後、歴代の総理及び大臣に対する事務次官・北 米局長等からのブリーフに使用された模様。
　　　＊同メモには、平成元年 8 月に栗山外務事務次官から総理、大臣に説明した際の同 次官作成メモが付されており、同メモの中には「双方の立場につき互いに詰めな いとの立場を理解。但し「密約」はなし」と記述されている。

The memo was made public on March 9, 2010. Wakaizumi Kei, Satō's emissary in secret talks with the Richard Nixon White House in the final stages of the Okinawa reversion agreement, revealed this compro-

mise in his memoirs, which were published in 1994 as 他策ナカリシヲ信
ゼムト欲ス and translated into English in 2002, under the title *The Best
Course Available: A Personal Account of the Secret U.S.-Japan Okinawa
Reversion Negotiations, ed.* John Swenson Wright (Honolulu: University
of Hawai'i Press, 2002).

39. U.S. Ambassador Edwin O. Reischauer stated in 1981 that the U.S.
government had long assumed that its ships armed with nuclear
weapons could transit Japanese waters and that this was not subject to
the prior consultation mechanism. *New York Times,* May 19, 1981,
https://www.nytimes.com/1981/05/19/world/nuclear-agreement-on
-japan-reported.html. The declassified U.S. documents can be found
here: https://nsarchive2.gwu.edu/nukevault/ebb291/doc05.pdf and
https://nsarchive2.gwu.edu/nukevault/ebb291/doc06.pdf.

40. For the internal Ministry of Foreign Affairs report, see Ministry of
Foreign Affairs, "*Gaimushō naibu chōsa hōkokusho*" [Ministry of Foreign
Affairs Internal Investigation Report], March 5, 2010, http://www.mofa
.go.jp/mofaj/gaiko/mitsuyaku/pdfs/hokoku_naibu.pdf. For the report
from the expert committee, see "*Yūshikisha iinkai ni yoru hōkokusho*
[Report by the Expert Committee]," March 9, 2010, http://www.mofa
.go.jp/mofaj/gaiko/mitsuyaku/pdfs/hokoku_yushiki.pdf). Foreign
Minister Okada Katsuya's exact words were

> 非核三原則というのは、これはやはり日本自身を核の脅威から
> 遠ざける、こういう考え方に立って行われているものだと私は
> 認識いたしますけれども、いざというときの、日本国民の安全
> というものが危機的状況になったときに原理原則をあくまでも
> 守るのか、それともそこに例外をつくるのか、それはそのとき
> の政権が判断すべきことで、今、将来にわたってそういったこ
> とを縛るというのはできないことだと思います。

The 2010 National Defense Program Guidelines, *Defense of Japan 2011,*
Japan, http://www.mod.go.jp/e/d_act/d_policy/pdf/guidelinesFY2011
.pdf.

41. Obama's Prague speech is available at https://obamawhitehouse.archives
.gov/the-press-office/remarks-president-barack-obama-prague
-delivered. Japanese media has reported that in 2009, Japanese government officials, including Vice Foreign Minister Akiba Takeo, requested

that the U.S. government maintain its theater nuclear forces capable of responding in Asia. *Asahi Shimbun,* May 14, 2018.

42. China has approximately twelve hundred short-range ballistic missiles and two hundred to three hundred medium-range missiles, according to the Department of Defense (*Annual Report to Congress: Military and Security Developments Involving the People's Republic of China 2017,* https://www.defense.gov/Portals/1/Documents/pubs/2017_China_Military_Power_Report.PDF). A 2017 RAND Corporation report on China's nuclear deterrent points out, "The only specific equipment priority that Xi Jinping mentioned in his [2016] remarks on the establishment of the Rocket Force called for 'strengthening medium-range precision strike forces,' which, in the Chinese lexicon, includes both medium- and intermediate-range systems." Eric Heginbotham et al., *China's Evolving Nuclear Deterrent: Major Drivers and Issues for the United States* (Santa Monica, CA: RAND Corporation, 2017), 115.

43. For media coverage of the policy debate on no first use, see David E. Sanger and Thom Shanker, "White House Is Rethinking Nuclear Policy," *New York Times,* February 28, 2010; Mary Beth Sheridan and Walter Pincus, "Obama Must Decide Degree to Which U.S. Swears Off Nuclear Weapons," *Washington Post,* March 5, 2010. The Nuclear Posture Review issued in April 2010 concluded that the United States was not prepared "at the present time to adopt a universal policy that the 'sole purpose' of U.S. nuclear weapons is to deter nuclear attack on the United States and our allies and partners, but will work to establish conditions under which such a policy could be safely adopted." See the full Nuclear Posture Review at https://www.defense.gov/Portals/1/features/defenseReviews/NPR/2010_Nuclear_Posture_Review_Report.pdf.

   For a scholarly review of this aspect of nuclear policy reform, see Michael S. Gerson, "No First Use the Next Step for U.S. Nuclear Policy," *International Security* 35, no. 2 (Fall 2010), 7–47.

44. The *Washington Post* first reported on this internal discussion of nuclear policy change in the final months of the Obama administration on July 10, 2016, and then followed with the report on the allied reaction on August 14, 2016. Included in this article was a report that Prime

Minister Abe had personally conveyed his concerns about a U.S. shift to no first use to Admiral Harry Harris of the U.S. Pacific Command. On August 20, 2016, Prime Minister Abe told the Japanese press that the *Washington Post* account of his conversation with Admiral Harris on no first use was false, and that President Obama's visit to Hiroshima made a strong statement on creating a world without nuclear weapons. He also said the United States has made no decision on a no first use policy, and the Japanese government would continue to work closely with them. The U.S. Pacific Command also denied that Abe and Harris had discussed nuclear policy at their meeting. See *New York Times,* update to August 14, 2016.

45. *New York Times,* September 5, 2016. Press conference with Deputy National Security Advisor for Strategic Communications Ben Rhodes on September 7, 2016, available at https://obamawhitehouse.archives.gov /the-press-office/2016/09/07/press-briefing-press-secretary-josh-earnest -and-deputy-national-security.

46. Heads of the Defense Agency Inō Shigejirō in 1959 and Norota Hōsei in 1999 reiterate this idea. See Sugio Takahashi, "Dealing with the Ballistic Missile Threat: Whether Japan Should Have a Strike Capability under Its Exclusively Defense-Oriented Policy," *NIDS Security Reports,* no. 7 (December 2006), 79–99, http://www.nids.mod.go.jp /english/publication/kiyo/pdf/bulletin_e2006_4_takahashi.pdf.

47. Maehara Seiji asked then head of the Defense Agency Ishiba Shigeru in the Diet Committee on National Security on March 27, 2003, "There is a question whether Japan need not possess capabilities of spear or whether Japan can rely on the United States for everything. On the issue of Iraq, one discussion is that if Japan does not support the United States [with Iraq], they may not help us in the situation of North Korea, but another is that it is uncertain whether they would come to our help even if we help them (on Iraq)."

In Japanese: "では、矛の能力は日本は持たなくていいのか、アメリカにすべて任せていっていいのかということがあると思うんですね。イラクの問題について、日本はアメリカを支援しなかったら北のときに協力してもらえないという議論があるのと反面に、協力してもいざというときに本当に協力してくれるかどうかというのはわからないという議論も反面あるわけです"

Ishiba responded by saying, "That is worth considering, honestly speaking." In Japanese, "私は検討するに値することだと思っています、正直申し上げて"

Lower House, Committee on Security, 156th Diet Session, March 27, 2003, http://kokkai.ndl.go.jp/SENTAKU/syugiin/156/0015 /15603270015003.pdf.

In December 2004, Ishiba reportedly ordered a study of this, including consideration of the government's position on Article Nine and of the U.S.-Japan alliance. A published analysis of the application of Article nine to the option of preemption is available: "Tairyō hakai heiki wo tōsai shita dandō misairu kyōika ni okeru senshu bōei no arikata" [The future of excusive self-defense posture under threat by ballistic missiles with weapons of mass destruction], December 2004, National Institute of Defense Studies. See also "[Kaku no kyōi] Nihon no yokushiryoku (5) Jieitai no kōgekiryoku wo shōten ni (siriizu)" [Threat of nukes: Japan's deterrence (5) with focus on self-defense force's offensive capabilities (series)], *Yomiuri Shimbun,* March 25, 2007.

Kuroi Buntarō, *Ishiba shigeru maehara seiji hoka ga shūchū kōgi! Nihon no bōei nanatsu no ronten* [Intensive lectures by Ishiba Shigeru, Maehara Seiji and other: Seven points of debate on Japan's defense] (Tokyo: Takarajimasha, 2005).

48. "Dandō misairu bōei no jinsoku katsu bapponteki na kyōka ni kansuru teigen" [Recommendations for enhancing ballistic missile defense promptly and fundamentally], Liberal Democratic Party's Policy Research Council, March 30, 2017, https://jimin.ncss.nifty.com/pdf/news /policy/134586_1.pdf. Former Minister of Defense Onodera Itsunori spoke about the proposal at the Sasakawa Peace Foundation USA's annual security forum in 2017, https://spfusa.org/event/fourth-annual -security-forum-u-s-japan-alliance-foundation-asian-security/.

49. This tension in alliances, between the fear of becoming entrapped in an ally's conflicts and the fear of being abandoned by an ally at a time of crisis, was articulated by Glenn H. Snyder in *Alliance Politics* (Ithaca: Cornell University Press, 2007).

50. For a fuller account of the East China Sea dispute and analysis of the rising tensions between Japan and China, see Sheila A. Smith, *Intimate Rivals: Japanese Domestic Politics and a Rising China* (New York:

Columbia University Press, 2015). For an account of how these tensions affected Chinese domestic politics, see Jessica Chen Weiss, *Powerful Patriots: Nationalist Protest in China's Foreign Relations* (New York: Oxford University Press, 2014).

51. Two U.S. policy makers, one in the National Security Council and another in the State Department, later wrote about this clash between Japan and China and the challenges it posed for the Obama administration. See Jeffrey Bader, *Obama and China's Rise: An Insider Account of America's Asia Strategy* (Washington, DC: Brookings Institution Press, 2012), and Kurt M. Campbell, *The Pivot* (New York: Twelve, 2016).

52. "Announcement of the Aircraft Identification Rules for the East China Sea Air Defense Identification Zone of the P.R.C.," *Xinhuanet*, November 23, 2013, http://news.xinhuanet.com/english/china/2013-11/23/c_132911634.htm. "Statement by Secretary of Defense Chuck Hagel on the East China Sea Air Defense Identification Zone," U.S. Department of Defense, November 23, 2013, http://archive.defense.gov/releases/release.aspx?releaseid=16392.

Ian E. Rinehart and Bart Elias, *China's Air Defense Identification Zone (ADIZ)*, Congressional Research Service, https://fas.org/sgp/crs/row/R43894.pdf. This report notes as follows: "After the PRC first announced the East China Sea ADIZ, it distributed its regulations internationally as a Notice to Airmen (NOTAM), which is a notice disseminated by an aviation authority to alert pilots of potential hazards that could affect the safety of their flight. Regarding commercial aviation, the State Department said on November 29, 2013, that the United States generally expects that U.S. carriers operating internationally will follow NOTAMs issued by foreign countries. The State Department also said that 'our expectation of operations by U.S. carriers consistent with NOTAMs does not indicate U.S. government acceptance of China's requirements for operating in the newly declared ECS ADIZ.'"

53. Minister of Defense Onodera Itsunori oversaw this guidelines review, and it was incorporated into the joint statement released at the October 3, 2013, meeting of the U.S.-Japan Security Consultative Committee, https://www.defense.gov/Portals/1/Documents/pubs/U.S.-Japan-Joint-Statement-of-the-Security-Consultative-Committee.pdf.

54. Secretary of State Hillary Clinton first expressed the U.S.-Japan security treaty's coverage of the Senkaku Islands to Foreign Minister Maehara Seiji on the sidelines of the UN General Assembly in September 2010, and she publicly reiterated it during a joint press conference with Maehara in Hawaii a month later, https://2009-2017.state.gov/secretary /20092013clinton/rm/2010/10/150110.htm. Secretary of State John Kerry restated this commitment in February 2014: https://2009-2017.state.gov /secretary/remarks/2014/02/221459.htm. President Obama affirmed it in Tokyo in April 2014: https://obamawhitehouse.archives.gov/the-press -office/2014/04/24/joint-press-conference-president-obama-and-prime -minister-abe-japan.

   President Donald J. Trump restated this U.S. policy in the joint statement issued when Abe visited Washington, DC, in February 2017: https://www.whitehouse.gov/briefings-statements/joint-statement -president-donald-j-trump-prime-minister-shinzo-abe/.

55. *New York Times,* March 26, 2016, https://www.nytimes.com/2016/03/27 /us/politics/donald-trump-interview-highlights.html.

56. For the full text of the Security Council resolution, see UN Security Council, 8019th Meeting, "Resolution 2371 (2017)" (S/RES/2371), Aug. 5, 2017, https://www.un.org/sc/suborg/en/sanctions/1718 /resolutions. Abe's address to the UN General Assembly on September 20, 2017, can be found at https://www.mofa.go.jp/fp/unp_a /page4e_000674.html.


## Conclusion

1. Former defense agency director-general Sakata Michita famously used the description "small but significant" to describe Japan's military and entitled his book on Japan's military role using that phrase. *Chiisakutemo ōkina yakuwari* [The Self Defense Force: Small but with A Significant Mission] (Tokyo: Asagumo Shimbunsha, 1977).

2. For comprehensive information about the types of missiles and missile technology that North Korea possesses, see the Center for Strategic and International Studies' Missile Threat database: https://missilethreat.csis .org/country/dprk/.

3. A report by the Pew Research Center shows a significant improvement in Japanese perceptions of the United States from the early 1990s into the 2000s; Bruce Stokes, "What Japanese and Americans Think about Each Other," March 20, 2013, http://www.pewglobal.org/2013/03/20/what-japanese-and-americans-think-about-each-other/. A majority of Japanese think the alliance relationship will stay the same or improve, even under the Trump administration. For more information about Japanese attitudes toward the alliance, see Craig Kafura, "Public perceptions and US alliances in the Asia-Pacific," *Pacific Forum CSIS*, no. 52 (2017), https://www.csis.org/analysis/pacnet-52-public-perceptions-and-us-alliances-asia-pacific-0.

4. For the transcript of the March 2016 interview, see *New York Times*, March 26, 2016, https://www.nytimes.com/2016/03/27/us/politics/donald-trump-transcript.html. Trump's suggestion that Japan pay 100 percent of HNS costs came at a rally in Des Moines, Iowa: "Trump Rips U.S. Defense of Japan as One-Sided, Too Expensive," *Japan Times*, August 6, 2016, https://www.japantimes.co.jp/news/2016/08/06/national/politics-diplomacy/trump-rips-u-s-defense-japan-one-sided-expensive/#.W1CniDpKi7o.

5. "Suga to Trump: U.S.-Japan Alliance to Stay," *Japan Times*, March 28, 2016. "Press Conference by Foreign Minister Fumio Kishida," Ministry of Foreign Affairs, Japan, March 29, 2016, http://www.mofa.go.jp/press/kaiken/kaiken4e_000252.html. Ministry of Defense, Japan, "Bōeidaijin kishakaiken gaiyō" [Minister of defense's press conference summary], November 11, 2016, http://www.mod.go.jp/j/press/kisha/2016/11/11.html. "Onodera Itsunori moto bōeishō nichibei dōmei e no rikai busoku kenen 'kore wo ki ni nihon dokuji no anpo giron wo'" [Former Minister of Defense Onodera Itsunori expresses concerns on the lack of understanding on the U.S.-Japan alliance and says, "This is an opportunity to discuss Japan's own defense thinking"], *Sankei Shimbun*, November 12, 2016. "Toranpu seiken to chihō saisei nado" [The Trump administration, local revitalization, and other issues], *Ishiba Shigeru Official Blog*, January 13, 2017, http://ishiba-shigeru.cocolog-nifty.com/blog/2017/01/post-46ef.html.

6. See Sheila A. Smith, "Behind Japan, 100%," *Asia Unbound*, Council on Foreign Relations, February 13, 2017, https://www.cfr.org/blog/behind

-japan-100; and Sheila A. Smith and Charles McClean, "Tokyo
Transitions to Trump," *Comparative Connections* 19, no. 1 (2017): 11–20,
http://cc.csis.org/2017/05/tokyo-transitions-trump/.

7. At a press conference with President Trump at the White House on
June 7, 2018, Prime Minister Abe expressed his determination to hold a
meeting with Kim Jong-un. "Remarks by President Trump and Prime
Minister Abe of Japan in Joint Press Conference," https://www
.whitehouse.gov/briefings-statements/remarks-president-trump-prime
-minister-abe-japan-joint-press-conference-2/.

# · FURTHER READING ·

Abe Shinzō. *Atarashii kuni e* [Toward a new country]. Tokyo: Bungei Shunjū, 2013.

Abe Shinzō. *Utsukushii kuni e* [Toward a beautiful country]. Tokyo: Bungei Shunjū, 2006.

Abe Shinzō and Okazaki Hisahiko. *Kono kuni wo mamoru ketsui* [The decisiveness needed to defend this country]. Tokyo: Fusosha, 2004.

Agawa Naoyuki. *Umino yūjō—Beikoku kaigun to kaijō jieitai* [Friendship at the sea—U.S. Navy and Maritime Self-Defense Force]. Tokyo: Chūkō Shinsho, 2001.

Aketagawa Tōru. *Nichibei gyosei kyōtei no seikjishi* [The politics of the U.S.-Japan Status of Forces Agreement]. Tokyo: Hōsei daigaku shuppankyoku, 1999.

Andelman, David A. *A Shattered Peace: Versailles 1919 and the Price We Pay Today*. Nashville, TN: Wiley, 2014.

Armacost, Michael H. *Friends or Rivals? The Insider's Account of U.S.-Japan Relations*. New York: Columbia University Press, 1996.

Armitage, Richard L., and Joseph S. Nye Jr. *The U.S.-Japan Alliance: Getting Asia Right through 2020*.

Armitage, Richard L., et al. *The United States and Japan: Advancing toward a Mature Partnership*. Washington, DC: Institute for National Strategic Studies, 2000. Washington, DC: Center for Strategic and International Studies, 2007.

Auer, James. *The Postwar Rearmament of Japanese Maritime Forces, 1945–1971.* New York: Praeger, 1973.

Bader, Jeffrey. *Obama and China's Rise: An Insider Account of America's Asia Strategy.* Washington, DC: Brookings Institution Press, 2012.

Berger, Thomas U. *Cultures of Antimilitarism: National Security in Germany and Japan.* Baltimore: Johns Hopkins University Press, 2003.

Berger, Thomas U. *War, Guilt, and World Politics after World War II.* New York: Cambridge University Press, 2012.

Berger, Thomas U., Mike M. Mochizuki, and Jitsuo Tsuchiyama, eds. *Japan in International Politics: The Foreign Policies of an Adaptive State.* Boulder, CO: Lynne Rienner, 2007.

Boynton, Robert S. *The Invitation-Only Zone: The True Story of North Korea's Abduction Project.* New York: Farrar, Straus and Giroux, 2016.

Campbell, Kurt M. *The Pivot.* New York: Twelve, 2016.

Catalinac, Amy. *Electoral Reform and National Security in Japan: From Pork to Foreign Policy.* New York: Cambridge University Press, 2016.

Cha, Victor. *Powerplay: The Origins of the American Alliance System in Asia.* Princeton, NJ: Princeton University Press, 2016.

Chanlett-Avery, Emma, and Ian E. Rinehart. *The U.S.-Japan Alliance.* Washington, DC: Congressional Research Service, February 9, 2016.

Chuma Kiyofuku. *Saigunbi no seijigaku* [The politics of rearmament]. Tokyo: Chishikisha, 1985.

Chunichi Shimbun Shakaibu, eds. *Samawah tayori-rikuji dai-10 shidan no iraku haken* [A message from Samawa—The deployment of the GSDF 10th division to Iraq]. Tokyo: Chunichi Shinbunsha, 2005.

Cronin, Patrick M., and Michael J. Green. *Redefining the U.S.-Japan Alliance: Tokyo's National Defense Program.* Washington, DC: Institute for National Strategic Studies, 1994.

*Defense of Japan 2018.* Tokyo: Ministry of Defense.

Drifte, Reinhard. *Arms Production in Japan: The Military Applications of Civilian Technology.* London: Westview Press, 1986.

Dutton, Peter A. *Scouting, Signaling, and Gatekeeping: Chinese Naval Operations in Japanese Waters and the International Law Implications.* U.S. Naval War College China Maritime Studies, no. 2. Newport, RI: Naval War College Press, 2009.

Fukuyama Takashi. *Chikatetsu Sarin Jiken—Jieitai Senki* [The sarin subway incident—Notes from the SDF front line]. Tokyo: Kōjinsha, 2015.

Funabashi Yoichi. *Alliance Adrift*. New York: Council on Foreign Relations Press, 1999.

Funabashi Yoichi. *The Peninsula Question*. Washington, DC: Brookings Institution Press, 2007.

Funabashi Yoichi and Barak Kushner, eds. *Examining Japan's Lost Decades*. New York: Routledge, 2015.

Ganguly, Sumit, Andrew Scobell, and Joseph Chinyong Liow. *The Routledge Handbook of Asian Security Studies*. 2nd ed. New York: Routledge, 2018.

Gotōda Masaharu. *Naikaku kanbō chōkan* [Chief cabinet secretary]. Tokyo: Kōdansha, 1989.

Green, Michael J. *Arming Japan: Defense Production, Alliance Politics and the Postwar Search for Autonomy*. New York: Columbia University Press, 1998.

Green, Michael J. *By More than Providence: Grand Strategy and American Power in the Asia Pacific since 1783*. New York: Columbia University Press, 2017.

Green, Michael J. *Japan's Reluctant Realism: Foreign Policy Challenges in an Era of Uncertain Power*. New York: Palgrave Macmillan, 2001.

Hara Yoshihisa. *Kishi Nobusuke—Kensei no seijika* [Kishi Nobusuke—A statesman of power]. Tokyo: Iwanami Shinsho, 1995.

Hara Yoshihisa. *Kishi Nobusuke shōgenroku* [Testimony by Kishi Nobusuke]. Tokyo: Chūkō Bunko, 2014.

Hara Yoshihisa. *Nichibei kankei no kōzu—Anpo kaitei wo kenshō suru* [Composition of U.S.-Japan relations—Examining security treaty revision]. Tokyo: NHK Books, 1991.

Hara Yoshihisa. *Sengo nihon to kokusai seiji—Anpo kaitei no rikigaku* [Postwar Japan and international politics—Power dynamics of security treaty revision]. Tokyo: Chūō Kōronsha, 1988.

Hashimoto, Akikazu, Mike M. Mochizuki, and Kurayoshi Takara, eds. *The Okinawa Question and the U.S.-Japan Alliance*. Washington, DC: Sigur Center for Asian Studies, 2005.

Hathaway, Oona A., and Scott J. Shapiro. *The Internationalists*. New York: Simon and Schuster, 2017.

Havens, Thomas R. H. *Fire across the Sea: The Vietnam War and Japan, 1965–1975*. Princeton, NJ: Princeton University Press, 2014.

Heginbotham, Eric, et al. *China's Evolving Nuclear Deterrent: Major Drivers and Issues for the United States*. Santa Monica, CA: RAND Corporation, 2017.

Hibako Yoshifumi. *Sokudou hittai—Higashi Nihon daishinsai rikujō bakuryōchō no zennikki* [Rapid response—The full diary of the chief of staff of the Ground Self-Defense Force during the East Japan disasters]. Tokyo: Manejimentosha, 2015.

Hirose Katsuya. *Kanryō to gunjin* [Bureaucrats and the military]. Tokyo: Iwanami Shoten, 1989.

Hosoya Yuichi. *Anpo Ronso* [Debating the U.S.-Japan Security Treaty]. Tokyo: Chikuma Shinsho, 2016.

Hughes, Christopher. *Japan's Foreign and Security Policy under the "Abe Doctrine": New Dynamism or New Dead End?* London: Palgrave MacMillan, 2015.

Hughes, Christopher. *Japan's Re-emergence as a "Normal" Military Power.* Adelphi Paper 368–369. London: Institute for International Strategic Studies, 2005.

Hughes, Christopher. *Japan's Remilitarisation.* London: Institute for International Strategic Studies, 2009.

Iio Jun. *Nihon no tōchi kōzō* [The structure of Japanese governance]. Tokyo: Chukō Shinsho, 2007.

Ikari Yoshirō. *Perushyawan no gunkanki: Kaijō jieitai sōkai butai no kiryoku* [Flying the military flag in the Persian Gulf: A chronicle of the Maritime Self-Defense Force minesweeping force]. Tokyo: Kōjinsha, 2015.

Inoguchi Takashi, G. John Ikenberry, and Yoichiro Sato, eds. *The U.S.-Japan Security Alliance: Regional Multilateralism.* New York: Palgrave Macmillan, 2011.

Inoue, Masamichi S. *Okinawa and the U.S. Military: Identity Making in the Age of Globalization.* New York: Columbia University Press, 2007.

Iokibe Makoto. *Daisaigai no jidai- mirai no kokunan ni sonaete* [The age of large-scale disasters: Preparing for Japan's future difficulties]. Tokyo: Mainichi Shimbun Shuppan, 2015.

Iokibe Makoto. *The History of U.S.-Japan Relations: From Perry to the Present.* Translated by Tosh Minohara. New York: Palgrave MacMillan, 2017.

Ishiba Shigeru. *Kokubō—Subete wo shirubeki tokiga kita* [The time has come to know everything about Japan's defenses]. Tokyo: Shinko Bunko, 2011.

Ishiba Shigeru. *Nihonjin no tame no 'shūdanteki jieiken' nyu mon.* [Allowing the right of collective self-defense for the Japanese people]. Tokyo: Shinkosha, 2014.

Ishiba Shigeru. *Nihon wo, torimodosu. Kenpō wo, torimodosu* [Restore Japan. Restore our constitution]. Tokyo: PHP Kenkyūsha, 2013.

Japan Saiken Inishiateibu [The Rebuild Japan Initiative], eds. *Gendai Nihon no Chiseigaku* [Contemporary Japanese strategic thought]. Tokyo: Chuo Koron, 2017.

Kaihara Osamu. *Nihon bōei taisei no uchimaku* [Behind the scenes planning for Japan's defense posture]. Tokyo: Jiji Tsūshinsha, 1977.

Kaihara Osamu. *Watashi no bōei hakusho* [My defense white paper]. Tokyo: Jiji Tsūshinsha, 1975.

Katzenstein, Peter J. *Cultural Norms and National Security: Police and Military in Postwar Japan.* Ithaca, NY: Cornell University Press, 1996.

Kitaoka Shinichi. *Gaikou to Kenryoku—Nihon Seijishi* [A political history of modern Japan: Foreign relations and domestic politics]. Tokyo: Yuhikaku, 2011.

Kokubun, Ryousei, Yoshihide Soeya, Akio Takahara, and Shin Kawashima. *Japan-China Relations in the Modern Era.* Translated by Keith Krulak. New York: Routledge, 2017.

Komamura Keigo. *Kenpō soshō no gendaiteki tenkai-kenpōteki ronshō wo motomete* [Contemporary turn of constitutional law litigation]. Translated by publisher. Tokyo: Nihon Hyouronsha, 2015.

Kōno, Masaru. *Japan's Postwar Party Politics.* Princeton, NJ: Princeton University Press, 1997.

Kubo Takuya. *Kokubōron* [On national defense]. Tokyo: PHP Kenkyūjo, 1979.

Kuroi Buntarō. *Ishiba shigeru maehara seiji hoka ga shūchū kōgi! Nihon no bōei nanatsu no ronten* [Intensive lectures by Ishiba Shigeru, Maehara Seiji, etc! Seven points of debate on Japan's defense]. Tokyo: Takarajimasha, 2005.

Lind, Jennifer. *Sorry States: Apologies in International Politics.* Ithaca, NY: Cornell University Press, 2008.

Morimoto Satoshi. *Futenma no nazo—kichi henkan mondai meisō 15-nen no subete* [The mysterious twists in the U.S. Marine Corps Air Station Futenma relocation plan]. Tokyo: Kairyusha, 2010.

Morimoto Satoshi. *Iraku sensō to jieitai haken* [Iraq War and Self-Defense Force dispatch]. Tokyo: Tōyōkeizai Shinpōsha, 2004.

Nagashima Akihisa. *'Katsubei' to iu ryugi—gaikou anzenshosho no riarizumu* [The Art of activating our U.S. ally—Foreign policy and national security realism]. Tokyo: Kodansha, 2013.

Nakajima Toshijiro. *Gaikō Shogenryoku—Nichibei anpo—Okinawa henkan tenanmon jiken* [Documenting Japan's diplomacy: The U.S.-Japan security treaty, the reversion of Okinawa and the Tiananmen incident]. Tokyo: Iwanami shoten, 2012.

Nakasone Yasuhiro. *Kokumin kenpō seitei e no michi—Nakasone Yasuhiro kenpōron no kiseki* [The path to establishing the Japanese people's constitution—The evolution of Nakasone Yasuhiro's thinking on the constitution]. Tokyo: Institute for International Policy Studies, 2017.

*NIDS China Security Report 2018*. Tokyo: National Institute for Defense Studies.

Nose Nobuyuki. *Bōeisho* [Ministry of Defense, Japan]. Shincho Shinsha, 2012.

Okada Haruo. *Okkaparu Ichidaiki—Hansen Heiwa ni Kaketa Giin Seikatsu 40-nen* [The diary of 'Okkaparu': Forty years as a Diet member working against war and for peace]. Tokyo: Gyokensha, 1986.

Oriki Ryoichi. *Kuni wo mamoru sekinin—Jieitai moto saikō kanbuwa kataru* [The responsibility for defending our country—Thoughts of a former chief of staff of the SDF]. Tokyo: PHP Shinsho, 2015.

Oros, Andrew L. *Japan's Security Renaissance: New Policies and Politics for the Twenty-First Century*. New York: Columbia University Press, 2017.

Oros, Andrew L. *Normalizing Japan: Politics, Identity and the Evolution of Security Practice*. Stanford, CA: Stanford University Press, 2008.

Ōtake Hideo. *Bōei seisaku to kokunai seiji* [Defense policy and domestic politics]. Tokyo: Sanichi Shobō, 1983.

Ōtake Hideo. *Nihon no saigunbi to nashonarizumu—Hoshu, riberaru, shakai minshu shugisha no bōeikan* [Japan's rearmament and nationalism: The defense views of Conservatives, Liberals, and Social Democrats]. Tokyo: Chūkō Shinsho, 1988.

Ozawa Ichirō. *Blueprint for a New Japan: The Rethinking of a Nation*. Tokyo: Kōdansha International, 1994.

Packard, George. *Protest in Tokyo: The Security Treaty Crisis of 1960*. Princeton, NJ: Princeton Legacy Library, 1966.

Pekkanen, Saadia M., and Paul Kallender-Umezu. *In Defense of Japan: From the Market to the Military in Space Policy*. Stanford, CA: Stanford University Press, 2010.

Pyle, Kenneth B. *Japan Rising: The Resurgence of Japanese Power and Purpose*. New York: Public Affairs, 2008.

Radford, Arthur W. *From Pearl Harbor to Vietnam: The Memoirs of Admiral Arthur W. Radford*. Stanford, CA: Hoover Institution Press, 1980.

Roehrig, Terence. *Japan, South Korea, and the United States Nuclear Umbrella*. New York: Columbia University Press, 2017.

Sado Akihiro. *The Self-Defense Forces and Postwar Politics in Japan*. Translated by Noda Makito. Tokyo: Japan Publishing Industry Foundation for Culture, 2017.

Sakamoto Kazuya. *Nichibei dōmei no kizuna—Anpo jōyaku to sōgosei no mosaku* [The bonds of U.S.- Japan alliance—The security treaty and search for reciprocity]. Tokyo: Yūikaku, 2000.

Sakata Michita. *Chiisakutemo ōkina yakuwari* [The Self-Defense Force: Small but with a significant mission]. Tokyo: Asagumo Shimbunsha, 1977.

Sakurabayashi Misa. *Umi wo hiraku—shirarezaru sōkai butai* [Paving the way across the seas—The must-read story of Japan's minesweeping forces]. Tokyo: Namiki Shobōo, 2008.

Samuels, Richard. *Securing Japan: Tokyo's Grand Strategy and the Future of East Asia*. Ithaca, NY: Cornell University Press, 2007.

Samuels, Richard. *Special Duty: A History of Japan's Intelligence Community*. Ithaca, NY: Cornell University Press, 2019.

Satō Masahisa. *Iraku jieitai 'sentōki'* [An SDF Iraq "war diary"]. Tokyo: Kōdansha, 2007.

Satō Yukio. *Sashikakerareta kasa—Beikoku no kaku yokushiryoku to nihon no anzen hosho* [Under an extended umbrella: U.S. nuclear deterrence and Japan's security]. Tokyo: Jiji Tsushinsha, 2017.

Schoff, James L. *Tools for Trilateralism: Improving U.S.-Japan-Korea Cooperation to Manage Complex Contingencies*. Herndon, VA: Potomac Books, 2005.

Schoff, James L. *Uncommon Alliance for the Common Good: The United States and Japan after the Cold War*. Washington, DC: Carnegie Endowment for International Peace, 2017.

Self, Benjamin L., and Jeffrey W. Thompson, eds. *Japan's Nuclear Option: Security, Politics, and Policy in the 21st Century*. Washington, DC: Stimson Center, 2003.

Shinoda Hideaki. *Shudanteki Jieiken no Shisoshi* [A historiography of the right of collective self-defense]. Tokyo: Shafuu Koosha, 2017.

Smith, Sheila A. *Intimate Rivals: Japanese Domestic Politics and a Rising China*. New York: Columbia University Press, 2015.

Smith, Sheila A., ed. *Local Voices, National Issues: The Impact of Local Initiative in Japanese Policy-Making*. Ann Arbor: University of Michigan Press, 2000.

Snyder, Glenn H. *Alliance Politics*. Ithaca, NY: Cornell University Press, 2007.

Soeya Yoshihide, Tadokoro Masayuki, and David A. Welch, eds. *Japan as a 'Normal Country'?* Toronto: University of Toronto Press, 2011.

Swaine, Michael D., Mike M. Mochizuki, Michael L. Brown, Paul S. Giarra, Douglas H. Paal, Rachel Esplin Odell, Raymond Lu, Oliver Palmer, and Xu Ren. *China's Military & the U.S.-Japan Alliance in 2030*. Washington, DC: Carnegie Endowment for International Peace, 2013.

Tamura Shigenobu, Takahashi Kenichi, and Shimada Kazuhisa, eds. *Nihon no Bōei Hōsei* [Japan's defense laws]. 2nd ed. Tokyo: Naigai Shuppan, 2012.

Tatsumi, Yuki. *Japan's National Security Policy Infrastructure: Can Tokyo Meet Washington's Expectations?* Washington, DC: Stimson Center, 2008.

Tatsumi, Yuki. *Japan's New Defense Establishment: Institutions, Capabilities and Implications*. Washington, DC: Stimson Center, 2007.

Tatsumi, Yuki, ed. *Strategic Yet Strained: US Force Realignment in Japan and Its Effects on Okinawa*. Washington, DC: Stimson Center, 2008.

Teshima Ryūichi. *Gaikō haisen—130 oku doru wa suna ni kieta* [Diplomatic defeat—13 billion yen disappears in the sand]. Tokyo: Shinchōsha, 2006.

Ueda Tetsu. *Sensōron* [Theory of war]. Tokyo: Marujyusha, 1989.

U.S. Department of State. *1952–1954, China and Japan*. Edited by David W. Mabon and Harriet D. Schwar. Vol. 14, pt. 2 of *Foreign Relations of the United States*, 1985.

U.S. Department of State. *1958–1960, Indonesia; Japan; Korea, microfiche supplement*. Edited by Madeline Chi, Louis J. Smith, Robert J. McMahon, and Glenn W. LaFantasie. Vol. 17/18 of *Foreign Relations of the United States*, 1994.

U.S. Department of State. *1958–1960, Japan; Korea*. Edited by Madeline Chi and Louis J. Smith. Vol. 28 of *Foreign Relations of the United States*, 1994.

Wakaizumi Kei. *The Best Course Available: A Personal Account of the Secret U.S.-Japan Okinawa Reversion Negotiations*. Edited by John Swenson Wright. Honolulu: University of Hawai'i Press, 2002.

Weiss, Jessica Chen. *Powerful Patriots: Nationalist Protest in China's Foreign Relations*. New York: Oxford University Press, 2014.

Williams, Phil. *The Senate and US Troops in Europe*. London: Palgrave Macmillan, 1985.

Yamazaki Taku. *YKK Hitsuryoku* [The hidden story of YKK]. Tokyo: Kodansha, 2016.

Yanagisawa Kyouji. *Kantei no Iraku sensou—moto bōeisho kanryō ni yoru hihan to jisho* [The Iraq War from the prime minister's office—The criticism and self-reflection of a former defense bureaucrat]. Tokyo: Iwanami Shoten, 2013.

Yoshida Shingo. *Nichibei dōmei no seidoka* [The institutionalization of the U.S.-Japan alliance]. Nagoya: Nagoya University Press, 2012.

Yōzō Kato. *Shiryoku—Jieitai shi: Keisatsu yobitai kara konnichi made* [A personal history of the history of the Self-Defense Force: From the National Police Reserve to today]. Tokyo: Seiji Geppōsha, 1979.

# · ACKNOWLEDGMENTS ·

Almost thirty years have passed since the end of the Cold War, and the geopolitics of Asia have made it far more important that Americans understand how our allies in that part of the world understand their security needs. As China becomes more assertive and militarily powerful and as North Korea has acquired weapons of mass destruction and the means to deliver them across Asia and indeed across the globe, U.S. security is increasingly under pressure from this changing Asia. How our closest ally thinks about its military is of great import to Asia's future, and to ours.

I have studied Japan's complex relationship with its military since my doctoral studies at Columbia University. There, James W. Morley never failed to challenge me as I grappled with the unique postwar circumstance of Japanese military restraint. I am immensely proud to be one of Jim's many, many students.

The Smith Richardson Foundation generously provided funding for this book, and I am grateful for the foundation's support. I owe an additional debt of gratitude to Allan Song, Senior Program Officer for International Security and Foreign Policy, who was also a student of James Morley's and a teaching assistant for Robert Jervis at Columbia.

He was a formidable mentor to a young undergraduate, and he has been over the years a deeply trenchant critic as well as a great friend. This book would not have been written without his encouragement and support.

My colleagues at the Council on Foreign Relations continue to be tremendous advocates of my work. I would particularly like to thank Richard N. Haass, president, for his continued belief in the importance of the U.S. partnership with Japan and in my work in the Japan program. I am indebted also to James M. Lindsay, director of studies, and Elizabeth Economy, director for Asia, for their encouragement and support. I must also thank two research associates who have worked tirelessly on this book: Ayumi Teraoka for her masterful research skills and Jeremy Fuller for his editorial deftness. Both exhibited remarkable grace under pressure. I want to thank our wonderful interns who ran down Diet debates and checked facts and footnotes over the years: Grace Ahearn, Masatoshi Asaoka, Kyle Bezold, Victoria Edwards, Joshua Fitt, Jiangtian Gong, Yuichiro Kakutani, Nick Kodama, Reina Sasaki, Yi Shen, Mikhail Skovoronskikh, Tsuyoshi Takahashi, and Hotaka Takeuchi.

My study group at the Council on Foreign Relations provided terrific critique and lively debate as I wrote this book. Their own work on Asia's geopolitics has informed my thinking about the region; I am indebted to them not only for their suggestions but also for their respectful critique of early drafts. Thank you especially to Patrick Cronin, Janine Davidson, Michael McDevitt, Michael Green, Michael Schiffer, James Shinn, Scott Snyder, and James Steinberg. I would also like to thank Admiral Dennis Blair for his careful reading of the manuscript and trenchant feedback on how to improve it. The *Asahi Shimbun* provided many of the photographs in this book, and I would like to thank Yamawaki Takeshi, former Washington, DC, bureau chief, and Kashiwagi Kazuhiko of the *Asahi* archives for their assistance.

As this book was years in the making, it is impossible for me to thank everyone I learned from in Japan. I have kept our conversations confidential, as they were intended, and have relied fully on open source material. Many of those described and cited in this book have given generously of their time and expertise. I have interviewed Ministry of Defense officials who have shared their analysis and experiences with me over the years. Japan's defense planners patiently described their policy goals, their assessment of Japan's security needs, and the institutional context within which they operate. The Ministry of Defense is still my first stop on virtually all my trips to Japan.

Today's SDF is very different from the military that hesitantly sought to consider how to contribute to global expectations of Japan in the Persian Gulf in the 1980s or to the first Gulf War in 1990. I was privileged to observe this transformation firsthand, and to the men and women of the SDF, I thank you for your frankness and your professional courtesy. Japan is also home to over fifty thousand men and women in the U.S. military, who serve closely with their Japanese counterparts. I must thank those in the U.S. military, especially at the Pacific Command (now the Indo-Pacific Command) and at U.S. bases across the Pacific who also gave generously of their time as I researched this book.

My father served most of his naval career in the Pacific, and we have enjoyed many, many conversations over the years about Japan and its military, and about his work during the Cold War. I have learned a great deal from him, not only about military operations but also about the values and principles that guide those who wear the uniform in our democracy. It is to him, with gratitude and love, that I dedicate this book.

# · INDEX ·

Abe Shinzō, 2–4, 12, 146, 149, 195–196, 201, 222, 233; on constitutional revision, 8, 14, 162–164, 167–171, 225; diplomacy with Southeast Asia and India and, 86; and the East China Sea, 116, 121, 124, 207–208; the Futenma base relocation issue and, 187; policy toward North Korea, 211–214, 235; reinterpretation of Article Nine by, 19, 79, 142, 155, 163–164; security reforms and, 14, 152–154, 156, 161, 236; the U.S.-Japan Alliance and, 209–210, 234–235

Afghanistan, 69, 132

Air defense identification zone (ADIZ): of China, 121, 207; of Japan, 125, 175

Air Self-Defense Force (ASDF), 119, 121; air defense operations around Japan, 116–117, 190; in Cambodia PKO, 64, 67; in humanitarian operations, 133–134, 139; role in BMD, 107, 115

Akashi Yasushi, 61, 65

Antipiracy, MSDF mission in the Gulf of Aden, 81–84, 88, 143, 193–194

Antiterrorism Special Measures Law, 79, 88

Armacost, Michael, 57

Article Nine, constitution of Japan, 29, 128–130; and Japan's contribution to international security, collective self-defense, 63, 132, 151–154, 156; postwar debate of, 129; reinterpretation in 2014 of, 79, 154–155, 161–164; revising of, 162–172, 225; the use of force and, 139–143

Ashida Hitoshi, 6–8, 27

Asia Pacific Economic Community, 234

Asō Tarō, 82–84, 193, 234

Auer, James, 28, 58

Aum Shinrikyō, gas attack on Tokyo Subway, 94–95; weakness in government response to, 98

Australia, 74, 85–87

Ballistic Missile Defense (BMD): Diet passes BMD response law, 107; readiness and missile destruction orders, 114–116, 194, 212; the U.S.-Japan Alliance and, 103, 159, 194

Banshō Koichirō, 76, 80, 119

Basic Policy on National Defense, 36–37

Burden sharing, 45–47, 174, 177, 179

Burke, Arleigh, 27–28

Bush, George W., and administration of, 71, 134, 201, 231

Cabinet Legislative Bureau, 31–32, 128–129, 161

China: anti-Japan protests (2012) in, 120–121; challenge to Japan's air defenses, 116–117; confrontation with Japan, 206–208; and the East China Sea, 215–216; military spending, 11; NDPG (2005, 2010) threat assessment of, 109–110; and the Taiwan Strait crisis (1996), 91–93, 215. *See also* East China Sea; Senkaku/Diaoyu Islands

Clinton, Bill, administration of, 90–91

Clinton, Hillary, 201, 209

Collective self-defense, 143, 150–162; Article Nine and, 129–130

Communist Party, Japan, 33, 184

Congress, United States, 45–47, 174, 177, 179

Constitution of Japan: Article Ninety-Six of, 166–167; Article Sixty-Six of, 34–35, 130, 144, 149; preamble and

international peace, 69–71; revision of, 162–172. *See also* Article Nine, constitution of Japan

Conventional strike capability, of Japan, 8, 16, 32, 101, 123–125, 159, 202–203, 237

Defense Agency, Japan, 28, 29, 40–41, 100–101, 108–109, 131, 134

Defense Exports, 86–87

Defense Intelligence Headquarters, 10, 108

Democratic Party of Japan (DPJ): and antiterror coalitions, 70–71, 82; on emergency legislation, 106; on the Iraq Special Measures Law, 136; on U.S. forces in Japan, 179–180, 185–186

Deng Xiaoping, 22

Deterrence: dynamic deterrence, 110–111, 204, 220; extended deterrence, 100, 173, 200–202, 205

Diaoyu Islands. *See* Senkaku/Diaoyu Islands

Diet: and antipiracy debate, 193; and Antiterror Law debate, 133; and constitutional revision, 166–169; and conventional strike debate, 203; and emergency legislation deliberations, 106; and Iraq Special Measures Law debate, 73, 136–137; and oversight of SDF debate, 148–149; and PKO Law debate, 62, 68; and postwar debate of Article Nine, 29–32, 129–131

Djibouti, 83–84

Dulles, John Foster, 36

UN Security Council, 67, 69, 82, 211, 235

U.S.-Japan Alliance, 151, 158, 173–219, 227–236; and abandonment fears, 205–219; in antiterror coalition, 69–78; and basing of U.S. forces in Japan, 181–189; and burden sharing, 45–47, 174, 177, 179; in the Cold War, 22–23, 36, 43, 51, 174–175, 190; and collective self-defense, 156; the East China Sea and, 17, 121–122, 207–208, 230–231; extended deterrence and, 100, 173, 200–202, 205; the Gulf War and, 57, 179, 229–230; and Japan's military capability, 36, 131; policy toward North Korea, 210–213

U.S.-Japan Defense Cooperation Guidelines; 1978, 44, 190; 1997 revision of, 191, 197; 2015 revision of, 121, 197, 208–209

U.S.-Japan Security Treaty: renegotiation of, 26, 174; the Senkaku Islands and Article Five of, 122, 207–209; 1960

U.S. Marine Corps, 52–53, 188–189

U.S. Navy, 47–49, 53, 86

Vietnam War, 37, 42, 176

Xi Jinping, and the East China Sea, 121

Yamaguchi Natsuo, 154–155, 202

Y Committee, 27–28

Yoshida Shigeru, 24–2